PULLING YOUR OWN STRINGS

Dr. Wayne Dyer is the author of *Your Erroneous Zones*, a record-breaking best-seller in the field of psychology. Following his own advice and through his enjoyment of working in the media, he has become a national television and press celebrity. He is a practising therapist and a former associate professor in the Graduate School at St. John's University in New York. He is the author or co-author of four other books and has written many professional and popular magazine articles.

PULLING YOUR OWN STRINGS

Dr. WAYNE W. DYER

Hamlyn Paperbacks

PULLING YOUR OWN STRINGS
ISBN 0 600 20061 2

First published in Great Britain 1979
by Hamlyn Books
Hamlyn Paperbacks edition 1979

Copyright © 1978 by Wayne W. Dyer
Portions of this work originally
appeared in *Family Circle*
Grateful acknowledgement is made for
permission to reprint *Pull Your Own Strings*
by Gayle Spanier Rawlings
Copyright © 1977 by Gayle Spanier Rawlings

Hamlyn Paperbacks are published by
The Hamlyn Publishing Group Ltd,
Astronaut House,
Feltham,
Middlesex, England

Reproduced, printed and bound
in Great Britain by
Cox & Wyman Ltd, Reading

To
Susan Elizabeth Dyer

before you I can think
aloud

Contents

3 Refusing to Be Seduced by What Is Over or Cannot Be Changed 49

4 Avoiding the Comparison Trap 69

5 Becoming Quietly Effective and Not Expecting "Them" to Understand   91

6 Teaching Others How You Want to Be Treated   119

7 Never Place Loyalty to Institutions and Things Above Loyalty to Yourself 147

8 Distinguishing Between Judgments and Reality 177

9 Being Creatively Alive in Every Situation 199

10 Victim or Victor? Your Present Victim-Profile Based on 100 Typical Situations 227

Foreword

by Susan Dyer

Much of what is expressed here pertains to my own personal development as a decision-maker and action-oriented adult.

As a teacher and counselor of the deaf I have worked with many young people who are more handicapped by their lack of self-confidence than by their physical disabilities, and we talk about the importance of feeling "in charge" of oneself before one can take charge of a situation. Then my students gradually assume the hard work of taking risks on their own, from such practical acts as ordering for themselves in restaurants, rather than waiting for a hearing companion to do it for them, to such internal psychological events as the decision of one junior-high student to move into college prep classes as the first member of her family to aim for such academic heights. Her challenge is great, but now so is her confidence.

Many of us with normal faculties have mentally handicapped ourselves and victimized ourselves by belief systems. We limit ourselves in search of security, never realizing how easily others can confine us further, using our limitations against us. One example from my life was conquering my allergies.

Hanging on to my allergies as an adult meant living up to a childhood label of being "delicate," which had given me a lot of attention in an active family. Prompt sniffling also got me out of many risky situations, such as outdoor sports (grass, trees, pollen), where I felt athletically inadequate, or social encounters in tightly packed parties where my allergic response to tobacco smoke was actually an attack of shyness. My allergist never spent a moment to check out any psychological maintenance system. He was content with my program of weekly office visits.

Once I began to determine that achieving independence meant not being delicate and not being a victim of my own fears of rejection, there was an end to injections and a beginning of touch football and new friendships.

Every day I encounter challenges. Daily examples include confronting authorities in the public schools to secure the best placement for deaf students, dealing with salespeople who give me poor service, satisfying relatives whose expectations for me are different from my own, and challenging the me I am, to become the me I choose to be.

This book is dedicated to me, and many of its examples came from me. All its messages are for me—and for you too! Read, grow, enjoy!

Introduction:
The Philosophy
of Non-Victimization

A little boy came home from school and asked his mother, "Mom, what's a *scurvy elephant?*"

His mother was perplexed, and inquired why he would even ask such a question.

Little Tommy replied, "I heard my teacher telling the principal that I was a *scurvy elephant* in the classroom."

Tommy's mother called the school and asked for an explanation. The principal laughed. "No, no. Tommy's teacher told me after school that he was a *disturbing element* in the classroom."

This book is written for people who would like to be completely in charge of their own lives—including the mavericks, rebels, and the "scurvy elephants" of the world. It is for those who will not automatically do things according to other people's plans.

To live your life the way you choose, you have to be a bit rebellious. You have to be willing to stand up for yourself. You might have to be a bit disturbing to those who have strong interests in controlling your behavior—but if you're willing, you'll find that being your own person, not letting others do your thinking for you, is a joyful, worthy, and absolutely fulfilling way to live.

You need not be a revolutionary, just a human being who says to the world, and everyone in it, "I am going to be my own person, and resist anyone who tries to stop me."

A well-known popular song tells us,

> Life is a beautiful thing . . .
> As long as I hold the string,
> I'd be a silly so and so . . .
> If I should ever let it go . . . .

This book is about not letting your own strings go. It is for those who feel strongly enough about not being manipulated by others that they are willing to put a stop to it. It is for those who want their own freedom more desperately than anything else. It is especially a book for those who have some driftwood in their souls, who want to move about on this planet with senses of being unrestrained.

Many people are more content to be regulated than to take charge of their own lives. If you don't mind having your strings pulled, this is not the book for you. It is a manual of change and how to make that change come about. It sets forth some very controversial and challenging ideas.

Many will see these views as counterproductive, and will accuse me of encouraging people to be rebellious and contemptuous of established authority. I make no bones about it—I believe that you must often be assertive, even pugnacious, to avoid being victimized.

Yes, I do think you often must be unreasonable, "insubordinate," to people who would manipulate you. To be otherwise is to be victimized, and the world is full of people who would love you to behave in whatever ways are most convenient for them.

A special kind of freedom is available to you if you are willing to take the risks involved in getting it: the freedom to wander where you will about life's terrain, to make *all* your own choices. The central insight must be that individuals have the *right* to decide how they will live their lives, and that as long as their exercise of this right does not infringe on the equal rights of others, any person or institution that interferes ought to be viewed as a victimizer. The book is for those who feel that their own personal lives are controlled too much by forces over which they in turn have little control.

Each person's life is unique, separated from every other life in the true experiential sense. No one else can live your life, feel what you feel, get into your body and experience the world the way you do. This is the only life you get, and it is too precious to let others take their own advantage of it. It is only logical that *you* should determine how you are going to function, and your functioning ought to bring you the joy and fulfillment of "pulling your own strings" rather than the pain and misery of victimization. This book is designed to help each reader achieve such total control over his or her own life.

Virtually everyone suffers some domination by others that is unpleasant and definitely not worth maintaining, let alone defending, as many of us unconsciously do. Most people know all too well what it is to be ripped off, manipulated, and pushed into behaviors and beliefs against their wills. The problems of victimization have become so acute and widespread that newspapers across the country have sprung into action with columns to help people who are being abused. "Action lines," "hot lines," and other such "public service" aids attempt to cut through the red tape which is a part of so much victimization, and they attempt to get results. Local television shows have consumer advocates and community ombudsmen to do some of the dirty work. The government has created agencies of protection, and many communities have agencies attempting to combat more localized forms of victimization.

But while all this is laudable and worthy, it still only scratches at the surface of victimization, and is largely ineffective, because it places the emphasis on blaming the victimizers, or on having someone else act for the victim. It misses the point: that people are victimized simply because they *expect* to be done in—and then, when it happens, they are not surprised.

It is almost impossible to victimize people who don't expect to be victimized, and who are willing to protest against those who want to subjugate them in any way. The problem of being victimized rests in *you*, not in all of those other people who have learned to pull your strings. This book puts the focus on you, the person who must do the resisting, rather than on someone else doing your resisting for you. It is written for one purpose: to be useful to the reader. I said to myself, "If they can't use it, leave it out." I have included case histories to give you more concrete ideas of how to avoid the numerous victim-traps I want to see you avoid, and some very specific strategies and techniques are suggested to help you out of deep-seated victim habits. Occasional quizzes are supplied to help you assess your own victim behavior, and I have concluded with a 100-item victim index, to which you can refer for further checking and guidance of your progress.

Each chapter after the first introductory one is organized around a major principle or guideline for not being victimized. Each contains anti-victim guidelines, examples of how the victimizers of the world work to keep you from using them, and then special examples and tactics to support you in assisting yourself.

Thus each chapter will take you through concrete steps to help you implement your own non-victim behavior.

I trust you will gain a great deal from reading this book. But if you believe the book will liberate you, then you are already a victim of your own illusions before you even start reading. You, and only you, must decide to take the suggestions and turn them into constructive, self-fulfilling behavior.

I asked a good friend and a very talented poet to write a special poem about being victimized as it is presented in this book. Gayle Spanier Rawlings succinctly sums up the non-victimization message in "Pull Your Own Strings."

Pull Your Own Strings
We are connected
in invisible ways
to our fears
we are the puppet
& the puppeteer,
the victims of our
expectation.
Silken threads pull,
arms & legs
flop & jangle.
We dance to the music
of our fears
bodies crouched inside
children hiding, pretending,
under that rock
behind that tree
someplace, everywhere
not what we control.

Pull your own strings
move into your body

> & to the beat of life
> cut your strings
> hold out your hand to
> the unknown,
> walk in the dark
> open your arms
> to the embrace of air,
> make them wings
> that soar.

GAYLE SPANIER RAWLINGS

Gayle's words convey the beauty of being free. May you learn to choose your own health and happiness, and practice some of that delicious soaring behavior.

All experience hath shown that mankind are more disposed to suffer, while evils are sufferable, than to right themselves by abolishing the forms to which they are accustomed.

DECLARATION OF INDEPENDENCE
JULY 4, 1776

Pulling
Your Own
Strings

1

Declaring Yourself as a Non-Victim

*There is no such thing
as a well-adjusted slave.*

You need never be a victim again. Ever! But in order to function as a non-victim, you must take a hard look at yourself, and learn to recognize the numerous situations in which your strings are being pulled by others.

Your antivictimization stance will involve a great deal more than simply memorizing some assertive techniques and then taking a few risks when other people conspire to manipulate or control your behavior. You probably have already noticed that Earth seems to be a planet on which virtually all the human residents make regular attempts to control each other. And they have evolved unique institutions which are highly accomplished at this regulation. But if you are one of those being governed against your will or better judgment, you are a victim.

It is quite possible to avoid life's victim traps without having to resort to victimizing behavior yourself. To do this, you can begin to redefine what you expect for yourself during your brief visit on this planet. You can start, I recommend, by expecting to be a non-victim, and by looking more carefully at how you behave as a victim.

WHAT IS A VICTIM?

You are being victimized whenever you find yourself out of control of your life. The key word is CONTROL. If you are not pulling the strings, then you are being manipulated by someone or something else. You can be victimized in an endless number of ways.

A victim as described here is not "first of all" someone who is taken advantage of through criminal activity. You can be robbed or swindled in much more damaging ways when you give up your emotional and behavioral controls in the course of everyday life, through forces of habit.

Victims are first of all people who run their lives according to the dictates of others. They find themselves doing things they really would rather not do, or being manipulated into activities loaded with unnecessary personal sacrifice that breeds hidden resentment. To be victimized, as I use the word here, means to be governed and checked by forces outside yourself; and while these forces are un-questionably ubiquitous in our culture, YOU CAN RARELY BE VIC-TIMIZED UNLESS YOU ALLOW IT TO HAPPEN. Yes, people vic-timize *themselves* in numerous ways, throughout the everyday business of running their lives.

Victims almost always operate from weakness. They let them-selves be dominated, pushed around, because they often feel they are not smart enough or strong enough to be in charge of their lives. So they hand their own strings over to someone "smarter" or "stronger," rather than take the risks involved in being self-assertive.

You are a victim when your life is not working for you. If you are behaving in self-defeating ways, if you are miserable, out of sorts, hurt, anxious, afraid to be yourself, or in other similar states which immobilize you, if you aren't functioning in a self-enhancing manner, or if you feel as if you are being manipulated by forces outside of yourself, then you are a victim—and it is my contention that your own victimization is never worth defending. If you agree, then you will be asking: What about relief from victimization? What about freedom?

WHAT IS FREEDOM?

No one is handed freedom on a platter. You must make your own freedom. If someone hands it to you, it is not freedom at all, but the alms of a benefactor who will invariably ask a price of you in return.

Freedom means you are unobstructed in ruling your own life as you choose. Anything less is a form of slavery. If you cannot be unrestrained in making choices, in living as *you* dictate, in doing as you please with your body (provided your pleasure does not interfere with anyone else's freedom), then you are without the command I am talking about, and in essence you are being victimized.

To be free does not mean denying your responsibilities to your loved ones and your fellow man. Indeed, it includes the freedom to make choices to be responsible. But nowhere is it dictated that you must be what others want you to be when their wishes conflict with what you want for yourself. You can be responsible *and* free. Most of the people who will try to tell you that you cannot, who will label your push for freedom "selfish," will turn out to have measures of authority over your life, and will really be protesting your threat to the holds you have allowed them to have on you. If they can help you feel selfish, they've contributed to your feeling guilty, and immobilized you again

The ancient philosopher Epictetus wrote of freedom in this line from his *Discourses:* "No man is free who is not master of himself."

Reread that quote carefully. If you are not the master of yourself, then by this definition you are not free. You do not have to be overtly powerful and exert influence over others to be free, nor is it necessary to intimidate others, nor to try to bully people into submission in order to prove your own mastery.

The freest people in the world are those who have senses of inner peace about themselves: They simply refuse to be swayed by the whims of others, and are quietly effective at running their own lives. These people enjoy freedom from role definitions in which they must behave in certain ways because they are parents, employees, Americans, or even adults; they enjoy freedom to breathe whatever air they choose, in whatever location, without worrying about how everyone else feels about their choices. They are responsible people, but they are not enslaved by other people's selfish interpretations of what responsibility is.

Freedom is something you must insist upon. As you read through this book, you will become aware of what at first may appear to be meaningless trifles of victimization imposed by others, but which are really efforts to seize your strings and to pull you in some direction that will end your freedom, however briefly or however subtly.

You choose freedom for yourself when you begin to develop a whole system of non-victim attitudes and behaviors in virtually every moment of your life. In fact, liberation, rather than slavery to circumstances, will become an internal habit when you practice freedom-commanding behavior.

Perhaps the best way to achieve freedom in your life is to remember this guideline: Never place TOTAL reliance in anyone other than yourself when it comes to guiding your own life. Or, as Emerson said in *Self-Reliance,* "Nothing can bring you peace but yourself."

In working with clients for many years, I have often heard the following kinds of laments: "But she promised me that she would come through, and she let me down." "I knew I should not have let him handle this matter, especially when it meant nothing to him and everything to me." "They let me down again. When will I ever learn?" These are the mournful regrets of clients who have allowed others to victimize them in one way or another, and consequently to encroach on their own freedom.

All this talk about freedom is not to imply that you should in any way isolate yourself from others. On the contrary, non-victims are most often people who love having fun with others. They carry themselves in uplifted, gregarious manners, and they are more secure in their relationships *because* they refuse to let their lives be run by manipulators. They do not need surliness or argumentative stances, because they have learned to feel from *within* that "this is my life, I experience it alone, and my time here on Earth is very limited. I cannot be owned by anyone else. I must be ever alert for any efforts to take away my right to be myself. If you love me, you love me for what I am, not for what you want me to be."

But how can such "healthy freedom" be pulled out of a past full of victim habits cultivated by the very victimizing tendencies of your society and your past?

GETTING OUT OF YOUR VICTIM HABITS

As a child you were often victimized simply by virtue of your stature within your family. Your strings were being pulled constantly, and while you complained privately, you also knew there was very little you could do to take control. You knew you couldn't support yourself, and that if you didn't go along with the program outlined by the big people in your life, there were very few acceptable alternatives available to you. All you had to do was try running away from home for twenty minutes to see how helpless you were on your own. So you went along, and you learned to accept your reality. In fact, having others dictate to you was a very sensible arrangement, since you really were incapable of carrying out any alternate "fantasies." And while you worked at attaining some independence, you were often content to let others do your thinking and life-directing for you.

As an adult, you may still be carrying many left-over habits from childhood, which made some practical sense then, but which set you up as an easy victim now. You may find yourself bulldozed by a "big person," and may have become so accustomed to taking it that you still let it happen, simply out of habit.

Getting out of your victim traps involves, above all, developing new habits. Healthy habits are learned in the same way as unhealthy ones, through practice—*after* you have become aware of what you are going to practice.

While you don't always have to have your own way in everything you do, you can at least expect not to be upset, immobilized, or anxious about anything that goes on in your life. By choosing to eradicate your internal upsets, you'll eliminate one big victim habit which is always self-imposed.

Eliminating victim traps in which you are held and controlled by others, or in which you are unnecessarily frustrated about the way your decisions are turning out, involves a four-part program of (1) learning how to size up your life situations, (2) developing a strong set of non-victim expectations and attitudes, (3) becoming aware of the most prevalent kinds of victimization in your life and in our culture, and (4) creating a set of principles which will guide you to detailed strategies for acting out a philosophy of life based on the unalterable notion that you are not going to become a victim. Numbers 1,

2 and 3 are briefly explored in this opening chapter. Number 4 is dealt with in the remaining chapters, which present successive guidelines for taking on your new non-victim stance.

SIZING UP YOUR LIFE SITUATIONS

Sizing up any potentially victimizing situation before you decide what to do about it is crucial to becoming a non-victim. Whenever you are about to enter into a social interaction, you must have your eyes wide open, so you can avoid being done in even before a possible drama of victimization has begun to unfold on you.

Sizing up your situation means being alert and developing a new kind of intelligence which just naturally keeps you from being abused. It means assessing the needs of the people with whom you will be dealing and anticipating what course of action will be best for you in attaining your own objectives—one of which should be getting along with people who are willing to respect where you stand. Before you even open your mouth or approach someone in a situation in which you could become a victim, you can forecast the kinds of victimizing behavior you might encounter. Effective "sizing-up" is crucial if you are to avoid circumstances which trap you into self-forfeiting actions.

For example, George is returning a defective pair of pants to the department store. He sizes up the clerk as surly and harassed. George is interested only in getting his money back, and not in an unpleasant encounter with a tired or angry salesperson. He knows that once he has had an unpleasant or, worse yet, unsuccessful encounter with the salesperson, he will find it much harder to persuade the manager, since he won't want to overrule the clerk, whose job is stubbornly to enforce the store's "no returns" policy. The clerk in turn may be a prime victim himself who has done nothing but enforce the company line on a policy he is paid to uphold.

So George simply goes straight to the boss, whose job it is to make exceptions to policy if he absolutely must. George may end up asking loudly if it is the store's policy to victimize its customers, but if he plays his cards right, in all likelihood he will get his money back, and never have to resort to any crass behavior.

The final chapter of this book deals with many typical everyday circumstances like this, and presents both victim and non-victim approaches to dealing with them.

Sizing up life situations means not only keeping your eyes open, but also having a set of plans and carefully carrying them out. If your initial plan, Plan A, fails, then you should be dispassionately able to shift into Plan B, Plan C, etc. In the case above, should the manager refuse to cooperate in refunding George's money, then he can shift into Plan B, which might involve talking to the owner, or writing a letter to the management echelons, or perhaps raising his voice (without becoming immobilized by anger), or faking extreme anger, or crying out loud, or staging a nervous breakdown right in the store, or pleading, or anything else.

Whatever your plan, you never invest your own self-worth in its ultimate success or failure. You simply shift gears when necessary, without becoming emotionally tied up. George's goal is simply to get his refund. Yours might be to obtain your tickets or have your steak cooked the way you want it. Whatever the goal, it is just something you want to accomplish, and whether you fail or succeed on a given day is no indicator of your own worth or happiness as a person.

Sizing up life experiences will be easier if you keep a sharp ear cocked for your own use of words and phrases, either in your private thoughts or in your speech, which almost always warn that you are asking to be victimized. Here are some of the more common ones you will have to trade in for better thoughts if you are serious about removing yourself from the victim column.

● *I know I'm going to lose.* This kind of mind-set will almost always guarantee you a place on anybody's tally sheet of available victims. If you decide to believe that you'll "win" what you deserve, you won't tolerate the thought of losing.

● *I get upset whenever I have to confront someone.* If you expect to be upset, then you will seldom disappoint yourself. Change this to, "I refuse to let someone else cause my upset, and I'm not going to upset myself."

● *The little guy never has a chance.* You are not a little guy unless you believe you are. This kind of thinking shows you have put yourself on the losing side against the person you have made into a big guy. Go into every situation expecting to attain your goals.

- *I'll show those bastards that they can't dump on me.* This may sound tough, but with this kind of attitude you will almost always lose. Your goal is not to show anyone anything, but to get whatever concrete benefit a victimizer is trying to do you out of. When you make your goal to "show them," you are already letting them control you. (See Chapter Five on being quietly effective.)

- *I hope they won't get mad at me for asking.* Your concern about them "getting mad" shows you are once again under their control. Once people know you are intimidated by their anger, they will use it to victimize you whenever it will work.

- *They'll probably think I'm stupid if I tell them what I did.* Here you have made someone else's opinion of you more important than your opinion of yourself. If you can be manipulated by others because they know you don't want to be thought of as stupid, they'll almost always give you the "you're stupid" look to victimize you.

- *I'm afraid I'll hurt their feelings if I do what I want.* This is another tack that will almost always end up with you carrying the dirty end of the stick. If others know they can manipulate you by having their feelings hurt, that is precisely what they will do whenever you get out of line or declare your own independence. Ninety-five per cent of hurt feelings are strategy on the "hurtee's" part. People will use their hurt feelings over and over on you if you are gullible enough to buy it. Only victims run their lives on the premise that they must always watch out for others' getting hurt feelings. This is not a license to be obstinately inconsiderate, but simply a basic understanding that people generally stop having hurt feelings when they realize that those feelings can no longer be used to manipulate you.

- *I can't handle this alone: I'll get someone who isn't afraid to do it for me.* Reactions like this will teach you nothing, and will positively hamper you in building your non-victim personality. If you let others fight your battles for you, you'll just get better at evading your own fights and reinforce your fear of being yourself. Moreover, when other people who are good at victimizing find you are afraid to confront your own challenges yourself, they'll simply bypass your "big brother" the next time and impose on you again and again.

- *They really shouldn't do this, it's not fair.* Here you are judging things by the way you would like the world to be, rather than the way it is. People simply *will act* in unfair ways, and your not liking it, or even complaining about it, will do nothing to stop them. Forget your moralistic assessments about what they shouldn't be doing, and instead say, "They *are doing this,* and I am going to confront it in the following ways to make sure they won't get away with it now and don't try it again."

These are just a few very common kinds of self-victimizing thoughts that will lead you down the path of personal ruin.

By sizing yourself and your culture up, you can (1) anticipate effectively, (2) eliminate self-doubts, (3) implement plans A, B, C, etc., (4) steadfastly refuse to be upset or immobilized at the progress you are making, and (5) persevere until you have emerged with what you were seeking. Be assured that you will be well on your way to eliminating at least seventy-five per cent of your victimization by adopting this strategy, and for the rest of the time, when you simply cannot attain your goals, you can learn from your behavior and get on with avoiding impossible circumstances in the future. At no time do you have to be hurt, depressed, or anxious when things don't go the way you would prefer, because that is the ultimate victim-reaction.

NON-VICTIM EXPECTATIONS

Generally speaking, you will become what you expect to become, and you will become a non-victim only when you stop expecting to be victimized. To do this you must begin to develop an attitude of expecting to be happy, healthy, fully functioning, and not abused, based on your *real* capabilities, and not on some ideal of your potential foisted on you by victimizing people or institutions. A good start is to consider four broad and critical areas in which you may have been taught to underestimate your capabilities.

YOUR PHYSICAL CAPABILITIES If you as an adult with good judgment can truly expect to be able to accomplish something with or through your body, virtually nothing can stand in your way; and in extreme situations, your body may reveal capabilities that verge on the "superhuman." Dr. Michael Phillips, writing in *Your Hidden Powers,* tells of an "elderly lady who was travelling with her son across the state by car. At one point in a fairly remote desert region, the car ran into difficulties and the son jacked it up and crawled underneath. The jack slipped and the car fell and pinioned him to the hot tarmac. The woman could see that unless it was removed from his chest, her son would suffocate within minutes." The woman had no time for expectations of not being strong, or failing, and as Dr. Phillips tells it, "Almost without a moment's thought, she grabbed the bumper and held the car up long enough for him to crawl out. As soon as he was clear of the vehicle, her sudden strength disappeared and she dropped the car back on the road. To have achieved such a feat meant that for at least ten full seconds she had lifted several hundred pounds; no small feat for a woman of less than 125 pounds." There are countless stories of such accomplishments. But the key to understanding them is that you can perform seemingly superhuman tasks when you expect to, or when you don't stop to believe that you can't do it.

You can avoid being victimized by your attitudes or expectations about your own physical health. It is possible to work at not expecting to have colds, influenza, high blood pressure, backaches, headaches, allergies, rashes, cramps, and even more serious illnesses such as heart disease, ulcers, and arthritis. Or you can say right now, as you read these paragraphs, that I am wrong and you simply can't help it. And my response to you is, What are you defending? Why should you go on defending those things as only natural, when as a result *your own defense system* will make you ill or immobilized?

What are your payoffs in defending such an attitude? Just begin to think that if you stopped expecting ill health in your life, if you began seriously to change your expectations, maybe, just maybe, some of it would go away. And if it doesn't work for you, then all you'll have is exactly what you have now—sickness, headaches, colds, etc. As a very wise man once said, "Instead of biting off my finger, look to where it's pointing." Your own attitudes can become the greatest medicine in the world, if you learn to make them work for you, rather than in the self-defeating fashion that is so typical in our culture. Dr. Franz Alexander, writing in *Psychosomatic Medicine, Its Principles and Application,* talks about the power of the mind: "The fact that the mind rules the body is, in spite of its neglect by biology and medicine, the most fundamental fact which we know about the process of life."

YOUR MENTAL CAPABILITIES   One of the most alarming research projects ever done in public education shows the danger of letting outside forces limit your expectations for learning achievement. In the 1960s a teacher was given a roster showing the actual I.Q. test scores of the students of one class, and for another class, a roster in which the I.Q. column had been filled in with the students' locker numbers. The teacher assumed that the locker numbers were the actual I.Q.s of the students in the second class, and so did the students when the rosters were posted at the beginning of the semester. After a year it was discovered that in the first class the students with high actual I.Q. scores had performed better than those with low ones. But in the second class the students with higher locker numbers scored significantly higher than those with lower locker numbers!

If you are told you are dumb and let yourself believe it, you will perform accordingly. You will be victimized through your own low expectations, and if you convince others as well, then you are in double jeopardy.

There is a genius residing in you, and you can expect to let its brilliance surface, or you can think of yourself as unfortunately ill-equipped by nature in the whole gray-matter area. Once again, the emphasis is on what you expect from yourself. You can believe it's going to be difficult to learn something new, and you'll find yourself experiencing the difficulty you predicted. You can expect never to learn a foreign language, for instance, and sure enough, you won't.

But in fact, the storage capacity of your grapefruit-sized brain is staggering—conservatively estimated at ten billion units of information. If you want to find out what you *do* know, Michael Phillips suggests this little exercise. "Suppose that you sat down with paper and pencil to write out everything you remembered, including names of people you know or have heard about, experiences from childhood on, plots of books and films, descriptions of jobs you've held, your hobbies, and so on." But you'd better have a lot of time for proving this point to yourself because, as Phillips goes on to say, "If you wrote 24 hours a day, you'd be at it for an estimated two thousand years."

Your built-in memory potential alone is phenomenal. You could train your mind, without much exercise, to remember all the phone numbers you use in a given year, to remember 100 names of strangers introduced at a party and recall them for months afterward, to describe in detail everything that happened to you in the past week, to catalog all the objects in a room after a five-minute visit, and to memorize any lengthy list of random facts. You are indeed a powerful person when it comes to using your brain and mental powers, but you may have a different set of expectations for yourself, which comes out in the following kinds of self-victimizing ways: "I'm really not very smart." "I never could remember names, numbers, languages, or whatever." "I'm not good at mathematics." "I'm a slow reader." "I never could figure out these puzzles."

All the above kinds of statements reflect an attitude that will keep you from achieving anything you might like to accomplish. If you traded those statements in for expressions of confidence and the belief that you can learn to do anything you choose, you would not end up the victim in a painful game of "one-downmanship" with yourself.

Your Emotional Capabilities   You have just as much of an inherent capacity for emotional genius as you do for physical and mental excellence. Once again, it all depends on what kind of expectations you have for yourself. If you expect to be depressed, anxious, afraid, angry, guilty, worried, or to suffer any of the other neurotic behaviors that I detailed in *Your Erroneous Zones,* then you will make these conditions regular parts of your life. You will justify them with self-sentences such as, "It's only natural to be depressed," or, "It's only human to get angry." But it is not only human; it is only neurotic to botch up your life with emotional trauma, and you can stop expecting these kinds of reactions from yourself. You don't have to have these erroneous zones in your life if you begin to live minute to minute and challenge some of the claptrap that many psychological mental-health workers spout. You are what you choose for yourself, and if you stop expecting emotional upset and instability, you will begin to take on the characteristics of a fully functioning person.

Your Social Capabilities   If you see yourself as clumsy, gauche, inarticulate, fumbling, shy, introverted, and so on, you have unsocial expectations which will be followed by appropriately unsocial behavior. Similarly, if you categorize yourself as lower, middle, or upper class, then you will very likely adopt the life style of one class, perhaps for an entire lifetime. If you expect that money will always be hard to come by, your attitude will often obscure any opportunity for changing your financial condition. You'll be content to watch others improve theirs and call them lucky. If you expect you will not find a parking place if you drive into the city, then you will not really look for one, and sure enough, you'll be able to say, "I told you we shouldn't have come into the city tonight." Your expectations for how you'll function in your social structure will largely determine what your life will be like. Think rich if money is what you want for yourself. Begin to picture yourself as articulate, creative, or as anything else you want to be. Don't be discouraged by a few initial letdowns; simply see them as learning experiences, and get on with living. The worst thing that can happen to you for having a new set of social expectations is that you'll stay where you are—and if you're there already, why not expect to be someplace better?

SOME TYPICAL VICTIMIZERS

Once you have begun to adjust your expectations to fit your real capabilities, you will have to deal with victimizers who keep you from fulfilling them. While it is possible to allow yourself to be victimized by virtually anyone in any social setting, some elements in our culture tend to be particularly troublesome. The six categories of victimizers described below will be alluded to in examples throughout the remainder of this book, in much the same way as problems with them crop up in your own daily living.

1. The Family   At a recent lecture I asked all 800 people in the audience to list the five most common situations in which they felt victimized. I received 4000 examples of typical victim situations. *Eighty-three per cent* were connected with the victims' families. Imagine, something like eighty-three per cent of your victimization may be due to your ineffectiveness in dealing with family members who end up controlling or manipulating you. And you must be doing the same to them!

Typical family coercions cited were: being forced to visit relatives, to make phone calls, to chauffeur people around, to suffer nagging parents, children, in-laws, angry relatives, to pick up after everyone, generally to be a servant, not to be respected or appreciated by other family members, to spend time with ingrates, to have no privacy because of family expectations, and on and on.

While the family unit is certainly the cornerstone of American social development, the main institution where values and attitudes are taught, it is also the institution in which the greatest hostility, anxiety, stress, and depression are learned and expressed. If you visit a mental institution and talk with the patients, you will find that virtually all of them have difficulty dealing with various members of their families. It is not neighbors, employers, teachers, or friends whom disturbed people have difficulty handling to the point where they have to be hospitalized. It is almost always family members.

Here is a brilliant little passage from Sheldon B. Kopp's latest book, *If You Meet The Buddha on The Road, Kill Him! The Pilgrimage of Psychotherapy Patients.*

It greatly upset the other members of Don Quixote's family and his community to learn that he had chosen to believe in himself. They were contemptuous of his wish to follow his dream. They did not connect the inception of the Knight's madness with the deadly drabness of his living amidst their pietism. His prissy niece, his know-what's-best-for-everyone housekeeper, his dull barber, and the pompous village-priest, all knew that it was his dangerous books that had filled Don Quixote's failing mind with foolish ideas and so made him crazy.

Kopp then goes on to draw an analogy between the aging Don Quixote and the influence of modern families on seriously disturbed people.

Their household reminds me of the families from which young schizophrenics sometimes emerge. Such families often give the appearance of hyper-normal stability and moralistic goodness. What actually goes on is that they have developed an elaborately subtle system of cues to warn any member should he be about to do something spontaneous, something that would topple the precarious family balance and expose the hypocrisy of their over-controlled pseudo-stability.

Your family can be an immensely rewarding part of your life, and it will be if you make it that way. But the other side of the coin can be a disaster. If you allow your family (or families) to pull your strings, they can pull so hard, sometimes in different directions, that they tear you apart.

Being a non-victim will force you to apply the guidelines of this book most specifically to the immediate members of your family. Family members who feel they own you, whom you feel obliged to defend simply because of a blood relationship, or who feel that they have a RIGHT to tell you how to run your life because of their kinships, must be set straight.

I am not encouraging insurrection within your family, but I strongly urge you to work hard at applying non-victim guidelines most strictly with those who will be the least receptive to your independence, that is, your relatives, be they your spouse, ex-spouse, children, parents, grandparents, in-laws of all descriptions, and relatives of every kind, from uncles and cousins to adopted family members. Your non-victim stance in life will be most seriously tested with this large group of relatives, and if you are victorious here, the rest will be a snap. Families are so tough because their members often feel they own each other, as though they've invested all their life's savings in each other, like so many shares of stock—which allows them to employ GUILT when it comes to dealing with insubordinate members who are turning out to be "bad investments." If you are allowing your family to victimize you, look closely to see if guilt isn't being used to make you stay in line and be "the way the rest of them are."

Many examples of effective non-victim family behavior are given throughout this book. You must arm yourself with the resolve not to be owned if you are to teach your family how you want to be treated. Believe it or not, they will eventually get the message, begin to leave you alone, and most surprisingly, they'll respect you for your declaration of independence. But first, dear friend, be warned that they will try every gimmick in their book to keep you as their victim.

2. THE JOB   Beyond the coercions of your family, you are very likely to feel victimized by the constraints of your job. Employers and bosses often believe that people who work for them automatically

give up their human rights and become chattel. So you may well feel manipulated on the job and intimidated by supervisory personnel or institutional rules and regulations.

You may hate your job itself and feel like a victim because you have to spend eight hours a day doing it. Perhaps you are forced to be away from loved ones because of your job commitments. Maybe you compromise yourself and behave in ways that you would not choose—if you could choose a different job. Perhaps you have trouble getting along with supervisors, or co-workers with whom you disagree. Excessive loyalty to your job—abdicating things like your personal freedom and family responsibilities for it—opens another huge avenue to victimization in job situations.

If your job expectations are frustrated or deflated, if you feel victimized by your job and its responsibilities, take some time to ask yourself what you are doing in a *job* that abuses you as a *person*.

A number of strong myths in the American ethic conspire to victimize you on the job. One is that you must stay at your job no matter what, that you could never get another one if you got *fired*. The very *word* makes it sound like you've been killed in some vengeful way. Another myth is that it is vocationally immature to change jobs regularly, let alone change careers.

Watch out for these kinds of illogical beliefs. If you buy them, they can lead you straight into being a job victim. The gold watch at the end of a fifty-year career with one company is no compensation if you disliked yourself and your job for lo those many years.

You are employable in hundreds of vocations. To be effective you cannot feel *constrained* by your present experience or training but must know that you can do a host of jobs, simply because you are a flexible, enthusiastic, and willing learner. (See Chapter 7 for a more complete treatment of job victimization.)

3. PROFESSIONALS AND AUTHORITY FIGURES People with fancy titles or positions of authority make it easy for you to victimize yourself. Doctors, lawyers, professors, executives, politicians, show-business and sports personalities, etc., have achieved far too inflated a status in our culture. You may find yourself unnerved especially in

the presence of "superpeople" who try to victimize you when you need their specialized services.

Most patients find it very difficult to talk to doctors about their fees, so they just pay whatever they are billed and console themselves with feeling ripped off. Many face unnecessary surgery because they are too abashed to seek out second or third surgical opinions. The ugly victim-syndrome shows itself again. If you can't talk to people about what they are charging you for services they are in business to provide, simply because you have elevated them so far above yourself that you cannot imagine their condescending to hear you, then you have set yourself up to be victimized every time you think about buying medical treatment, legal advice, education, etc. By conceding special titles like "doctor," "professor" or "sir" to these people, you are constantly putting yourself in inferior positions. The only result is that you feel victimized, and may well *be* victimized, because you cannot deal with them on equal footings.

To avoid the victim snares of authority figures, you have to begin seeing them simply as human beings, no more important than you, who perform tasks they have been highly trained for, and for which you are therefore paying very highly. Remember that if anyone ought to be elevated in importance it is the person being served, the one paying the freight. You cannot give any person more esteem than you give yourself and expect to be treated as an equal. If you are not treated as an equal, you are a victim who must look up, ask permission, wait in line, hope for some nice treatment from your supervisor, trust that you won't be overcharged or done in by someone who won't discuss his charges, or does so in a patronizingly hasty manner.

But all of this happens because you let it happen. Professional or authority figures will respect you if you *command* their respect, while treating them with courtesy for their professionalism, but never reacting with awe for their "superhuman" status or allowing them to victimize you in any other way.

4. BUREAUCRACIES   Institutional machinery is a giant victimizer in our country. Most institutions do not serve people very well but use them in highly depersonalized ways. Particularly abusive are government and non-profit monopolistic bureaucracies such as public

utilities. Institutions like these are complex, multitentacled monsters with endless forms, departments, red tape, and employees who don't give a damn—or if they do, are as powerless as those they're trying to serve.

You know how involved it can be to attempt to renew a driver's license or to spend a day in traffic court. You have probably gone through tax-assessment procedures that have taken months or years and involved endless levels of bureaucrats, only to find out you never had a chance in the first place. You know what it is like to have an obvious error in a phone or electric bill corrected. You know too well the vastness of the clumsy machinery involved in getting a computer to stop sending you threatening letters about a bill that never should have been sent. You may also have experienced the long, long lines at unemployment offices, the inconsiderate clerks and the mindless questions and the endless paperwork in quadruplicate, with very little emphasis on what you as a human being are going through. You have heard grizzly stories of people's dealings with Social Security administrators or tax auditors. You know about our glorified court system, which takes years to adjudicate simple things like divorces, and how passionless the maze of people you deal with about a simple traffic violation can be.

The bureaucracies of our world can be deadly for public citizens to handle. Yet they are run by public citizens, who for some reason adopt bureaucratic personalities once they sit behind their desks.

You can adopt some strategies against the big victimizers built into bureaucracies, but bureaucracies themselves are exceedingly difficult, if not impossible, to change. You must really be observant to escape their gnashing jaws.

The most effective strategy is avoidance whenever possible, that is, refusing even to participate in bureaucracies' victimizing games. Understand that many people need attachments to institutions in order to feel important. Therefore, you never let yourself get angry. Look at all your dealings with these organizations as challenges which have nothing to do with you. Henry David Thoreau called for "simplicity, simplicity, simplicity! I say, let your affairs be as two or three, and not a hundred or a thousand." But the monsters our society has created in the name of serving the people are the furthest thing from simple. Our bureaucrats would not only scoff at a man who would live at a pond for two years, but would send him letters and issue him notices about why he couldn't stay, and insist that he buy fishing, hunting, occupancy, and water-use licenses.

5. THE CLERKS OF THE WORLD   If you have spent much time observing how our culture works, you will have noted that by their very job descriptions, many clerks (not all) exist to victimize you in uncountable ways.

Often when you confront clerks with complaints, you are just wasting your breath. Clerks are there to see to it that *you* obey *their* companies' policies, to enforce rules and regulations expressly intended to keep you from skirting the prescribed ways of doing things.

Most clerks have no vested interest in treating their clienteles fairly. A clerk who has sold you shoddy goods doesn't really care if you get your money back, or if you shop somewhere else. Clerks are often doing their jobs if they can keep you from talking to someone who could help you, and besides, they are notorious for taking pleasure in using their companies' "power" to put you down. Clerks love to say, "That's our policy, I'm sorry." "I'm really sorry, but you'll have to send us a letter." Or, "Stand in that line." "Come back next week." "Just plain go away."

Perhaps the best way to deal with the clerks of the world is always to remember these five words: A CLERK IS A JERK!

No, not the person behind the role of clerk; he or she is intrinsically a wonderful, unique, important person, who becomes jerky when turned into a policy enforcer paid to victimize you. Avoid clerks, and deal with people who can be of service to you. If you tell the clerks at a large department store that you'll never shop there again, do you really think they care? Of course not. They view their job as a take-home salary, and whether you like that store is of very little consequence to them. This is not a sour view at all—why should clerks care? Their very role demands that they not care, and they are paid to keep you from violating policies that would cost their employers money, time or effort. But you don't have to deal with them, unless you enjoy being victimized.

By all means, be respectful of people who work as clerks. Perhaps you do it for a living yourself (as I did for many years). But when it is time for you to be effective and to get what you believe you deserve from a department store, insurance company, grocery store, government agency, landlord, school, etc., then start your journey with the attitude that you are not going to be victimized by any clerks, whom you can view as roadblocks to your goals.

6. YOURSELF Yes, you. Despite all the people in the five categories above, and the infinite number of other victimizers and categories of them we could mention, *you* are the one who decides whether you'll be hurt, depressed, angry, worried, afraid, or guilty about anything or anyone in this world. Beyond being upset when people don't behave toward you the way you would prefer, you can victimize yourself in hundreds of ways. Here are some of the more typical categories of self-victimization which you can tackle by yourself:

• *Your training.* You are victimizing yourself if you are still doing what you were once trained to do if you don't enjoy it any longer. If you are forty years old and working as a lawyer or a mechanic *just* because some seventeen-year-old decided that was what you should do, then you are a victim of training that was originally supposed to give you the freedom of a job option you didn't originally have. How often do you trust the judgment of a seventeen-year-old in terms of how you ought to run your life? Well, then, why be stuck with your own seventeen-year-old decisions when you are no longer seventeen? Be what you want for yourself today. Get new training if you aren't happy with yourself and your work.

• *Your history.* You can be a victim of your very own history if you do things because you've always done them that way—for instance, if you are married because you've already invested twenty-five years in your marriage, even though you are miserable today. You may be living someplace you don't like simply because you've always lived there, or because your parents lived there. You may feel you will lose a part of yourself if you "move away" from any large part of your past.

But whatever you've been until today is already over. If you still consult what you've done in the past to decide what you can or can't do today, you are very likely victimizing yourself by ruling out whole realms of present-moment freedom just because you never got around to enjoying them in the past.

• *Your ethics and values.* You may well have adopted a set of ethical beliefs which you know very well don't work for you, and needlessly work against you, but you continue to abide by them anyway, because they define what you've come to expect of yourself. Perhaps you believe you must apologize for speaking or thinking in contrary ways. Or perhaps you believe that lying is *always* bad. Perhaps you've adopted some sexual ethics that keep you from enjoying your sexuality. Whatever the case, you can examine your ethics on a regular basis and refuse to continue to victimize yourself by holding onto beliefs that just plain don't work.

• *Your behavior toward your body.* You can become very self-destructive toward your body and become the ultimate victim—a corpse. Yours is the only body you'll ever get, so why make it something that isn't healthy, attractive, and wonderful to be around? By letting yourself get fat through improper diet or lack of exercise, you victimize yourself. By allowing your body to become addicted to pills such as tranquilizers, or alcohol, or tobacco, you are a very effective self-exploiting victim. By not giving your body adequate rest periods or by fouling it up with stress and tension, you are allowing yourself to be victimized. Your body is a powerful, well-tuned, highly efficient instrument, but you can abuse it in so many ways by simply rejecting it, or fueling it with low-caliber fuels and addictive substances that will only demolish it in the end.

• *Your self-portraits.* As we have already seen in connection with your capabilities, your own self-images can contribute to your being victimized in life. If you believe that you can't do something, that you're unattractive, that you're not intelligent, and so on, you will also believe that others see you that way, and you will act that way, and even *be* that way. Working at healthy self-images is crucial if you are to avoid being a knee-jerk victim, with responses as predictable as when the doctor smacks your knee with a little hammer.

IN CLOSING

If you use your imagination, you will find innumerable ways to victimize yourself. But by applying your imagination in constructive ways, you can, by the same token, find the means to eliminate your victim status. The choice is up to you.

2

Operating from Strength

Fear itself does not exist in the world. There are only fearful thoughts and avoidance behaviors.

WHERE DO YOU STAND? TWENTY-ONE-ITEM TEST

Do you typically behave from positions of weakness, or of strength? The very first guideline for being a non-victim is: Never operate from weakness. Below is a twenty-one-item questionnaire (arranged by the categories of common victimizers treated in Chapter One), which you can use to assess whether you regularly operate from weakness or strength.

FAMILY

Yes   No

_____   _____   1. Do you find yourself just "going along" with what others in your family want to do, and resenting it?

_____   _____   2. Are you the person designated to chauffeur, "pick up after others," or generally run your life on "their" schedule?

_____ _____ 3. Do you find it difficult to say NO to your parents, spouse or children, and to express your feeling about it?

_____ _____ 4. Are you often afraid to tell relatives that you don't want to talk on the telephone without making up excuses?

JOB

_____ _____ 5. Do you avoid asking for promotions and presenting strong cases for your requests?

_____ _____ 6. Do you shun confronting your superiors when you have differences of opinions with them?

_____ _____ 7. Do you find yourself doing menial tasks on the job and disliking this role?

_____ _____ 8. Do you always work late when requested, even when it interferes with something important in your personal life?

PROFESSIONAL AND AUTHORITY FIGURES

_____ _____ 9. Is it difficult for you to call your doctor or dentist by his first name?

_____ _____ 10. Do you find yourself "just paying the bill," even when you believe you've been charged too much?

_____ _____ 11. Is it difficult for you to tell someone with "status" how you feel when they have let you down?

_____ _____ 12. Do you just accept your grades from a professor, even if you feel you deserve something better?

BUREAUCRACIES

_____ _____ 13. Do you end up waiting in lines when you deal with government agencies?

_____ _____ 14. Do you avoid asking to see supervisors when you have been abused?

_____ _____ 15. Do you avoid confronting bureaucrats who you know are giving you doubletalk and being evasive?

THE CLERKS OF THE WORLD

_____ _____ 16. Do you do as you're told when clerks tell you that you have to obey policies such as "no returns"?

_____ _____ 17. Is it hard for you to tell clerks to their faces that you are feeling abused?

_____ _____ 18. Do you find yourself sitting at restaurant tables that you dislike and not asking for better ones?

YOURSELF

_____ _____ 19. Do you avoid conversations with strangers?

_____ _____ 20. Do you find yourself unwillingly donating to panhandlers, talking to sidewalk weirdos and wanting to escape, etc.?

_____ _____ 21. Do you find yourself asking permission to speak or to do things?

If you responded yes to any of these, it is indicative of your victimization as a result of operating from weakness.

A NEW LOOK AT STRENGTH

Being strong in no way implies being powerful, manipulative, or even forceful. By operating from strength, I mean leading your life from the twin positions of *worth* and *effectiveness*.

You are always a worthy, important human being, and there is never any reason to conduct yourself, or allow others to pull or push you, in any direction in which your basic merit as a human being is challenged. Moreover, in any situation you have a choice between

(1) being effective and reaching your goals, or (2) being ineffective and, ultimately, being restricted from doing what you desire. In most cases—not all, but most—you can be effective, and in *all* cases, you can operate from the position of your own intrinsic worth as a person.

In dealing with your self-worth, remind yourself that by definition it must come from yourself. You are worthy not because others say so, or because of what you accomplish, or because of your achievements. Rather, you are precious because you say so, because you believe it, and most importantly, because you ACT as if you are worthy.

Being a non-victim starts with the principle of saying and believing that you are valuable, but it is put into practice when you begin behaving as if you are worthwhile. This is the essence of strength, and of course, of not being a victim. You can't act out of needs to be powerful or intimidating, but you must act from strength which guarantees you will be treated as a worthy person simply because you believe down to your very soul that you do count.

Being effective is not a universal given, as is your own self-esteem. At times you will not attain your goals. Occasionally you will find people irrationally impossible to deal with, or encounter situations where you'll have to back off or compromise to avoid being further victimized. You can, however, cut these "losses" down to an unavoidable minimum, and more important, you can eliminate totally the emotional upsets of being thwarted now and then.

Being effective simply means you apply all your personal resources and use all available strategies, short of stepping on others, to achieve your objectives. Your own worth and personal effectiveness are the cornerstones of operating from strength.

Keep in mind that a breakdown of the word *invalid,* meaning a physically weak person, comes out *in valid*. By living your life from a position of emotional weakness you are not only a loser most of the time, but you virtually invalidate yourself as a person. "But," you may ask, "why would I ever do a thing like that to myself?"

FEAR: SOMETHING THAT RESIDES IN YOU

Most of the reasons you'd give yourself for not operating from strength involve some kind of fear of "what will happen if . . ." You may even admit that you are often "paralyzed *by fear*." But what is it that you think comes from somewhere out of the blue and im-mobilizes you? If you started on a scavenger hunt today and you were told to bring back a bucket full of fear, you could look forever, but you'd always come home empty-handed. Fear simply does not exist out there in the world. It is something that you do to yourself by thinking fearful thoughts and having fearsome expectations. No one in this world can hurt you unless you allow it, and then of course you are hurting yourself.

You may be victimized because you've convinced yourself that some person won't like you, or that some disaster will befall you, or that there are any of thousands of other excuses, if you do things your way. But the fear *is internal,* and is supported by a neat little system of thoughts which you cleverly use to avoid dealing directly with your self-imposed dread. You may express these thoughts to yourself in sentences like the following:

I'll fail
I'll look stupid.
I'm unattractive.
I'm not sure.
They might hurt me.
They might not like me.
I'd feel too guilty.
I'll lose everything.
They might get mad at me.
I might lose my job.
God won't let me into heaven.
Something bad will probably happen if I do.
I know I'll feel awful if I say that.
I won't be able to live with myself.

Thoughts like these betray an internal support system and main-tain a fear-based personality which keeps you from operating from strength. Every time you reach inward and come up with one of these fear sentences, you've consulted your weakness mentality, and the victim stamp will soon be evident on your forehead.

If you have to have a guarantee that everything will be all right before you take a risk, you will never get off first base, because the future is promised to no one. There are no guarantees on life's services to you, so you'll have to toss away your panicky thoughts if you want to get what you want out of life. Moreover, almost all your fearful thoughts are purely head trips. The disasters you envision will rarely surface. Remember the ancient sage who said, "I'm an old man, and I've had many troubles, most of which have never happened."

A client once came to me for counseling with a chronic fear problem. As a little girl in Canada, Donna had one time walked four miles home because she was afraid of what the bus driver would say to her because she didn't know where to put the money, and was afraid to ask. She related how she had operated from fear throughout her childhood—so terrified, for instance, of giving oral book reports that she literally made herself sick with high temperatures and uncontrollable vomiting which kept her out of school when it was her turn to speak in front of the class. As an adult she had gone into bathrooms at parties and not permitted herself to relieve her bladder because she feared people would hear her urinating and laugh.

Donna was a bundle of self-doubts. Fear ruled her life. She came for counseling because she was tired of being victimized by her own fears. After several sessions in which I encouraged her to take on some "easy risks," she began to learn firsthand the antidote to eliminating fear. She started small, by simply telling her mother that she would not be able to come over the following week. For her this was a major step. Eventually she began to practice confronting clerks and waitresses when she felt she was being given poor service. Finally she agreed to give a five-minute talk to one of my university classes. She sweated internally about her debut, but she went through with it.

It was amazing to see the transformation that took place in Donna as she developed fear-challenging behavior. She was sensational in front of the class, and not one person even detected her nervousness and self-doubt. Furthermore, Donna today (some three years later) has become a Parent Effectiveness Trainer and she currently gives her own workshops for large audiences throughout metropolitan New York. No one can believe she was once a tote bag full of fears. She tossed them aside by effectively challenging the folly of her internal fear-support system, and by taking risks, which is now natural and fun for her.

The brilliant English author and lexicographer Samuel Johnson once wrote,

All fear is painful, and when it conduces not to safety, is painful without use—Every consideration, therefore, by which groundless terrors may be removed, adds something to human happiness.

Johnson's words are still vital some two hundred years after he wrote them. If your fears are groundless, they are useless, and removing them is indispensable for your happiness.

EXPERIENCE AS AN ANTIDOTE TO FEAR

Donna's case history illustrates one of life's most significant lessons: You cannot learn anything, undermine any fear, unless you are willing to DO something. Doing, the antidote to fear and most self-defeating behavior, is shunned by most victims who operate from weakness. But the maxim of education that makes the most sense to me is:

I hear: I forget.
I see: I remember.
I Do: I understand.

You will never know what it feels like to get rid of a fear until you risk behavior that confronts it. You can talk to your therapist until you turn into a frog, you can brood until your teeth itch and your brain sweats, and you can listen to friends tell you there's nothing to be afraid of until your cochlea collapses, but you'll never truly understand until you *do*. Just as no one can teach you fear, no one can teach you not to be afraid. Your fears are your own unique sensations, and you alone are going to have to challenge them.

At a beach I once heard a mother yell at her child, "Don't you go into that water until you know how to swim!" How about that for the logic of learning? It's like saying, "Don't try to stand up until you know how to walk," or, "Stay away from that ball until you know how to throw it." If other people want to stop you from doing and expect you to learn without it, you'll have to see that as their peculiar problem. If big people got away with it when you were a child, and you blame that for your immobilization from fear today, then you are really stuck. What they did to you as a child can never be undone, so if you use that as your excuse for not doing now, you're always going to be the same victim. Understand your childhood experience as the result of your parents having done what they knew how to do, and get on with doing what you know how to do in changing yourself today. You just have to get out there, grovel around, fail a lot, try this, change that—in a word, experiment. But can you really imagine that experimenting and experiencing, will *decrease* your wisdom and chances for success? If you refuse to give yourself the necessary experiences, you are saying to yourself, "I refuse to know." And refusing to know will make you weak and assure your victimization by others.

You can't know strength unless you are willing to test yourself—and if all tests always succeeded, there would be no need for them, so you can't stop testing whenever you fail. When you get to the point where you are willing to attempt anything that seems worthwhile to YOU (not them, you), then you will understand experience as the antidote to fear. Benjamin Disraeli, the witty nineteenth-century English statesman and author, said it quite succinctly in his earliest writings:

> Experience is the child of Thought, and Thought is the child of Action. We cannot learn men from books.

First you think, and then you do, and only thirdly do you know. And that is how you challenge all the timidity that keeps you a victim.

COURAGE: A NECESSARY COMMODITY FOR NON-VICTIMS

Willingness to confront fear is called courage. You will find it very hard to overcome your fears unless you are willing to muster up some valor, even though you will find that you already possess it if you are willing to realize it.

Courage means flying in the face of criticism, relying on yourself, being willing to accept and learn from the consequences of all your choices. It means believing enough in yourself and in living your life as you choose so that you cut the strings whose ends other people hold and use to pull you in contrary directions.

You can make your mental leaps toward courage by repeatedly asking yourself, *"What is the worst thing that could happen to me if . . . ?"* When you consider the possibilities realistically, you will almost always find that nothing damaging or painful *can* happen when you take the necessary steps away from being a knee-jerk victim. Usually you will find that, like a child afraid of the dark, you are afraid of nothing, because nothing is the worst thing that could happen to you.

Take my old friend Bill, an actor who was afraid to audition for a part in a Broadway play. I asked him to think about the worst thing that could happen to him if he failed. He started to break down his own fear when he answered, "The worst thing that could happen is that I wouldn't get the part I already don't have."

Failing generally means ending up where you started, and while it may not be utopia, it is certainly a situation you can handle. After the "worst-thing" method had shown Bill the absurdity of his fears, they disbanded and he performed beautifully in the audition. He didn't get that particular part, but four months later, after numerous auditions, he finally wound up with a role in a play. Action was the only way for Bill to break out of his victimization and get a role he desperately wanted. While he may not have *felt* brave, he mustered up the pluck to *act*. Cora Harris, the American author, said it this way,

The bravest thing you can do when you are not brave is to profess courage and act accordingly.

I like the idea of professing courage, because the important thing to do is act, rather than to try to convince yourself of how brave you are or aren't at any given moment.

UNDERSTANDING YOUR OPERATING-FROM-WEAKNESS DIVIDENDS

Any time you catch yourself paralyzed by fear—in a word, victimized—ask yourself, "What am I getting out of this?" Your first temptation will be to answer, "Nothing." But go a little deeper and you'll ask why people find it easier to be victims than to take strong stances of their own, to pull their own strings.

You can seemingly avoid a lot of risks, avoid ever "putting yourself on the spot," by simply giving up and letting others take control. If things go badly you can blame whoever *is* pulling your strings, call them bad names, and neatly avoid your own greater responsibility. At the same time you can conveniently avoid *having* to change; you are "free" to remain a "good little victim," getting regular dividends of phony approval from the victimizers of the world.

The payoffs of weakness almost all come out of your avoidance of risks. For fuller descriptions of the total payoff systems for almost all neurotic behaviors, consult *Your Erroneous Zones,* but here, keep in mind that it is crucial for you to always be appraised of your own reward system, self-defeating though it may be, as you work toward improving the quality of your life in every behavioral and mental dimension.

NEVER PLACE ANYONE'S HEAD ABOVE YOUR OWN

If you are ready to give "operating from strength" a serious go, you will have to stop placing other people above yourself in value and worth. Whenever you give another person more prestige than you give yourself, you have set yourself up to be victimized. Sometimes placing heads above your own has been sanctified in social custom, as in the use of props and titles, and you may have to break custom to make your point. People who are good at victimizing often insist that you concede them their titles, and then proceed to call you by your first name.

A cardinal principle for all adults is, *Always deal with people on a first-name basis unless they make it clear that they need to be addressed in some other way.*

Tom, a neighbor of mine, understood the wisdom of dealing with people on a first-name basis, and on principle he refused to hand out titles when doing so would put him at a disadvantage. One day he went to his son's school to talk with the principal about changing his son's class. The boy's teacher had obviously been insensitive to the boy's needs, and a more effective class was available. Tom knew the school's policy was no changing of classes, even though it was being enforced at the expense of his son's education.

The principal (consciously or not, it doesn't matter) employed a variety of power games designed to put Tom on the defensive. To begin with, the principal sat behind a large desk, and left Tom a chair that was too small and without anything that Tom could "hide" behind. When the secretary brought Tom in, the principal acted very busy. He had very little time for this trifling matter. And most importantly, the secretary introduced him to Tom as Mr. Clayborn.

Tom had asked the secretary before the meeting what the principal's first name was. She had responded, "Why, I'm not even sure. He's just always been Mr. Clayborn. After all, he is the principal of the school."

So Tom's very first question to Mr. Clayborn was, "What is your first name?"

The principal paused for a moment. He had never encountered such an opening from a parent, and he knew that he was dealing with someone who was not, like all the others, going to accept a shaky position.

"Robert," he replied.

Tom asked, "Do you prefer Robert or Bob?"

"Uh . . . Bob," the principal replied, and Tom had won two most important points—because he resolutely refused to be intimidated by the ploys of power, and particularly by the use of titles.

Tom didn't have to beat the desk in winning his right to be dealt with as an equal. He carried himself as a person who believed in himself, and he saw the "principal's status" as a factor to be dealt with rationally. He did not let himself get trapped, victimized, by giving his own esteem away to someone who would gladly ignore it. By the way, Tom got the transfer for his son. In this case he was effective largely because he believed he was worthy and acted so, and because strategy had put him in a position of strength from the opening of the encounter.

The weapon of a title is particularly strong in the hands of people who are paid directly to serve you. (Public-school officials, for example, you pay indirectly, through government.) Your banker, landlord, doctor, dentist, lawyer, etc., are *people with whom you do business.* If you do not feel comfortable dealing with them on a first-name basis, you ought to ask yourself why. Could it be that you really don't believe you are significant enough to go around calling important people by their first names?

I've found that I have been able to operate on a first-name basis with *everyone* in my life, and it has never caused me, or anyone else, any embarrassment or hard feelings. If your boss wants and needs to be given a title, then by all means give it—but let the need obviously come from him or her, not from you. If you serve these people's needs by letting them have titles, then waltz right into title-dispensing—but never without asking yourself, "Whose need am *I* serving?" If you *have* to do it, then you are placing their heads above your own.

You can also elevate others to prominence by sending unmistakable signals that you are willing to be duped. It is just plain easier to sucker someone who expects it than to foil someone who expects never to be victimized. You may send out victim signals unconsciously, so you have to watch your victim profile carefully. Do you appear under shadows of your own recrimination and self-put-down? Do you start out apologizing for taking people's time—silently telling them their time must be more valuable than yours? Ask yourself why anyone else's time should count more. It shouldn't, unless that person counts more—and of course that is up to you.

The only time you might go along with elevating others above yourself is when it will work as an act in a good strategy. If assuming a "poor me" stance will elicit favorable treatment for you, for instance, then by all means, go into the act if you can. But pretending to elevate others should be a rare tactic used only when nothing else will work, and since it means sending out signals to the other person that say, "Victimize that poor soul," you have to be positive it won't backfire. If you plan to get your greedy landlord to reduce your rent by playing helpless, make sure that sympathy for the helpless is the *only* definite point of vulnerability in your particular landlord's mercenary armor. If you're wrong, you may get an increase instead of a reduction, since he knows you'll scrape the money up somewhere, and assumes you don't have the backbone to fight the increase. If the landlord knows he has to deal with someone who believes in herself and is not to be browbeaten, who is determined and will stand up and fight effectively, rather than with malice, then he will be more likely to respect her wishes. The "poor little me" act can be used, but use it only sporadically, and with a great deal of sizing up beforehand.

A final word about not being obnoxious is in order. *Strength* is a word I use with a great amount of prethought. I've been careful to define it in explicit terms. Being cantankerous, unruly, obnoxious, deceitful, and the like is not advocated, since it will almost always turn away the very people you want to have help you. I am, of course, supportive of being able to be obnoxious if it is called for on extreme occasions, which I will talk about in later sections. You just don't have to be passive or weak as you walk through your life steps, and that is really the fundamental lesson of this chapter. Be a worthy, effective, self-important you, rather than a sniveling permission-seeking victim who believes that everyone is more important than you are.

ISN'T IT IRONIC—PEOPLE RESPECT STRENGTH

If you really want to be respected, take a hard look at those who are so expert at getting respect. You will quickly deduce that you will not gain anyone's respect, including your own, by operating from weakness. You must set aside the idea that people will not like you if you behave assertively.

Time after time, parents have confided to me that the child in their family they most admire is the one they never quite succeeded in taming. While the parents may have tried hard to get the child into line, to conform, they had to admit they had a rebel on their hands. They may have cursed that kid, tried punishment, bribery, guilt or whatever, but they just couldn't get acquiescence.

When parents reveal these things to me in counseling sessions, I almost always detect a gleam of admiration as they recount the "horrors" of trying to raise a mutinous child. But when I confront them with their suppressed respect, the reply is almost always the same, "Yeah, I guess I really *do* respect that kid . . . he [she] has the kind of moxie I always wished I could muster."

Virtually all families have "unmanageable" members—and while the entire families will often conspire to make them more compliant, they cannot extinguish the natural glimmers of respect and awe they feel at their rebels' refusals automatically to be like everyone else.

Whenever you find yourself standing up for what you believe and wondering what everyone else is thinking, rest assured that if you took a private poll, you would find almost everyone secretly pulling for you, and admiring your attitude of toughness. People have developed special affinities for underdogs, and we often find ourselves rooting hard for those who are given very little chance of succeeding. So not setting your goals according to which ones will win the immediate approval of others may, paradoxically, help you get their approval in the long run—and no one is denying that it feels better to receive approval than to be rejected. It might just be comforting to know that the people whose approval you are most concerned about are much more prone to respect you when you behave from your own convictions than when you simply tag along and do what is expected of you.

Cathy was a client of mine who relayed how she learned this lesson firsthand. She was scheduled to attend a convention seminar for which she had preregistered to assure herself a seat. But when she arrived at the meeting, the instructor told her it was overbooked, and she would have to settle for a substitute meeting in another building.

Cathy was full of resolve, and although it had not been her habit, several months of counseling had encouraged her to be more assertive and take more risks. She confronted the instructor in front of the whole group and insisted that she be admitted. When the instructor attempted to dissuade her with evasive language and a lot of "yes-buts," she refused to budge. Finally the instructor conceded and told her to stay, but asked her please not to tell the registrar, since she was violating a load limit that had been arbitrarily set by the management.

After several hours in the seminar, the topic of Cathy's intractable behavior came up. She related that she had feared everyone would think her a pernicious boor who had bulldozed her way in where she wasn't wanted. But on the contrary, virtually all the seminar members revealed how proud they were of her, how they had secretly been pulling for her, and how they wanted to learn from her how to take those same kinds of non-victim risks in their own lives.

Cathy was flabbergasted as she told me about this incident.

"Imagine," she said, "people were actually asking *me* for help—and I'd always thought of myself as cautious and timid!"

In *Man and Superman* George Bernard Shaw summed up the internal feeling of strength and self-satisfaction that comes from taking risks:

> This is the true joy in life, the being used for a purpose recognized by yourself as a *mighty one;* . . . the being a force of Nature instead of a feverish selfish little clod of ailments and grievances complaining that the world will not devote itself to making you happy.

Indeed, a *mighty one* is a most apt description of how you'll feel when you think enough of yourself to tackle the world on your own terms.

SAMPLE DIALOGUES AND SPECIFIC TECHNIQUES TO HELP YOU OPERATE FROM STRENGTH

You now know that strength is the name of the game, that people will respect you more for being vigorous, and that your debilitating fears are self-imposed. You also know you'll need courage to turn down the self-defeating rewards of being non-assertive. But courage is something you must choose in the face of every challenge, not an attribute you can obtain forever.

Below are some strategies which will help you deal with others from positions of strength and confidence in typical "victim situations" that confront all human beings.

• From this moment on, try to stop automatically asking anyone permission to speak, to think, or to behave. Eliminate supplication, in favor of declaration. Instead of, "Would you mind if I asked you a question?" use, "I'd like to know if . . ." For, "Would you mind terribly if I brought this back for a refund?" try, "I'm bringing this back because I am dissatisfied." And replace, "Is it all right, dear, if I go out for an hour?" with, "I'm going out, dear, is there anything that you'd like me to do for you?" Only slaves and prisoners must ask permission, and as I said at this book's outset, the "well-adjusted slave" is a myth.

• Look directly into the eyes of the people you talk to. When you look down or to the side, you send signals that you really aren't sure of yourself and put yourself in a prime position to be victimized. By looking directly at the person, even if you are nervous, you send the message that you are not afraid to deal with the person up front.

• Your posture and body language should also communicate self-confidence and personal strength. Stand as tall as you are. When you sit, avoid slouching. Don't cover your face with your hands or clutch yourself nervously. If you think confidently, you can also eliminate twitches, grimaces, and even blushing. And speak in a firm rather than subdued or weak voice.

• Work on your own language, particularly at eliminating empty pauses and incessant "uh-huhs," "hmmms," and "you-knows." These habits broadcast insecurity and stifle effective communication. If necessary, talk more slowly and deliberately. If you decide to be conscious of your language you can change your weak speech almost overnight.

• If someone asks you for a loan, whether of money, materials, time, or talent, which you don't want to give, you must be prepared to operate from strength, or you will immediately become a victim. Practice saying to yourself, "I'd rather not be a lender," or, "No, I really don't like to be a creditor." You don't have to make up a lot of fancy excuses, or beat around the bush about it, and then end up making the loan anyway and feeling victimized. Simply state outright what you are going to do and you'll find (1) that you won't be harassed, because you've made your position clear right from the beginning, and (2) your friends and relatives will very likely end up respecting you more for your straightforwardness. If you are afraid friends will hate you just because you've exercised your right not to do something you know you'll be unhappy with, ask yourself, "Do I really want friends who will reject me for being myself?"

Friends are not people who insist that you be other than what you choose to be. But parasites will dislike you when you don't let them feed off you. Here the "worst thing that can happen" to you is that someone who wants to use you won't like you, and will probably stay away from you in the future. And what's so terrible about that? Of course if you don't mind lending, then by all means, lend: just do it effectively.

• Call people to whom you are accustomed to giving titles by their first names. Even if you only do it once with your dentist, doctor, lawyer, etc., try it to see what the results will be, and then ask yourself if your fears of doing it had any basis. And if you should decide not to be a first-name-basis person at all, know in your own heart (by having done it) that you always have the option. If you are anxious, afraid, or even unable to do it, then examine very closely why you should feel so uneasy about so simple a thing as calling another human being by his name. Then get over your fear and do it. You'll probably find yourself feeling very good about your new-found confidence, and none of the disasters you have imagined are likely to happen.

• If you are a non-smoker and can't stand smoke, muster up the courage to say something when other people's smoking bothers you. You don't have to be nasty; just speak from strength. "I would appreciate it if you'd not smoke right now." You're not asking a smoker's permission to ask them not to smoke; you are saying what you would like. If they refuse, which in some situations they have a right to, then you can exercise your own option to get up and move. But you never have to just sit there and allow yourself to fume, inside and out. What is the worst thing that could happen? The smoker could go on smoking, which he or she is already doing. But nine times out of ten, smokers will respect your request. Very few will just sit there and arrogantly smoke once they know they are being bothersome. If they really want to smoke, they can and will go somewhere else for a few minutes.

• Learn to use your anger or hurt effectively, rather than letting them victimize you. If your little child insists on playing in the street and you want to make it clear that you won't tolerate such behavior, by all means raise your voice, act angry and forceful, but be sure you are doing it for effect. If you walk away from such an episode with your heart beating faster, your blood pressure raised twenty points, full of internal rage, you have been victimized by the behavior of a child who doesn't even know better. Instead, you can be firm and walk away from the situation saying to yourself, "Hey, I was terrific, I really let her know that I meant business, and I'm not the least bit upset." By operating from your own personal strength you avoid ulcers, hypertension, rage, anxieties, and so on, simply by using your skills effectively.

• When dealing with funeral directors, don't let them use your grief to victimize you. State right out what you want, what you're willing to spend, and if they use the tactics of guilt on you, simply walk out, with the remark that you'll talk when they are willing to listen.

The tactic of refusing to talk with people who won't hear what you're clearly saying, and walking a short distance away, is most effective. When they come after you with apologies, tell them you just won't waste your time talking to people who refuse to acknowledge your desires.

Hearing you and then suggesting the direct opposite of what you've said is a victimizer's best weapon. But you don't have to buy it, and absenting yourself is the most efficient way of teaching someone by your behavior, rather than with meaningless verbal exchanges.

• Never be afraid to go over someone's head in order to be heard. College professors who dangle grades as threats, tax auditors who use intimidation by exploiting your ignorance of complicated laws, public-utilities personnel who threaten you with their bigness, etc., all have superiors to whom they must answer. A simple phone call, or a well-written letter, sent via registered mail to the president, chairman, or whomever, is a very effective antidote to being victimized by people in positions of power. Once you see that pressing any encounter with people who are responsible to superiors is going to result in your losing, make it clear that you will not hesitate to go over their heads—and then, by all means, if necessary, follow through.

• Work at being dispassionate when dealing with potential victimizers. Never let them know you are anxious, afraid, or intimidated. Always remember not to confuse your worth and happiness as a person with your ultimate victory or defeat in any encounter. View your "win-lose" situations as games you can have fun at, rather than constantly telling yourself, "This means a lot to me." Resolve to be effective and go into such encounters with game plans, but *always* work at suppressing outward signs of fear or intimidation. Once an adversary sees that you view an encounter as crucial to your life and therefore upsetting to you, you can be pushed into saying things you don't mean, and even behaving irrationally. Far better simply to send out signals of determination which keep people from even imagining that they can control your emotions with their behavior. And lo and behold, as you practice not letting others control your emotions, you'll begin to take over control of yourself, which will lead to far more fulfillment for yourself—and yes, to many more victories.

• When applying or being interviewed for a job, never let yourself say things like, "I'm really not sure if I could handle this," or, "I've never had any training for this, but I think I could learn." You can just as well say to yourself, and convey to the person to whom you are applying, that you can learn to do anything, because you have already tested yourself in so many different situations that you know you have the flexibility to handle the job. Be enthusiastic about yourself and your qualifications, and don't hesitate to let your interviewer know that you are a person who can learn readily. While a few interviewers who are easily threatened by strong people might be turned off by your self-confidence, you can usually size them up quickly, and the vast majority will appreciate self-confidence as a trait that will be immensely useful to their firms. If you do encounter a weak-kneed interviewer, tell the president of the company about it, and request another shot with a different interviewer. This kind of perseverance will work for you far more often than it will fail.

• Never be hesitant to talk in personal ways about yourself. Challenge the fear that anyone can hurt you by finding out "personal" facts about your life; the old fear of the "other person hurting me" is about ninety-nine per cent fallacy. If you are free to express yourself about virtually anything, and aren't visibly offended when this or that topic surfaces, you will be far stronger than if you keep numerous little pockets of off-limits sensitivity about yourself. While it is not necessary to reveal your private sexual fantasies, or to haul all the skeletons out of your closet, you can certainly eliminate the idea that people will destroy you if they find out what kind of a person you really are.

Be candid about yourself. Share yourself when you feel like it. Get rid of the idea that you can't reveal yourself because it's dangerous. If you don't want to be revealing that is one thing, but if you fear it, that is quite another. And you will find it healthy to practice challenging all the reasons why you say you don't want to talk about yourself. If you've been shy all your life, if you've cried easily, been easily intimidated, overly aggressive, or anything, just what can anyone do with that information that will hurt you? Almost every answer you give will turn out to be one of those internal disasters. Will your boss fire you? Hardly. But even if you *did* get fired, there are other jobs. Will people spread rumors about you? Probably not. But if they do, why should you run your life on the basis of what others say? And people will spread rumors even if you don't like it or never say a thing, so why stifle yourself to avoid their gossip?

 • If you suspect that someone you are paying for service is trying to victimize you by not doing what they've promised, such as fixing your car a certain way, then decide to stay and observe them doing it—provided this doesn't further victimize you by wasting too much of your time.

Have servicemen show you evidence that they've done what they said they would do, and don't believe for a second that you must sign a blanket agreement in advance to pay whatever they charge. Tell them in advance that you don't want a new oil filter, or sure enough, you'll get one, whether you need one or not. Be firm about asking for explanations of charges you feel are unjustified. In a restaurant, if a waiter overcharges you, take it up with the management, and do not tip the waiter, if you feel it was not 100% accidental. (Waiters will ALWAYS apologize profusely and claim overcharges were not intentional.) You can simply refuse to reward incompetence *or* attempted rip-offs.

Get in the habit of checking every invoice you receive. If you find an overcharge, let the company know precisely how you feel about it, and refuse to do business with people you feel are cheating you. And send a formal complaint to your local Better Business Bureau or Consumers Protection Agency. A two-minute letter to one of these organizations will help put a stop to such practices. You might believe overcharging is rare and usually accidental, but I have found that restaurant bills are frequently incorrect, and that about ninety per cent of the "mistakes" in my bills happen to be overcharges. Apparently the laws of statistical probability do not apply to these "mistakes." When you see it happening to you, let the management know immediately, and follow your complaint up with determination if you are inclined to make a point. If not, just let the management know you won't pay the charge and you won't bring your business back to them.

• When you are told you must wait some ridiculous length of time for furniture delivery, car delivery, etc., don't be victimized by accepting the dealer's assumption that you must get what you want at his convenience, or his word that no one else can get it for you any faster. If it's a car you want or need soon, check out automobile dealerships in other localities, and even other states if necessary. Let the slow-delivery sales people know that you are not interested in any such wait, and deal specifically with the management, rather than with clerks. Let the management know you will go to the competition if they can give you a quicker delivery date. Talk to wholesalers and even manufacturers to see if you can get special speed-up service. Never pay in advance, and get a commitment in *any* contract that you can get your minimal deposit returned if the dealer does not live up to the details of the contract. You don't have to be picky, simply firm and strong, and not just another one of those victims who says, "Oh, only ten weeks to wait. That's the way it'll have to be, I guess, even though I wanted it sooner."

A client of mine, when told that he couldn't get delivery on a car in New York for eight weeks, called a dealer in Michigan and learned he could get one out there in four days, for $300 less than the New York price. He drove twelve hours for the pick-up, and had a pleasant vacation trip saving money on his new car.

Virtually any situation can be turned into a victory if you don't expect to be victimized, and won't accept it.

• Refuse to pay for poor quality or poor service as a rule, on principle. If your restaurant salad tastes like straw, or your pie is dried out, or whatever, simply point it out, and ask to have it subtracted from your bill. If you get a waiter or cashier who acts incredulous, then calmly deal with a "non-clerk," and you will find yourself a non-victim.

If you are ever billed for something you didn't order, or you are overcharged, just don't pay the bill, and don't be intimidated by dunning letters or threats of credit-rating loss. They can't hurt you out there if you won't let them, and your refusal to pay for defective materials and service is one way to keep the victim stamp off your noggin.

SUMMARY THOUGHTS

You can get yourself operating from strength by beginning to place total reliance in yourself, and not placing others in positions of authority above you. You are asking to be victimized when you place total reliance in someone else to control your life properly. If you seize or make your own opportunities, rather than waiting for success to come along, and go after your objectives without staking your personal emotions on the outcome, you'll be on the non-victim bandwagon before you even recognize it. One little statement wraps up the contents of this chapter: "If you are paying the fiddler, make sure he is playing your song."

3

Refusing to Be Seduced by What Is Over or Cannot Be Changed

Progress and growth are impossible if you always do things the way you've always done things.

One major victimizing tactic repeatedly used in our culture employs references to things about which you can do nothing, or behaviors and events which are now history. You can learn to avoid these monumental victim-traps simply by refusing to let yourself be sucked into discussions of such things, by becoming aware of how others will attempt to divert your attention and throw you on the defensive with complaints about past acts you cannot ever change, and by rejecting the peculiar brand of non-logic they are trying to tie you up with.

I have always maintained that we can learn a great deal from animals, without reducing ourselves to operating on pure instinct as they must because of their reasoning limitations. Walt Whitman wrote poignantly of his love for animals in *Leaves of Grass:*

I think I could turn and live with animals, they are so placid and self-contained.
I stand and look at them long and long.
They do not sweat and whine about their condition.

They do not lie awake in the dark and weep for their sins,
They do not make me sick discussing their duty to God,
Not one is dissatisfied, not one is demented with the mania of owning things,
Not one kneels to another, nor to his kind that lived thousands of years ago,
Not one is respectable or unhappy over the whole earth.

Somehow animals are unable to go around focusing on things that are over. While they are deprived of some beautiful memories, they are mercifully incapable of needless brooding and recrimination, and can only consult the present for living now. To remove yourself from the victim ledger, you will have to take a little clue from animals, and begin a program of (1) realizing or reminding yourself what kinds of things you cannot change, (2) becoming aware of how others will try to use the past to victimize you, (3) seeing how you use your own past to victimize yourself, and (4) implementing some specific non-victim strategies whenever you see victimizing behavior by yourself or in others.

SOME THINGS THAT YOU CAN DO NOTHING TO CHANGE

The most obvious thing about which you can do nothing now is your past behavior. Everything that you ever did is simply over, and while you can almost always learn from it, and sometimes change effects that are continuing into the present, you cannot undo what you have done. Therefore, any time you find yourself quarreling about how you should or shouldn't have done something, instead of discussing how you can grow from your past errors or what can be done *now,* you are a victim in a no-escape pitfall. To chew old cud endlessly, to be reminded of how you did this or that, and how you should have done it, or to agonize over how you might have done it, are all victim responses you can challenge. Since you can only live in the present moment, it is preposterous and self-negating to let yourself be hurt about what used to be.

In addition to your own past, there are many other things you are incapable of changing, which consequently are logically fruitless for you to be upset about. You can either learn to accept things you can't circumvent, or continue being neurotically disturbed over them. Some of the things you should explicitly realize that you can't do anything to change include:

• *The weather*.

It might seem needless to tell you that you can't change the weather, but ask yourself how often you have been upset about the temperature, the winds, the rain, a storm or whatever. This is pure and simple victimization of yourself. Of course you don't have to pretend that you like "inclement weather," but being even mildly immobilized by it is something you may as well decide against.

• *Time moving fast or slowly*.

Time will always move at exactly the same pace, whether you like it or not. You get twenty-four hours each day, and you can complain forever that present time seems to be going too fast or slowly, but all you will get for your trouble is a little bit older.

• *Taxes*.

Go ahead and knock yourself out about things like high taxes, and your only reward will be a K.O. and some present-moment stress. Taxes will always be, and furthermore, they will always be too high. You can work at minimizing your tax bite, vote for low-tax politicians, or whatever, but upsetting yourself about taxes is just an exercise in futility.

• *Your age*.

You just can't change how old you are. You can certainly change your appearance, attitudes, dress, and even how old you feel, but you're stuck with your age. To complain constantly about being old won't change a thing except to make you feel even older, more tired, creaky, arthritic, etc., than you are.

• *Other people's opinions of you*.

Once again, what other people think of you is totally up to them. People will pretty much believe as they want, whether you like it or not, and although you can do your best to treat them as you'd like to be treated or to reason with them, you can't afford to compromise yourself in attempts to sway them. If you can't ultimately determine what they are going to think of you, then there assuredly is no logic in being upset about their opinions, unless you believe their view of you is more important than your own self-image.

- *Historical events.*

To be distressed about the outcome of an election, a war, a debate, a storm, or whatever, will only immobilize you. The same goes for large-scale social evils in the present. Consider "the present war in . . ." No matter how much you dislike it, man is an aggressive creature who uses war as a means to establish his power because he doesn't trust his mind enough to use reason. People have always fought each other, and if they continue to do so today somewhere on the globe, it should come as no surprise. Certainly you don't *have* to fight in *any* war, and you can do what you can to wipe the scourge of war from this planet. But to be wretched, distraught, unhappy because other people choose to fight, is self-victimizing. You can't stop wars, plagues, famines, etc., by feeling guilty or miserable. so quietly consider why you would ever make such foolish and self-abolishing choices.

- *Your height and general physical presence.*

Most of what you see is what you get. Complaints about things like your body type, your height, your ears, toes, breasts, genital size, etc., are more self-victimizers which will give you nothing but upset. Liking what you are given is as much a matter of choice as changing what you can by reducing, muscle-building, etc. What you can't change, you'd better learn to love—a lot!

- *Other people's illnesses.*

People you know and love will get sick. You will be a victim if you immobilize yourself at these times, and you'll also improve your own chances of joining your loved ones on the sick list. By all means help them, be there if you choose, comfort them, but don't tell yourself things like, "This shouldn't be happening," or, "I can't bear to see her this way." Your own strength will serve as a model for others, and may even help them want to get better. But your gloomy demeanor will hurt everyone involved, especially you.

- *Death.*

As much as some people try to deny it, no one gets off this planet alive. Life, in fact, is a terminal disease. We have developed a mystique about death which labels it as something to be feared, to be cursed, and to be disconsolate about when it comes to our loved ones or comes near to us, as it inevitably must. But our morbid attitudes about death are largely cultural and learned, and you can change yours, for attitudes of realistic acceptance. Remember Jonathan Swift's words about death:

It is impossible that anything so natural, so necessary, and so universal as death, should ever have been designed by Providence as an evil to mankind.

• *The way nature is.*

Nineteen-year-old Jennifer whined, "I don't like this picnic on the beach, there's too much sand everywhere!" Beaches are simply sandy, rocks are hard, ocean water is salty, and rivers have currents. You will always be a victim unless you accept natural things and stop griping when you run smack into reality as it is. Every time you find yourself complaining about something in nature, you might just as well be wishing that you were on Uranus.

So much for recognizing some of the innumerable things which will always be as they are. It is undeniably admirable to work at being an agent of change in the world. But learn to pick your spots, and not to victimize yourself with frustration and present-moment sorrow by making ridiculous judgments about things which will never be any different. Leave it to Ralph Waldo Emerson to say it in just a few short, meaningful words in his essay *Prudence,* written around 1841:

Do what we can, summer will have its flies. If we walk in the woods, we must feed mosquitoes.

More than 120 years later, there are still flies in the summer, and mosquitoes in the woods.

THE "YOU SHOULD HAVE" VICTIM TRAP:
HOW AND WHY IT WORKS

Whenever anyone tells you, "You should have . . ." look out for victimization. A "should-have" will not change a thing you've done, but it can be used to get you to admit that you were wrong, and to avoid dealing with you about what can be done now. As long as a potential victimizer can keep conversation focused on your past behavior, you can be certain you will not get what you are looking for now.

Here's an example showing how this little victimizing game works.

Arthur moved into his home on a Friday afternoon and called the public-utility lighting company to request that his electricity be turned on. The clerk he made his request to responded, "You should have called us on Wednesday. It's too late to do anything now."

Arthur was about to be victimized if he let himself be dragged off on this tangent, which was completely illogical because he'd had no way of knowing that the company's "policy" was to require two days' notice before turning anyone's electricity on—and besides, on Friday, there was no way for him to go back to Wednesday and make the call, so being told that *he should have* was as ludicrous as it was useless. But Arthur knew these kinds of things get said over and over, recognized the trap, knew the company *could* turn his electricity on that day if the right person gave the order, and requested to talk with a supervisor before he got bogged down with the clerk receptionist. Arthur explained his case to the supervisor in detail, and had his lights on that evening, even though the receptionist had assured him it was "impossible."

The "you should have" gambit is used virtually every minute of every day, especially in offices around the world, by people who want to tie you up for their convenience. It works because potential victims don't recognize it when it is coming, and therefore are trapped into feeling guilty or irresponsible themselves. Most people are all too willing to wallow around in the past anyway, and so are all too prone to let victimizers abuse them with diversions on the subject of behavior that never even occurred. When people use the "you should have" tack, they are usually interested in having you feel bad for their own ends, and not in helping you learn from your past mistakes or correct your ignorance. Once they have you feeling bad or stupid, it's easy to convince you that they can't possibly help you, and you're set up for, "I'm sorry, but there's nothing I can do now. You should have . . ." And if you buy it, off you go, a good little victim, done in by your not recognizing the trap that was so neatly, though perhaps not deliberately, set for you. It is easier to punish someone who unconsciously agrees he should be punished, and "you should have" is designed to make you think just that.

"You should have" is used over and over again on children to keep them feeling guilty and so keep them in line. "You should have told me this morning, Dennis, if you wanted to build your rabbit cage in the cellar. It's too late now, because I just finished cleaning up down there, and I don't want another mess for a while." Dennis knows there was no earthly way he could have predicted when his father would clean the cellar, and no sense to his father's "you should have." But he is unable to use his own logic with his father, who once he has started on this tack will use his anger or bigness to victimize Dennis even more.

The only strategy for avoiding the "you should have" trap is to decline to participate in the ritual by focusing on what actually *can* reasonably be done in the present. When someone tells you, "You should have," you can respond with, "Are you asking me to go back in time and do what you claim I should have done, or can we talk about what really can be done right now?" If you simply can't get someone like Arthur's clerk-receptionist off the "you should have" gambit, and have to go over his or her head, you might well stop a superior from playing it on you by starting off with, "I'm trying to get my electricity turned on [or whatever] today, but your clerk only wants to talk about yesterday [last week, last year]."

OTHER COMMON TACTICS USED TO KEEP THE FOCUS ON WHAT IS OVER

George Noel Gordon (Lord Byron), the famed English poet, once wrote, "No hand can make the clock strike for me the hours that are passed." Yet that is precisely what the folks who would victimize you attempt to do with their multitude of strategies concentrating on past behavior, of which "you should have" is merely one of the most common and powerful. Below are seven typically past-focused sentences which are almost always used to get people to be good little victims and take their "punishment."

- *"Why did you do it that way?"*

Asking you to explain or justify past behavior in detail can effectively keep the focus of discussion from shifting to the present, where it might do some good. Any answer you come up with will generally meet with scorn, disapproval, and a new request for you to expand your defensiveness further. Watch out for that magic word *why*; it can keep you retreating forever.

- *"If only you had consulted me first."*

It may be true that if you had consulted the person first, things would have turned out better, but it may equally be false, because perhaps the person would not then have told you what he now (with the benefit of hindsight) says he would have told you. He may just be jumping on a free chance to look good at your expense. And besides, it's too late now to have consulted him first then, so if he's trying to help you now with this commonly employed sentence, he can only help you feel guilty for behaving without consulting him—probably so he can proceed to do you in by whatever method he pleases, since he's "proved" that you deserve it.

- *"But we've always done it this way!"*

This neat little trick implies that any time you stray from your past "accepted" behavior, you should feel bad, and admit that you've not only violated someone else's rights, but your own as well. (What right have *you* to change?) If you can be made to admit that you shouldn't do anything you haven't done before, then you get the axe for any new behavior with no questions. Right?

- *"If you said it before, why don't you mean it now?"*

This is the logic of forever, meaning that if it suits their purposes, people will try to hold you to everything you've ever said, even decades later, and even though you may have changed as situations may have changed, and the whole world may have turned upside down. But if you are behaving contrary to what you once said, then you are immoral, unconscionable, dastardly, unethical; you take your choice, or fill in another appropriate slander. If you can be made to feel bad for having changed, then you will very likely revert back and hold yourself to what you originally said, even if you don't mean it now—which will, of course, make your victimizer happy—and effective!

- *"If only I hadn't done that."*

This is the "review neurosis," in which you hurt yourself in the present moment by reliving past errors in judgment; you literally curse yourself for having done something a certain way. You can also victimize yourself with the opposite, "If only I had done this," which is equally silly. Plainly, it is impossible now to have done anything differently then, and jostling it around in your head will do nothing but waste your present moments.

- *"Why, just yesterday we had an example similar to yours."*

Here is a ploy that service people often use. By telling you what happened in a case similar to yours, they seduce you into agreeing with them that you really should just accept the garbage that is being dumped on you, because "just yesterday" they victimized someone else into accepting it.

- *"Whose fault was it?"*

By retracing all of the steps where something has gone wrong and assigning blame to everyone involved, anyone who wants to can keep the focus off doing something constructive. Fault for things that are over, other than for financial-remuneration purposes, is a waste of time. If it gets determined that Herby was forty per cent at fault, Michael thirty-five per cent, and the remaining twenty-five per cent split four ways, so what? By staying back there in fault-finding patterns, you can spend the better part of your life dispensing blame and meting out guilt for things that are already over.

Below are the same seven sentences, and what you might expect instead from a non-victimizing person.

Victimizing Sentence	*Non-Victimizing Sentence*
Why did you do it that way?	What have you learned from doing it that way?
If only you had consulted me first.	It might be better if you would consult me first in the future.
But we've always done it this way!	You're different now and this is hard for me to accept.
If you said it before, why don't you mean it now?	You led me to believe something different, and it's painful for me.
If only I hadn't done that.	I see what went wrong, and won't repeat that error.
Why, just yesterday we had an example similar to yours.	What can I do for you?
Whose fault was it?	How can we avoid this in the future?

Relatives will use victimizing sentences like the above to get you to be the person they want you to be. Family members will use them to justify punishment they are about to dole out, or to keep rebellious members from straying too far afield. Merchants who want you to pay without even questioning will use these tactics, as will clerks and receptionists who are paid to keep you from emerging with your own goals at the expense of the company they so fervently serve. Victimizers use these tactics to avoid logic, to escape the present moment, to intimidate, to manipulate, and to win. As soon as anyone you're trying to deal with hauls out a reference to the past, you can ask yourself whether it's victimizing or not, and be prepared to react accordingly. Here is one example—

Several years ago Sam ordered some municipal bonds from a salesman by telephone, and was promised they would be delivered by a certain date. When they arrived a week late, Sam refused to sign for them. On the telephone the salesman, who had just lost a large commission, tried to tell Sam he couldn't do that, because he *should have* called when the bonds didn't arrive on time. So Sam would just have to accept them. "Why didn't you call me?" he kept repeating.

Sam's response was, "You think I should explain myself? You really feel that it was MY responsibility to call you when *you* were late?"

The salesman soon gave up and ended up with the bonds.

YOU CAN VICTIMIZE YOURSELF BY WALLOWING AROUND IN YOUR OWN PAST

While other people are definitely willing to use past references to manipulate you as they choose, you can also do quite a job on yourself in this regard. Perhaps you, like many others, are living today based upon your earlier beliefs, and they no longer even apply. You may feel trapped by your past, but be unwilling to let go and start afresh.

Joanne, a client who came to me for counseling because she was always nervous and anxiety-prone, confided that she could not get through a day without feeling tense. She revealed how she was always blaming her parents for her unhappy childhood. "They wouldn't let me have any freedom. They constantly monitored my behavior. They made me the nervous wreck I am today." These were Joanne's laments, even though she was fifty-one years old and her parents were both deceased. She still hung on to what had happened thirty-five years before, so helping her free herself from a past she couldn't change was the main aim of the counseling sessions.

Through examining the futility of hating her parents for doing what they believed to be right, and putting all those experiences where they belonged—in the past—Joanne soon learned to abolish her self-defeating blame of her dead parents. She saw that even as a young teenager she had made decisions to let her parents' overprotectiveness disturb her, and that had she been more assertive as a youngster, she wouldn't have been so victimized. She began to believe in her own powers of CHOICE, that she had been choosing her own misery all along, and that she was self-destructively continuing this habit. By eliminating those victimizing connections to a past she could never change, Joanne literally freed herself from her anxiety.

As you assess past influences on your own life, make sure you're not hanging onto the belief that anyone else is responsible for what you are feeling or doing, or even failing to do, today. If you catch yourself blaming your parents, grandparents, the hard times, or whatever, for your present troubles, keep this little sentence in your mind: "If my past is at fault for what I am today, and the past cannot be changed, I am doomed to stay as I am." Today is always a brand-new experience, and you can decide now to chuck out all the unpleasant things you remember about your past, and make *this* moment a pleasant one.

The simple truth about your parents is, *They did what they knew how to do. Period.* If your father was an alcoholic or he abandoned you as an infant, if your mother was overprotective or uncaring, then that is what they knew how to do at the time. Whatever unfortunate things might have happened in your youth, you have very likely made them much more traumatic than they were at the time. Young children usually adapt to anything (unless it is horribly debilitating) and they don't go through their days whining or feeling sorry for themselves that their parents are this or that way. They pretty much accept their families, their parents' attitudes, etc., as they are, just like the weather, and they get along. Their heads are filled with the wonder of the universe, and they are creatively having a good time, even in the face of what others would call miserable conditions. But in our culture adults often analyze their pasts repeatedly and remember terribly abusive experiences, lots of which they never really had.

When clients are preoccupied with finding out from their pasts why they behave as they do today, I tell them to pick two or three of their favorite explanations from some list like the following, use them if they need to, and then get on with making new choices today. These are some of the most common reasons from the past that people use to explain why they are the way they are today. After spending a great deal of time and money in therapy surveying their past, most people discover some of these things.

My parents were irresponsible.

My parents were too inhibited.

My mother was overprotective.

My mother was underprotective.

My father abandoned me.

My father was too strict.

Everyone did everything for me.

No one did anything for me.

I was an only child.

I was the oldest of ———

I was the youngest of ———

I am a middle child.

Times were really tough.

Times were too easy.

I lived in the ghetto.

I lived in a mansion [big, fancy house, etc.].

I had no freedom.

I had too much freedom.

We were too religious.

There was no religion in the home.

No one would listen to me.

I had no privacy.

My brothers and sisters hated me.

I was adopted.

We lived in an area where there were no other children.

[And so on.]

Whatever reasons you select, keep in mind that it is a myth that there are *truthful* interpretations of anyone's past. The best any therapist can give you are his or her hunches, which will promote your self-understanding if you believe they are true. The truth is not in the hunch, but in your being satisfied that it is helpfully correct. While I grant that you can develop insight into yourself by examining your past, the fact is that the insight itself won't change the past *or* present, and that blaming your past for what you are today will just plain keep you stuck.

Most great thinkers have forgotten the past, except for experience or history that could help them, and live totally in the present, with an eye toward improving the future. Innovators never say, "We've always done it this way, and therefore we can't change it." Never. They learn from the past, but they do not live there.

Shakespeare alludes to the folly of consuming yourself with the past in several of his plays. At one point he admonishes, "What's gone and past help, should be past grief." And in another of his lines, he reminds us that "things without remedy, should be without regard; what is done, is done."

The art of forgetting can be essential to the art of living. All those dreadful memories you've so carefully stored away in your brain are hardly ever worth recalling. As the master of what stays in your brain, you don't have to choose to keep them. Rid yourself of those self-crippling memories, and most importantly, give up the blame and hatred you harbor for people who were only doing what they knew how to do. If their treatment of you was really horrible, then learn from it, vow not to treat others that way, and forgive them in your own heart. If you can't forgive them, then you will be choosing to continue to be hurt, which will only victimize you all the more. Moreover, if you don't forget and forgive, you will be the only person, I emphasize, *the only person,* to suffer. When you approach it from this point of view, why should you continue to hang on to a victimized past if it only victimizes you all the longer?

STRATEGIES TO STOP YOURSELF FROM BEING VICTIMIZED BY REFERENCES TO THE PAST

Your basic strategy for avoiding past-oriented victim traps is to be alert, "see them coming," and sidestep them before you put so much as a toe into the quicksand. Courage and assertive behavior will see you through once you've sized up the situation. Below are some guidelines for facing down people who are intent on hauling you into the paralyzing mire of past references.

• Whenever someone tells you things have always been one way, or reminds you how others behaved in the past, for the purposes of victimizing you in the present, try asking, "Would you like to know if I care about what you are telling me right now?" This will disarm any potential victimization before it even gets under way. If the person says, "All right, do you care?" you simply answer, "No, I'm interested in talking about what can be done now."

• When people you have to deal with personally use "you should have," "just last week," etc., so they won't have to hear what you're saying, try walking away a short distance: create a little "stand-off." You teach people with your behavior, not with your words, so *demonstrate* that you are determined not to talk about things that are over when they turn into reasons why you must be a victim now.

• Work at eliminating victimizing references to the past from your own speech, so that you don't teach others to use them on you. Be conscious of avoiding, "You should have," "Why did you do it that way?" and other such gambits which victimize your friends and relatives. Your example will show what you are asking of others, and your requests to be spared this kind of victimization will not be met with, "Look who's talking!"

• When someone starts off with, "You should have," try telling the person, "If you can get me a round-trip ticket back to the time you're talking about, I'll gladly do what you say I should have done. But if you can't . . ." Your "opponent" will get the message that you are wise to the trap, which is more than half your battle. Alternately, you can try, "You are right, I should have." Once you've agreed, the responsibility is on your "adversary" to deal with you in the present.

• If someone asks you why you did something a certain way, give your best *brief* response. If the person argues that your reasons were wrong, you can say that you agree or disagree at the moment, BUT you thought you'd been asked to *explain* your reasoning at the time, and not to justify what you did. And if necessary, you can add, "If you don't like my explanation of why I did it, perhaps you'd like to tell me why *you* think I did it, and we can talk about your views, rather than mine." This kind of straight talking will quickly teach others that you will not succumb to their usual victimizing ploys.

• When you sense that someone is upset with you and is using the typical past-oriented entrapments to manipulate you, instead of trying to give you their feelings at the moment, force the issue with, "You're really disappointed in me right now, aren't you?" "Wow, you're more upset than I thought you would be." "You're angry because you feel I've let you down." The focus will shift to the real problem, which is the person's present distress. This strategy of "labeling" present feelings also defuses other people's opportunities to victimize you.

• If you feel that you really were wrong or inconsiderate in a situation being discussed, don't be afraid to say, "You're right, and the next time I won't do it that way." Simply saying what you've learned is so much more effective than feeling you have to defend and relive your entire past endlessly.

• When someone close to you—a mate, a dear friend—starts

dragging up an incident from your past which you know is painful to that person, and which you feel has already been talked through more than enough, try to keep the focus on his or her feelings, rather than being seduced by the "how could you have . . .?" or the "you shouldn't have!" routine. If the person insists on repeatedly blaming you, don't respond with a lot of words which will only intensify the pain, rather use a gesture of affection—a kiss, a touch on the shoulder, a warm smile—and then go away for a bit. By showing affection and then leaving, you can teach others by your behavior that you are with them, but you just aren't going to be victimized by reliving the hundred other times the matter was discussed in the past, which only ended up in hurt feelings.

- Vow to learn from the past rather than to repeat or talk about it endlessly, and discuss your resolution with those you feel are your greatest victimizers. Lay down the ground rules that you'd like to have understood from now on. "Let's not harp on each other for things that are over, and let's work at pointing out to each other, without malice, when we see this occurring." With your spouse or someone similarly close, you can even come up with a non-verbal signal, like a tug of the ear, to use when you feel the past-reference victimization starting.

- When someone starts to tell you about the good old days, or how they did things when they were young, or whatever, you can respond with, "Actually, because you've been around longer, you've had longer to practice and reinforce doing things ineffectively, *as well as* longer to learn from experience. So the fact that you've always done things a certain way doesn't prove that I should be more like you and do them that way also." A simple statement like this conveys to the potential victimizer that you are alert to the gambit, and that you just don't run your life based upon the way other people used to run theirs.

- Don't place so much stock in memories that you do things just so you'll be able to remember them. Work at enjoying the present as it happens. And then, rather than using up your future moments reminiscing, you can be concentrating on new pleasant experiences. Not that memories are neurotic, but they really take a backseat to more delicious present moments. Check out what Francis Durivage wrote in this regard:

"They teach us to remember; why do not they teach us to forget? There is not a man living who has not, some time in his life, admitted that memory was as much of a curse as a blessing."

● Work hard at eliminating your own complaints about things you can do nothing to change—things like those listed earlier in this chapter. Check yourself whenever you hear these useless complaints habitually popping up in your mind or conversation until you are able to stop playing these self-victimizing games on yourself. Keep track of your success with a daily log if necessary.

● Silently forgive everyone you think has wronged you in the past, and vow not to keep on victimizing yourself with remembrances of evil or "private vengeance" thoughts that only hurt you. If possible, write or phone someone you've refused to talk with and start afresh. Holding old grudges only keeps you from enjoying many potentially rewarding experiences with people just because they may once or twice have made mistakes that affected you. Who hasn't made mistakes like that? And remember, if you are upset today by their past behavior, then they are *still* controlling you.

● Work actively at risk-taking—assertive, confronting behavior—with as many people as possible. Set aside time to tell people what you are feeling now, and explain when necessary that you won't continue to argue about things that can't be changed. Be a risk taker with people, or be a victim: the choice is yours.

SUMMARY THOUGHTS

Our minds are capable of storing an incredible amount of data. While this is a blessing in many ways, it can also be a curse when we find ourselves carrying around memories which can do nothing but hurt us. Your mind is your own; you have that terrific capacity to push its victimizing memories out of it. And with determination and alertness, you also have the power to help others stop victimizing you.

4

Avoiding the Comparison Trap

*In a world of individuals,
comparison is a senseless activity.*

TEN-ITEM TEST

Take this little questionnaire before you begin reading this chapter.

Yes	No	
_____	_____	1. Do you often wish that you looked like someone else whom you adjudge to be beautiful or attractive?
_____	_____	2. Do you always want to know how others have performed on tests you've taken?
_____	_____	3. Do you use words like "normal" and "average" to describe yourself?
_____	_____	4. Do you tell your children (or yourself) that they can't do things just because others aren't doing them?
_____	_____	5. Do you strive to be like everybody else so that you will fit in?
_____	_____	6. Do you say to others, "Why can't you be like everybody else?"

_____   _____   7. Do you find yourself jealous over the accomplishments of others?

_____   _____   8. Do you set your personal goals based upon what other people have achieved?

_____   _____   9. Do you give in when someone says to you, "This is the way everybody gets treated, you're no exception."

_____   _____   10. Do you have to see what others are wearing before you decide on your own clothes, or if you are satisfied with your own appearance?

Any yes responses indicate that you are a victim of a very common ailment in our world: comparing yourself with others to determine how you should conduct your own life.

It takes a great deal of self-confidence for people to consult their internal resources to determine what *they* want to do, and when people don't have that self-esteem, they use the only other standards available—comparisons with others, which virtually everyone is willing to use, because they are so effective at keeping folks in line. To get out of the trap of this constant comparison shopping, you will have to develop a strong enough belief in yourself (which you can choose to put into effect minute to minute in your life), and implement some of the strategies outlined in this chapter.

But first you will have to see that it is impossible to be like everyone else and still be your own person. Ralph Waldo Emerson understood this better than anyone I've ever read. In *Self-Reliance* he said,

> Whoso would be a man, must be a non-conformist. He who would gather immortal palms must not be hindered by the name of goodness, but must explore if it be goodness. Nothing is at last sacred but the integrity of your own mind.

Those are mighty powerful words, but they are not the most popular of sentiments. Nonconformity is by definition not sanctioned by the majority of people, who *as* the majority, set standards for conforming.

While blatant nonconformity simply for its own sake is not herein advocated, it is certainly important to look closely at yourself and your very personal aspirations, and appreciate the absurdity of running your life on the basis of comparisons with others, if you are to avoid string-pulling of this most severe variety. People who are interested in having you be as they are, or as they want you to be, will repeatedly remind you of how others are doing things to give you solid examples to follow. Resist their suggestions, along with your own temptation to look outside yourself for models.

YOU ARE UNIQUE IN ALL THE WORLD

The first step out of the comparison trap is to realize that *there is only one you*, and you take that you wherever you go. As the old maxim says, "Wherever I go, there I am." No one is even remotely like you in terms of your innermost feelings, thoughts, and desires. If you accept this notion, then you will want to take a hard look at why you would use anyone else's example as a reason for your doing or not doing anything.

Our culture is composed of people (all unique themselves) who all too often are threatened by anyone who is different. Of course, we often look back in history at people whose uniqueness made them great, and praise them. There is a popular football coach, for instance, who uses Emerson as a model in his public speeches. But anyone who studies the coach and Emerson realizes that Ralph Waldo wouldn't last an hour at the training camp. All of the coach's talk about being a nonconformist, not having heroes, and being your own person, somehow doesn't jibe with his not permitting "his" players to talk to the press, handing out little identity decals for them to place on their helmets as external rewards for doing things well, acting as spokesman for everyone, and the like. Similarly, people like Jesus, Socrates, Gandhi, Sir Thomas More, and even quite recently Harry Truman and Winston Churchill, were all scorned for their crazy individualism in their own times, and then deified later on, when it was safe to do so.

We use things like "normal curves" in our classrooms to decide who is "fitting in" and who isn't. We use standardized instruments to measure everything about people, in pursuit of the sacred "average." Frederick Crane once said, "Mediocrity finds safety in standardization." Yet despite all the pressures on you and the constant reminders that you must be the way other people are, you can never, ever do it. You will still perceive, think and feel in your very own unique way. If you understand the motivation of others in using external references, which is solely to control your behavior, and exercise power over you, then you can begin putting a halt to this form of victimization.

THE CONCEPT OF EXISTENTIAL ALONENESS

In addition to realizing that you are unique in this world, you must also accept that you are always alone. Yes, alone!

No one can ever feel what you are feeling, whether you are surrounded by hundreds of thousands of people, or making love with one person, or by yourself in a closet. Your inevitable "existential aloneness" simply means that your human existence is unavoidably predicated on your being alone with your own unique feelings and thoughts.

Your recognition of your existential aloneness can either be very freeing or highly enslaving, depending upon what you choose to do with it. But in either case, you will not ever change it. You *can*, however, *choose* to make it a freeing experience by making it work for you, as I have encouraged many clients to do.

Consider the example of Ralph, a forty-six-year-old executive who came to me for counseling some years ago.

Ralph's confrontation with his existential aloneness had come suddenly. He told me how he had been sitting in his living room one evening staring at his wife, who was preoccupied reading the newspaper, oblivious to the swirling vortex of thoughts in his head. All at once he had the eerie feeling that this person to whom he had been married for twenty-four years didn't even know him, that she was like a total stranger sitting there in his living room. He realized for the very first time that this person would never, ever know the private inner workings of Ralph.

The feeling was very spooky, and Ralph didn't know quite what to do with it, except to seek counseling. In our early sessions he felt that he *had* to do something about it, like get a divorce or run away. But as he came to grips with this fundamental truth about what it means to be a human being, he learned to see his fundamental aloneness from a totally different perspective—a freeing perspective, if you will. Since his wife could never feel what he was feeling, he should stop expecting her to understand him and "be with him" all the time. Conversely, he realized that his wife was existentially alone too, and so he could relieve himself of the burden of always trying to be as one with her and experience what she was feeling, which led to needless guilt when he failed. Armed with this insight, he could stop his infernal, self-dooming quest for someone to feel what he was feeling, and could get on with pulling all his own strings. He could also eliminate his wasteful expectations for his wife and get off her back, too.

Before long, Ralph felt like a new man—all because he had been freed from the senseless attempt to have someone join him inside his own unique body and mind.

It is important to see how Ralph might have turned his insight of existential aloneness into disaster, as so many people do, by telling himself that he was a prisoner of his human condition, and that no one would ever understand him. He had done a lot of complaining that his wife "didn't understand" him before coming to me for counseling, and his sudden intuition that she was in one way a "stranger" could have aggravated that behavior and made the situation seem hopeless. But as we examined existential aloneness together, Ralph recognized the futility of trying to get anyone to be with him internally, that while people can share many things, and get very close to each other, the plain truth is they can only know each other's surfaces. Their inner beings are strictly off-limits by virtue of their very humanity.

Existential aloneness can be a source of great strength as well as a source of big trouble. Whenever you even get tempted to use other people's lives as models of how you should run your own, think of this line by Henrik Ibsen, the nineteenth-century Norwegian dramatist: "The strongest man in the world is he who stands most alone."

Now you can interpret this as an antisocial, selfish attitude, if that is what you wish to do—or you can look hard at what is dictated by the parameters of your own reality. The fact is that the people who have had the greatest impact on mankind, who have helped the greatest number of people, are those who have consulted their own inner feelings, rather than doing what everyone else said they should do. In this context, strength means being able to stop trying to get everyone else to feel what you are feeling, and stand up for what you believe.

To go back to my former client Ralph: He still recalls that moment in his living room as one of the most important of his life, because not only did it get him into counseling and give him the freedom to halt his lifelong, albeit futile, effort to have his wife and children feel what he was feeling, it also gave him the strength to be himself in a more powerful and positive way. He still believes that no man is entirely an island who can function as an antisocial hermit, but he now knows, by virtue of having experienced it, that internally we are islands unique unto ourselves, and that coming to grips with that idea will help all of us build bridges *to* others, rather than erecting barriers by being upset when we see that others are not like us.

THE DESTRUCTIVE ART OF SELF-COMPARISON

Once you have gained the above-mentioned insights, however, you will have to contend with the fact that you have very likely become highly adept at the self-comparison game. It is virtually a universal malady, afflicting all but the staunchest of resisters. People are taught by our culture always to look outward for their behavioral cues, and consequently "comparison vision" dictates most of our judgments. How do you know if you are intelligent? You compare yourself to others. How do you know if you are stable? Attractive? Worthy? Happy? Successful? Fulfilled? By checking out how others around you are doing and then deciding where you fit on the comparison scale.

You may even be at the point where you can't see any alternatives for self-judgment besides measuring yourself by "common standards." But indeed, you are ignoring a much more important barometer for your self-measurements, which is *your own* satisfaction with the way your life is going. You don't *have* to look outside yourself for self-assessment. How do you know if you are intelligent? Because you say and know you are, because you can do the things you want to do. Are you attractive? Yes, by your own standards, which you'd better set for yourself, before you find that *you've chosen* to accept someone else's standard of attractiveness—at *your* "victimized" expense.

The self-comparison game is deadly because in it your assessments of yourself are always controlled by something outside you which you in turn cannot possibly regulate. The game robs you of any internal security, since you can never be sure how others will judge you. Comparing yourself can be very seductive, since it eliminates all the risks that go with standing alone. And of course, you can generate a lot more superficial "acceptance" by comparing yourself to others and working at being more like them.

But you can also become a particularly lost and helpless victim by employing this method of running your life. Perhaps you secretly dream of doing something "different"—wearing your clothes in a new style, dating an older or younger person, or anything "out of the ordinary." If no one else is doing it, then you are trapped.

If you *happen* to end up doing things the way a lot of other people are doing them, there is certainly nothing wrong with that. But if you *have* to look to the other people to decide what you should be doing, then you are definitely caught in the self-comparison victim trap. Again, you don't have to be a nonconformist at every opportunity just to prove that you refuse to be a victim. In fact, such a "compulsive" nonconformist is just as victimized by others as the conformist, when he looks at the way people conform and then purposely sets out to be exactly the opposite. Use your own inner "common sense" when it comes to deciding what you want, without *needing* to be like everyone else—if only because you are a unique person and couldn't be "just like all the others" even if you really wanted to be.

The first concrete step out of the victimization-by-self-comparison maze is to stop whenever you catch yourself using comparison terminology: As always, take practical steps to control your own bad habits, whether in thinking to yourself or in dealing with (and sending signals to) others.

THE EVEN MORE DESTRUCTIVE ART OF ALLOWING YOURSELF TO BE COMPARED

While you can readily go to work to eliminate your own destructive comparison-habits and develop internal standards for evaluating your life, you may find it much tougher to halt the incessant bombardment of victimizing comparisons directed at you by others.

It is easy to victimize people who are willing to do things—or more aptly, have things done to them—because everyone else plays by *the rules* that allow such treatment.

In many cases (probably most), it is perfectly all right for you to be treated just like everyone else. But when you are ill-treated under a "policy" that should be flexible enough not to victimize anyone, you are up against a person who will feel good only if he can victimize you.

The clerks of the world are among the *most* addicted to taking advantage of people in this way. You'll recall from Chapter One that A CLERK IS A JERK! (Not the person, but the role.) This is because clerks are paid to enforce policies their employers want "everybody" to swallow, and so clerks find it second nature to say, "Just look at that lady, she's not complaining," or, "Everybody gets treated the same." But keep in mind that clerks are hardly alone in using these tactics.

The way clerks in particular tend to employ the comparison-to-others game is illustrated in these two little scenarios, which also show how two acquaintances of mine dealt with the situations by sizing them up and applying successful strategies:

• *The pancake lady.* Chuck entered a pancake house and was shown past an empty booth to a tiny table in front of an exit door, with a hard chair, a door handle at his back, and a draft to blow on his pancakes.

He told the hostess he'd prefer to sit at the booth they had passed. She told him it was reserved for parties of more than one person. He insisted on sitting elsewhere. So she said, "It's our policy, sir. Everyone else goes by it. See that man over there? He's not complaining."

She was right. The shivering man eating cold pancakes in front of another door was *not* complaining. "So what?" Chuck asked. "I'm not complaining either. I'd just like to eat the meal I'm prepared to pay for at a pleasant table. If it's such a problem for you, I'd like to see the manager."

"He isn't in."

"Well, there are several empty booths. Why should I be uncomfortable?"

Chuck didn't want to get nasty and walk out. That would have made him even more of a victim, because he was hungry and didn't have time to drive elsewhere. And if he could help it, he didn't want to move to the booth and force the pancake lady's hand, because he sensed *she* might stage a nasty scene. Nor was he in the mood to pay her off with a tip. So he decided to have some fun and stage a little nervous breakdown.

He continued to plead with her to be reasonable, but as she became even more haughty, he started twitching. His arm began shaking "uncontrollably" and his face contorted.

"What's wrong, sir?" Suddenly the pancake lady was thrown off her guard.

"I don't know," Chuck replied, his speech halting. "When these things happen to me I just go crazy." He got a little louder and more noticeable.

A supervisor miraculously appeared. "For god's sake, Alice, let him sit in the booth!"

End of study. In this case Chuck got in some acting practice, hurt no one, and really enjoyed his hot pancakes in a comfortable booth. He gave the hostess a sly wink when he left, and of course, left no tip, just so as not to reinforce her victimizing behavior on others.

• *Sarah* was riding her bicycle one day when she noticed a sign on a grocery-store window: "Orange Juice, Three Quarts for a Dollar." That was a good deal, so she stopped and a few minutes later arrived at the checkout counter with six quarts of orange juice, which she proceeded to pack into two bags, one inside the other.

The cashier saw what she was doing and announced indignantly, "I'm sorry, dear, no double-bagging. It's against our policy."

Sarah replied, "Your policy doesn't work in this case. You see, I'm taking this home on a bicycle, and if I don't have a double bag, I'll have orange juice all over myself, or all over the road, before I get home."

The cashier became incensed. Sarah detected that the clerk felt her very worth as a person was at stake. "No double-bagging!" she insisted.

Sarah knew the policy was important, and that ninety-nine per cent of the time it should be followed to cut down America's absurd waste of paper, even though the store might have adopted it just to save money. But she wasn't going to let it victimize her in this situation.

The cashier reminded her that no one else double-bagged, so why should she? And what made her think her case was so special? (Even though Sarah had already told her quite reasonably.) And so on about what everyone else did. So Sarah asked her if it was all right to put three quarts in one bag and three in another, and she said it was! But putting the same two bags inside each other was not.

Confronted with this wonderful example of a clerk's logic, Sarah asked to see the manager, who quickly saw how silly his clerk was being. Off Sarah rode with her double-bagged package. She escaped being victimized, but the cashier didn't. She was furious, slamming things around when Sarah left—all because Sarah had decided not to be abused by the silly execution of a policy when an exception was clearly called for.

In a recent issue of *Time* magazine, the following little tale is told of how Joe DiMaggio once went in to ask for a raise. "After my fourth season, I asked for $43,000 and General Manager Ed Barrow told me, 'Young man, do you realize Lou Gehrig, a sixteen-year-man, is playing for only $44,000?' " There it is, the call to the other-directed reference as an excuse to victimize. Once you accept that logic, you can be brutally victimized forever, just because "everybody else is." Really top-notch victimizers nimbly haul out this strategy whenever they feel they are about to lose an element of the control they have over you.

Clerks and other functionaries will often put pressure on other people to join them in enforcing their company's policies. If a sign says no talking, and your children or someone else's are talking, the "enforcer" will often give you a look which means, "Why don't you enforce the no-talking ban?" But if the no-talking ban happens to be foolish and predicated on the belief that small children should act like grown-ups, then you would be a fool to enforce it and join in the victimizing policy.

On a recent winter's day, John was swimming in the heated outdoor pool of a hotel where he was a guest. There was a sign that said no splashing or ball-throwing, even though the pool was covered with thousands of plastic balls to keep the heat from escaping into the cold air. When several children, who weren't even John's, started throwing the balls and splashing, the attendant asked *him* to enforce the policy. There were no other adults around to be bothered, and enforcing the policy wasn't John's job anyway, so he replied, "I personally don't *believe* in the policy. I think a swimming pool ought to be a place where children can have fun. They're not bothering me or anyone else. If you want them to stop, you'll have to get in here and stop them yourself. I wouldn't dream of it." The guard was incensed, somehow feeling it was John's obligation as an adult or a hotel guest to take sides against the children, but he did get into the water and "do his job."

John thought the children had clearly been victimized, and that was against *his* policy. So he went to the manager, told him who he was, and said he thought the policy itself was silly and the attendant irrational in enforcing it. "I'll tell you," he said, "I'm not going to bring *my* family to stay in this hotel as long as that policy is continued. Come to think of it, there are other hotels for me to stay in when I'm by myself, too." The result: The manager changed the policy that very moment. The sign was taken down, and the attendant told to use better judgment in simply assuring that all guests could enjoy the pool as they wanted, as long as they did so safely and without bothering others. As the manager realized, a policy originally designed to accommodate customers seemed more to alienate them, and he wasn't in business for that.

One of the favorite gambits of people who are intent on victimizing you is to tell you about "the lady who was here last week." Of course it can just as easily be "the man," "the couple," or "the people," but for some reason "the lady" seems to get the most exercise. If you are questioning your bill, you will hear all about *the lady* who had to pay twice as much, so you should feel lucky you're getting off so cheaply. If you can't have a good seat in a nightclub, there was *the lady* who had to sit in the corner by the toilet—but *she* still enjoyed the show. If your goods are two weeks late, there was *the lady* who had to wait four months.

People will haul "the poor lady" out of their little victim-bags whenever they want to get you to feel guilty about demanding to be treated decently. Watch out for her, because when you see her being brought out, you are about to be given a dose of victim pills to be swallowed with a manufactured story.

Perhaps you yourself are a clerk, or someone else in a position to victimize others with the senseless enforcement of policies which don't have meaning in certain circumstances. (Mankind has yet to devise a rule that never requires exceptions.) Undoubtedly, you find yourself victimized in turn by some of your colleagues in abuse when you are tempted to make reasonable exceptions. Your lament is almost always the same. "If I do, I'll lose my job," or some other horrible thing will happen. Of course, this is not only false, but throughout the ages it has been the ultimate cop-out used by history's most infamous victimizers.

You never have to enforce policies loudly or emotionally, and you can generally overlook them if they simply don't apply to some particular person's situation. That is, the occasions that call for flexibility should be evident to your common sense. You don't have to advertise your "overlooking behavior," and you will find that overlooking is easy when you don't put your self-worth on the line to enforce any one policy all the time. If you find yourself enforcing policies that victimize others on a regular basis, and you don't like it, then ask yourself why you would ever make one particular job, for instance, more important than your own feelings of worth.

Had Emerson been around nowadays, he might well have repeated to the devoted comparison-artists and policy-enforcers of the world,

Every individual nature has its own beauty . . . and each mind hath its own method—A true man never acquires after rules.

If habitual victimizers were capable of applying this reasoning in their own lives, they wouldn't have such pressing personal needs to "enforce the rules." I do not imply that a person who happens to work as a clerk cannot be his or her own person. Not so. But the clerk's job so often demands that the person victimize others that it does tend to attract people who are willing to boost their egos by enforcing "the rules" on others no matter what. Many of these people remain clerks all their lives.

On the other hand, many people "clerk" for the sole purpose of gaining the experience, money or whatever, and do not identify their own self-worth with their enforcement of victimizing policies. They are quietly effective and they know how to look the other way when it is sensible to do so. If you ever find yourself "clerking" for a living, remember, it's up to you which kind of clerk *you* want to be.

Lately I have taken to watching a gentleman who has taken on a position as a school-crossing guard at a busy intersection I often pass. I have noticed that he likes to wait until there is traffic coming before he lets children cross the road—even if he has to have the children bunch up on the sidewalk when the road is clear. He then walks out into the middle of the road and exercises his power by stopping traffic when it comes, so he can let the children cross. He is a classic example of the functionary who measures his self-worth by how much control his job can give him over others. Of course he is victimizing drivers with unnecessary delays, but this is probably the only source of power over others in his life. Very little harm is really done, but the illustration is clear. When people get their feelings of worth by exercising power over you, or anyone else, you can bet they will do all they can to get their habitual exercise. If you were to confront this crossing guard and point out that he is needlessly inconveniencing people by making them stop when he could just as easily escort the children across the street while there is no traffic, he would very likely reply, "Everybody else stops, and nobody else complains. What's the matter with you? Don't you like children?" As usual, the references to others and the appeals to absurdities are designs he uses, consciously or not, to keep the focus off *his* behavior, and to keep you as his victim.

OTHER COMMON COMPARISON TRAPS

Below are some more of the sentences most commonly employed to victimize you by focusing on others. Watch for those which you use frequently, or which others use to keep you from reaching your own goals.

- *Why aren't you more like . . . ?*

This is an invitation for you to dislike yourself and succumb to victimization because you aren't behaving as some other "model" person is. This ploy is particularly effective when used by authority figures to control their "subordinates": employees, children, etc.

• *Nobody else is complaining!*

This tactic is used by anyone who hopes to keep you in the same status as "all the others" who are too timid to assert their rights.

• *What if everybody in the world behaved like you?*

Victimizers will try to make you ashamed of yourself by telling you that you are promoting anarchy in the world if you demand your rights. Of course you know that all people won't stand up for themselves, and even if they did, the world would be a far better place, since no one would step on anyone else by abusing such abstract moral questions as "What if everybody in the world . . . ?"

• *You should be satisfied with what you have.*

This clever little comparison device is usually accompanied by something like, "Your grandparents never had anything," or, "There are starving children in Albania," and is designed to engender guilt—for your wanting what you believe you deserve—on the basis of what others have not had in the past or don't have now. This technique implies that you should never stand up for yourself in your particular situation because people in other situations have had or are having difficulties. If you can be conned into feeling guilty about things you had no part in and can do nothing about, your victimizer will have proved that you never have a right to anything your grandparents didn't have, or the people in Albania don't have, etc.

• *Don't make such a scene! You're embarrassing me.*

This tack is used to get people to behave in self-forfeiting ways, rather than effectively, just because the speaker can't stand public confrontations. It is used especially to teach young people to put more stock in what others think—which ultimately helps them to distrust themselves, have low self-esteem, and seek out therapy.

• *Why can't you be more like your brothers and sisters?*

More people are troubled in their adult lives because of incessant comparisons with siblings than any other kinds of comparison. Children cannot develop senses of individuality and self-worth when they are expected to be anything like other members of their families. Each person is unique and ought to be treated that way.

• *They want it this way. They don't allow that. That's the way they do things. Etc.*

Watch out for the magic "they," which pops up when victimizers want to give you the impression that some all-powerful authority has dictated the terms you are supposed to live by. If the speaker can't tell you who *they* are, then for all you know *they* don't exist—and you would be rather foolish to live by *their* rules!

• *This is what God wants me to do.*

There are many people who believe that they have special pipelines to God, and when these lead them to victimize others, it is just God's way of saying to the others, "Tough for you." In the Saturday, December 12, 1976, edition of the *Miami Herald,* the coach of the New York Jets football team was quoted as explaining to the press why he wasn't going to fulfill the final four years of his signed contract and legal obligation. "I can't give pro football my heart. God did not put Lou Holtz on this Earth for that." And so, having said that it was God's will, he proceeded to take another job in another part of the country. It intrigues me that football coaches believe that God has so little to do that she is concerned about who is coaching what teams.

SOME STRATEGIES FOR OVERCOMING YOUR VICTIMIZATION BY COMPARISON

As with the use of other guidelines presented in this book, your strategy will require you to size up your situations, avoid being caught off guard, and be prepared with a counteroffensive that will defuse any victimizing effort. Here are some of the kinds of techniques you will have to keep in mind when dealing with people who try to use comparisons with others to keep you from attaining your objectives, or to manipulate you into doing what they want you to do.

• In any confrontation where someone is using references to other people he has victimized and expecting you to go along, remember that his comparisons have nothing to do with you as a person; he would do the same to anyone. Refuse to be upset and you will be well on the way to avoiding these often insulting efforts at victimization.

• When you are offered someone else's example as an argument why you should do something you don't want to do, try asking, "Do you think I care about some customer you had last week?" Or, "Why would I want to hear about how you've dealt with other people?"

Don't shrink from asking such questions: Your victimizer is willing to ask much more of you.

Try interrupting people the instant they bring up comparisons to use against you. Simply say, "Hold on a minute. You are using other people's examples as reasons why *I* should be a certain way, and I am not any of those other people." Such a straight-from-the-hip approach, while you might be unaccustomed to it, must be used despite your quivering insides. Once you've tried it a few times, you'll find it easier to be confronting, and you'll notice that once the regular victimizers in your life see that you mean business, they will cease their futile efforts. Remember, they only do what they do because it works. When it no longer works, they won't do it.

- Practice using sentences that begin with "you" for these situations. "You think I should be more like Sally?" Or, "You think I should be doing things the same way as everyone else?" By leading with "you," you convey that you are not internalizing the person's efforts, and that you are well aware of what he or she is saying. Deliver these statements with a sense of incredulity and bewilderment that the person would even think such things.

- If all else fails, practice ignoring references to others. Simply don't respond to them. This tactic is particularly effective with family members. If you get very quiet whenever anyone tells you that you should be doing things the way others are doing them, your silence will probably be noticed. When people inquire, tell them you've tried everything else to get them to stop manipulating you by comparing you, so you've just decided not to react when they persist. They may get huffy (as a tactic to get you to stop), but they will also get the message.

- You can also reverse the above strategy; for example, "I'm glad you mentioned *the lady* last week who didn't complain, because I wanted to tell you about the mechanic I met last week who charged less than you do!" Or, "If you keep telling me I should be a fashion model like cousin Liz, I'm going to tell you that you should be as generous as Uncle Harry!" It won't be long before your victimizer will see how wise you are to the game.

- More specifically, you can label what your victimizer is doing and show him that you know how he feels: "You're upset, and you're comparing me with someone else so I'll stop trying to do what *I* believe in." Any up-front statement like this which hits the nail on the head will convey your own non-victim position and set the stage for honesty instead of evasiveness or more meaningless comparisons.

• Stop yourself from dealing with victimizers such as clerks the moment you recognize they are unwilling or unable to help you, which will be as soon as they insist that "they," "everybody," "the lady," "the policy," etc., are the standards by which you must be treated. If you continue the conversation even for a moment after you have that insight, you will ultimately dig yourself a deeper hole to climb out of. If you are talking with a lawyer, an IRS agent, a doctor, or whomever, and suddenly realize that you know more than the supposed "expert," dismiss yourself politely and head for someone who can answer your questions or be of help. If you don't get out of these situations when you suspect that you should, you'll almost always end up a victim of others' intentions, be they decent or evil.

• When you confront a potential victimizer who uses comparisons, ask yourself, "What do I want from this encounter?" rather than, "What the hell does he think he is doing here, telling me I should be like someone else?" With this kind of a self-dialogue, you will be looking for your opportunities, as opposed to being seduced by your anger at the tactics you are observing. Once you realize what you want, you can busy yourself at achieving it, rather than focusing on the victimizer's behavior.

• Always assess a potential victimizer's needs as you steer clear of comparison traps. Ask yourself, "Does he [or she] need to feel powerful, understood, important, respected?" If you can see a way for the person to get something out of the encounter, to "save face," then you stand a better chance of not being victimized. If you encounter a hotel captain, maitre d', etc., whom you can clearly see needs to feel important, you can remark on what a job it must be for him to keep things running smoothly (thereby communicating that you expect them to run smoothly for you). If there's a good opening for more casual or personal banter, try asking how long he's been on this job. (If a short time, he must have learned fast; if a long time—well then, he's got a lot of experience.) When you can get people on your side, they will be much more willing to serve and much more reluctant to victimize.

• If you find that certain people in your life habitually try to pull your strings with comparisons and other-directed references, pick a time when you are not upset about them behaving in this way, and discuss it. Ask them to work on it. Such simple requests at neutral times will usually be more effective than ranting and raving when you find yourself angry, which just teaches others to "compare" you more, since you have given them evidence that they are controlling you with this tactic.

• Practice some "surprise" reactions of your own that you can use with a smile, and without fear, when you see the comparison-victimization game in action. "You just compared me to someone I don't even know and who isn't here to verify what you are saying. If you can't deal with me here and now, then go get the person you're talking about and relive whatever you want with her. But why tell me about it?" You can try specific statements like, "The policy just doesn't work in this case!" or more general comments like, "Mediocrity thrives on standardization." Such pithy aphorisms, which you can make up yourself, are excellent defusing tools that can stop the other person short, derail his victimizing train of thought, and put you in charge of the discussion.

• If you feel someone is playing victimizing games on you, don't be afraid to go into an act of your own. Remember Chuck's "nervous breakdown" with the pancake lady. If someone insists that you act like someone you're not, you can oblige by "acting" like whatever person you want to—which in your case will be whoever will get the results you want. "Acting" is one of those tricks in *your* bag which you haul out just for fun, and because it works when used sparingly.

• Don't forget to catch yourself when you are in the victimizer's seat. The best way is to listen to yourself talk and arrest those comparisons before they get out of your mouth, so you don't reinforce this same behavior in those who are close to you. Excise those "be like her [him]" sentences. Get rid of *the lady* and all her downtrodden relations when you are talking to others. Stop asking your children to be like their sisters and brothers, and treat them as unique people. Stop using yourself as a reference for others. Eliminate sentences such as, "You don't see me doing that to you!" Or, "I don't do those things, so why should you?" Don't give others the chance to say, "Well, you did it to me." If *you stop doing it,* that silly excuse will also evaporate.

• Be persevering in your efforts to avoid being compared with others. Don't just mention a habitual victimizer's games once and then give up. Be adamant for as long as it takes to get your message across. Your perseverence will pay off.

• Get rid of all your idols, or other people whose lives you want to model yours after. Be your own hero. Don't ever expect to be like anyone else. While it is fine to admire the accomplishments of others, you must keep in mind that they are or were just as unique as you. If you always want to be like other people or duplicate their accomplishments, then you make it far easier for victimizers to use those other people as references when they want you to get back in line.

• Perhaps most important, try to make all your encounters happy, fun and challenging experiences, rather than battlegrounds in which you place your very humanity on the line. *Have fun* seeing how effective you can be. If you succeed in this but don't invest your entire self-worth in the process, you'll also be much more successful at eliminating the victim stamp from your cranium. On the other hand, if you plow through life and all your encounters with deadpan seriousness, you set yourself up as a person used to being victimized: "You're just asking for it." People who don't try so hard, who relax and enjoy, are by far the most effective at what they do. Just watch how easy any champion makes his craft appear. It is largely because he has made his techniques natural, and is never rattled into pushing himself, into feeling that he "has to succeed." Generally when the champions get tight and push, they fall behind, but when they take it easy, they take it.

FINAL THOUGHTS

Albert Einstein once reported, "Great spirits have always encountered violent opposition from mediocre minds." What a hunk of truth that is. If you want to achieve your own greatness, to climb your own mountains, you'll have to use yourself as your first and last consultant. The only alternative is for you to listen to the violent opposition of virtually everyone you encounter.

The masses will always compare you to others, since that is their weapon of manipulation and enforcer of conformity. Your antivictimization stance will involve your steady refusal to use others as comparative models for yourself, as well as your learning how to defuse the victimizing efforts of others to compare and so control you.

5

Becoming Quietly Effective and Not Expecting "Them" to Understand

Loving relationships work because there is no work.

TWELVE-ITEM TEST

You will never win if you have to prove that you are the winner. That is what this chapter on becoming quietly effective in your life pursuits is all about. Your answers to the test below will indicate how quietly effective you are now.

Yes No

1. Do you get upset when you can't get a point across to other people?

2. Do you have to announce your accomplishments to others?

3. Do you have to tell others whenever you've defeated someone at something?

4. Do you find yourself easily offended by other people's behavior or language?

5. Do you have difficulty lying, even when it would be more sensible and practical to do so?

_____ _____ 6. Is it hard for you to assert your own needs for privacy without feeling guilty?

_____ _____ 7. Do you find yourself being dragged down by the sour dispositions of other people?

_____ _____ 8. Do you find yourself saying or thinking, "He [she] doesn't understand me," a lot?

_____ _____ 9. Do you feel that suffering is natural, and that you are supposed to suffer on this earth?

_____ _____ 10. Do you find it difficult to walk away from people you find annoying, such as drunks or fast-talkers?

_____ _____ 11. Do you explain yourself a lot, and resent having to do it?

_____ _____ 12. Do you spend a lot of time analyzing your relationships with your friends and relatives?

Yes responses indicate areas of victimization you can go to work to eliminate. If you have to explain yourself to others, trying to make others understand you *all the time,* or if you are always trying to prove your worth to people through your behavior and your words, then you are a victim of the "not being quietly effective" malady.

BECOMING QUIETLY EFFECTIVE

What does it mean to be quietly effective? The word being stressed here is *quietly,* since we've talked in detail in earlier portions of this book about the significance of being effective. Being *quietly* effective means that you don't have to tell anyone else about your victories to make them meaningful to you. While it is quite often appropriate to tell others about your life happenings, you will become a victim if you NEED to inform others before you can be satisfied yourself. Once you put the word *need* into your vocabulary, you are at the mercy of the other people's recognition of you—and then if they refuse to recognize your value or your achievements for whatever reasons, you will collapse and they will end up pulling your strings.

Being quietly effective also means that you don't have to rub your fellow man's face in your victories. If you have to do such things, you will find others retaliating, trying to frustrate you in one way or the other. The most important key to being quietly effective lies in how you feel about yourself. If you have self-confidence, then pleasing your*self* will be enough, since the self you are pleasing is worthy. But if you lack self-esteem, then you will look to others for a verification of your esteem, and this will be where you get yourself into trouble. Once you *have* to get that reinforcement from without, you are volunteering for victim status.

A typical example of a "loudly ineffective" person was Daryl, a bright counseling client of mine in his late thirties, who had lost his job several years before, when his company had gone bankrupt. He sought out counseling because he was getting nowhere in looking for a job or even supporting himself. As he put it, "I've just been unable to make the right contacts, and I'm afraid I may just go on searching forever."

In counseling sessions it soon came out that Daryl was the world's greatest name-dropper. It was virtually impossible for him to talk without bringing up his associations with this or that big shot, most of which were manufactured in his head. Daryl also bragged to everyone about his accomplishments, and when he didn't accomplish much, he invented more stories. In short, Daryl found it difficult to keep things to himself *or* feel his own sense of inner pride. He needed others to recognize him or he wouldn't feel right.

When Daryl began to look at his need to be important in other people's eyes, he saw that it came from a real feeling of worthlessness, which in turn had come from his losing his job and persistently viewing himself as a failure. He had believed so much that his worth came from his performance, that even when he was no longer performing because his *company*—his employer—had failed, his worth disappeared. He then sought to compensate by proving to everyone else "how great he was." But everyone saw through him, and he became a victim of his own low self-esteem. When he name-dropped, his friends would just ignore him. When he bragged about himself, he would similarly alienate his friends and family. He began to extricate himself from his trap through learning to keep his victories to himself and by consciously working at avoiding bragging, boasting and "look at me" behavior. Once these behaviors subsided, he was more pleasant to be around, he began to have greater self-confidence, and most importantly, he stopped being victimized by his own attitudes and behaviors.

A WORD ABOUT PRIVACY

When you begin to develop your self-confidence, you will stop expecting everyone to want to hear your stories, as well as find solitude more acceptable. Your privacy is a very important part of your life, and it is necessary to your own sense of well-being. Wanting to have everyone understand and share everything that you think, feel, say and do is a self-victimizing attitude.

Additionally, not feeling a need to be understood, and keeping some things private, are ways of avoiding being pulled around by other people. While this is not an argument for hermit behavior, it is a suggestion to take a hard look at your own personal right to your privacy, and to look even harder at those who would attempt to victimize you by encroaching in those areas, or even worse, denying your privacy. Henry David Thoreau, who lived alone for almost two years at Walden Pond, wrote about his feelings of privacy in *Walden,*

> Men frequently say to me, "I should think you would feel lonesome down there, and want to be nearer to folks, . . . I am tempted to say . . . "Why should I feel lonely? Is not our planet in the Milky Way? I find it wholesome to be alone the greater part of the time. To be in company, even with the best, is soon wearisome and dissipating. I love to be alone.

While we are not all Thoreaus, and this is the twentieth century, his observations are still most appropriate today. You do not have to be around others, or to always have others sharing and understanding you, in order to be fulfilled. In fact, you will find yourself a victim if you have these kinds of expectations, or if you allow others in your life to visit expectations on you. It takes an element of courage to insist on your privacy, particularly when other people insist that your desires for privacy are rejections of them. But trying to explain this to most people is an exercise in futility. You simply have to exercise your rights with behavior, and by doing it often enough, you will be teaching them how you want to be treated. If you talk about it, and analyze it to death, then you will very likely feel victimized and end up forfeiting your privacy anyhow.

YOU WILL NEVER BE UNDERSTOOD
ALL THE TIME

You will recall from the last chapter's discussion of existential aloneness that no one can ever understand you all the time, nor can you ever understand anyone else all the time. Your spouse will do things that you don't understand, your children will be bewildering perplexities virtually all of their lives, politicians will say and do things that you would never believe, and people will go right on being disappointing and disappointed until the world becomes flat. If you expect people to understand everything you say and do, you will not only feel disappointed most of the time, but you will be victimized as well. Here are a few very important concepts that you can think about as you work at adopting a stance of being quietly effective in your life.

SHRUGGING IS A VIRTUE   Learn to overlook things. Don't feel you have to be noisy about other people's attitudes and behaviors that you might find irritating but aren't hurting you. Simply shrug your shoulders and forget about it. If you're at a party you don't like, you can say to yourself, "Everyone else in this room may feel compelled to make small talk and dress in their phony ways, but I don't have to, and I'm glad." You can either leave, or enjoy yourself for being so quietly effective, or whatever. But you don't have to make a big deal about their behavior, get noisy, offensive, and end up hurting yourself and having everyone else hurt as well. A shrug and a "So what?" *to yourself* and you've handled the whole thing. This is the mark of the non-victim, not a phony, just a person who has no needs to let everyone else know where he is all the time.

BEING OFFENDED IS A VICTIMIZING CHOICE   You need never be offended again, either by put-downs directed at you or by things in the world that you may have become accustomed to "finding offen-

sive." If you don't approve of someone else's behavior or language, ignore it, particularly when it has nothing to do with you. By being offended and upset, by saying things like, "How dare he say that!" or,
"He has no right to make me upset like this!" or, "I am offended
when I see weirdos," you are victimizing yourself with the conduct of
others, which is tantamount to having your emotional strings pulled
by the very people you dislike. Shrug it off, ignore it, look the other
way, ask yourself whether it's really that bad at all; or if you want to
work at changing it, by all means do so. But don't choose the victim
position of being offended and upset about it.

ANALYZING A RELATIONSHIP TO DEATH CAN VICTIMIZE YOU   If
you feel you *have* to sit down and "work on" your relationships, particularly your marriage, on a regular basis, you may be participating
in a more neurotic exercise than you think. Working on relationships
often involves long conversations about things, trying to understand
each other's motivations, and vowing to be with each other emotionally all the time. These things may be fine occasionally, but if
they become a regular part of the relationship, they become straining,
frustrating, and just plain tiresome. Who wants to go off to work all
day, and then come home and work some more on a relationship?
Look again at what you defend before you pass this attitude off as insensitive. The most beautiful relationships I've ever observed are
those in which people accept each other for what they are, rather
than analyzing everything they do.

Fifteen-year-old lovers are not immature, they just accept everything about each other. They look into each other's eyes simply loving what they see. No analysis of why, or demands that each understand the other. But if they get into a real "mature" relationship, they
might talk to each other like this after five years of marriage: "Why
did you do that?" "You're not the same person I thought you were!"
"Why don't you do what I want you to do?" "You didn't ask me if it
was all right!" Look again when you call real love "infatuation," and
assess how much you accept the loved ones in your own life for what
they are.

While sharing thoughts and feelings can be a beautiful experience and I encourage it if it's not "pushed" as a regular duty, I
believe a great many relationships are overanalyzed nowadays, and

this is why for many couples, being together is more torment than passion. The facts are that you are two different people and that you will never completely understand each other, nor would you ever want to, if you thought about it. So why not work at accepting one another for what you are, and put the skids to all of that hashing, rehashing, analyzing and trying to "work on" your relationship. Let each other be unique, and as Kahlil Gibran said, "Let there be spaces in your togetherness."

ARGUING IS NOT WORTH DEFENDING The old saw that people argue with each other as a sign of their love ought to be seriously challenged when the arguing leads to your becoming a victim in any way. You can be seduced into an argument with someone, find yourself all upset, your blood pressure up, your ulcer seeds planted, moving toward violence, and then leave the situation, calling that normal. But it is not normal, it is self-defeating victimization.

Repudiate the idea that arguing is always healthy. While a good wingdinger can be fun when no one gets hurt, this is not generally possible with argumentative people, people who really need to argue. They are boorish to be around, with their punishing language and volatile outbursts, and *everyone* involved usually ends up as a victim.

When you are arguing with someone who doesn't understand you, you'll be surprised how often you'll find your argumentation reinforcing the non-understanding and helping the other person to believe even more strongly in his own point of view. The argument only cements his obstinacy—and yet you are likely to defend such arguing as worthwhile.

Hank recently got out of his car in a parking lot and accidentally bumped the door of a car next to him. A man jumped out of the other car, his face red and flushed, spoiling for a fight. "What the hell do you think you're doing?" He desperately wanted Hank to argue with him, so he could reinforce his anger and ultimately pick his fight.

But Hank wouldn't buy it. "Hey, look, I was careless and inconsiderate. I know how you feel. I don't like people bumping my car door, either. If there's any damage, I'll pay for it."

Hank's calm behavior defused a potentially explosive situation. The other driver calmed down himself in a moment. "I don't know why I'm so upset at *you*. I've been having a really bad day. But I didn't mean to be so hostile over such a small thing. There isn't even any damage. Forget it." They ended on a handshake.

The moral is clear. If you allow yourself to be seduced into arguments, expecting to *make* people understand your position, you'll almost always end up the victim. Even if you "win" a heated argument, physical strain on you should be enough to make you realize that you haven't really won. You can try to prove you are the winner with behavior that engenders ulcers, high blood pressure, and heart disease if you wish—or you can avoid such arguments and keep your sanity and your health.

LYING IS NOT ALWAYS IMMORAL In your efforts to have everyone understand or approve of you, you may well have adopted a very rigid stance on lying—never allowing yourself to partake of such an "evil practice."

Take another look. Do you find yourself victimized by habitual truth-telling-at-all-costs? You may well agree with the common observation that if, for example, you were about to be executed by Nazis unless you could convince them that you weren't Jewish, and you happened to be Jewish, you would hardly be obligated to tell the truth. In such *extreme* cases, people agree that you don't owe any special allegiance of truth to your enemies. In fact, it is considered effective behavior to trick them any way that you can. So you are not against lying in all circumstances, but you probably define very narrowly the circumstances in which you believe it to be ethical. So what you really need to do is give more thought to *defining your grounds* for lying. Is it sensible to avoid lying when you know the truth will be damaging to others? Are your principles (your policies) more important than the people they were designed to serve? Look hard at these questions and ask yourself whether you are being victimized by your rigidity.

A client of mine who was sixty-one years old came to me confounded by the fact that she could not get a job, despite the fact that she was a capable, well-trained stenographer. She complained about being discriminated against by employers who would not hire her because of her age. When I encouraged her to put down a different age and fight their discrimination with her own weapon, she was aghast. "That would be lying," she said.

Of course I knew that was precisely what it was. This client had been refused seven jobs by insensitive, discriminating employers who were even disobeying the law—and yet she continued to victimize herself with her principle of never lying. Ultimately she "stretched the truth" and told an interviewer she was fifty-five (she looked like she was forty-five) and was hired. She demonstrated her effectiveness on the firing line and was promoted to supervisor in just six months. However, if her silly taboo had persisted, she would never have given herself a chance to get the doors to her working life open again.

Another question to ask yourself about lying is, "What constitutes a lie in my eyes?"

Suppose you have information about yourself that you believe you have a right to keep private. It is just plain nobody else's business. Along comes someone who asks you to reveal that information, who feels he has a right to invade your privacy. That person will want you to feel it is a kind of lie if you want to "hide" information that you feel you have a right to keep private. He will want you to feel guilty about not "being able" to reveal that information. But do you really have any responsibility to tell him? Of course not. Are you in any way lying when you say, "That happens to be none of your business?" How could you be? Every court of law in the world gives people the right to refuse to answer questions on grounds of possible self-incrimination, and especially if you feel people are likely to use what you tell them against you, you don't owe them anything.

People will not always understand you; that is the theme of this chapter. Look carefully at your stance on lying, and see if you are not victimizing yourself, or being victimized, by letting others control your behavior through your compulsive truth-telling. Once you tell the truth, and another person is hurt or you are hurt, do you think you have helped others to understand you?

There are risks in opening up the topic of lying, since many, many people take the position that lying at any time is bad—something to feel guilty about—even if it is justifiable under certain circumstances. I obviously do not support indiscriminate lying. But if by truth-telling, you end up a victim because you are revealing information about yourself which ought to be private by your own definition, then you are behaving in a self-defeating manner, and you might want to reexamine your attitudes. Further, if lying is the only or best tactic you can use to get out of a victim trap, don't be afraid to consider it. Would any prisoner of war plotting to escape tell his captors if he is asked, "Are you planning your escape?" He would lie, and you would very likely endorse it. Well, look at your own prisoner behaviors during commonplace inquisitions and make your own assessments. Suppose a burglar asked you at gunpoint, "Do you have any money hidden in this house?" You obviously wouldn't insist on the truth at your own expense in this case. You need never be *manipulated* by others into revealing private information, nor victimized because of blind devotion to the truth.

THE ABSURDITY OF HAVING TO PROVE YOURSELF

Having to prove yourself to others means being controlled by the others to whom you must show the proof. Quietly effective behavior involves no such need for proving yourself. As a child, you were full of "watch me" behavior. You wanted everyone, mostly your parents, to watch as you practiced diving into the pool, or skating backwards, or riding your bicycle, or whatever new experience you were having with growing wiser. You needed those eyes on you then, because you developed your self-concept on the basis of how significant "other people" reacted to you. But those days are over. You are not a developing child who must be noticed or who must constantly prove himself—unless you are one of those adults who still covets the approval of virtually everyone you meet.

Having to prove yourself to everyone will victimize you a great deal in your life. You will find yourself upset when others don't notice you enough or when they disapprove of you, or most victimizingly, when they don't understand you. Consequently, you will strive even harder to get them to understand, and when they see you doing this, they will be able to exercise even more power over you. An example of this occurred with a friend of mine, who was trying to convince his wife that his playing touch football on Sunday afternoon was his right, and that it was not his responsibility to stay home and entertain her. She simply didn't understand how he could want to throw a football around with a group of sweaty men when he could be with her, especially since he hadn't been with her all week. The more my friend talked, the more it became evident that his wife did not understand him. Before long, he was arguing with her about her not understanding him, and he ended up not playing ball that afternoon. Not only was the afternoon shot, since he and his wife were not speaking, but she still didn't understand him wanting to play football. A triple victim-move on his part. If he had understood that she would never understand his desire to play ball with the guys, and that it was okay for her not to understand, then he would have avoided the trap of trying to prove to her that he was still an all-right guy even though he wanted to do something that she didn't understand.

The converse of your feeling that you have to prove yourself is other people expecting you to do so. It is not uncommon for you to hear, "What made you do that?" or, "Oh, yeah, prove it," or some similar sentiment. Once again, you must be on the alert for having to prove anything to anyone. You can be quietly effective at times like these, and simply have an internal consultation with yourself which goes, "Do I really have to prove anything to this person? Will my proving myself make things any better? Maybe I'll just *pass* on this, and let him think whatever he chooses." This is particularly important when you are dealing with strangers. Did you ever stop to consider how foolish it is to prove yourself to a total stranger, and spend time trying to convince him of the rightness of your position? This is generally done because you are trying to convince *yourself*, and you are using your listener (victim) as a mirror.

Soon you'll learn to love your quiet victories. During an intermission at a recent concert, Kevin went out to the refreshment stand in the lobby and bought four sodas for the group he was with. He turned around to take them back inside and then noticed a sign on the wall next to the entrance: ALL SOFT DRINKS MUST BE CONSUMED AT THE CONCESSION STAND.

There Kevin stood with four drinks in his hands, and a series of options. He knew the security guard standing by the entrance was just hoping he would try to get past him, so he could stop him and assert his own self-worth by "doing his job."

Kevin could drink all four sodas, give some away, throw some away, leave them all behind and work his way back through the crowd to get his companions, argue with the guard that people couldn't be expected to see the sign until *after* they'd bought their drinks, and that he should overlook Kevin's "smuggling" the drinks in and have the sign moved. But as he was thinking, he saw a way to achieve a quiet victory. He spotted a door behind the concession stand which led to an alley that ran alongside the building. He slipped out and saw an open exit door near the front of the hall where his group was sitting. So he went down the alley, into the crowd far enough to hail his friends, and they retired to the street to drink the sodas.

Had Kevin needed to say to the guard, "There I did it, nah, nah," he would have ended up a loser in this little minidrama just by wasting his time on a nasty scene. But sizing up the situation and finding a solution in a few seconds let him emerge as a non-victim, without hurting anyone, and without having to prove his superiority to anyone.

With all cases like this, tact is a very important consideration. Being tactful involves not making it easy for other people to hurt themselves, and consideration for their feelings and responsibilities. When you have to prove yourself, you often lack tact and become boorish as well as victimized. Here is my favorite story about tact, as told by one of the greatest of all storytellers, John Steinbeck:

> Two men were meeting in a bar when the subject of Green Bay, Wisconsin came up. The first man said, "It's a real nice place." The second responded, "What's nice about it? Only things ever come out of Green Bay are the Packers and ugly whores." "Now, wait just one minute, you sonofabitch," said the first man. "My wife is from Green Bay." "Oh," the other replied. "She is? *What position does she play?*"

PROVING YOURSELF AMONG RELATIVES AND FRIENDS

The primary family is one social unit in which it is particularly important for you to practice proving yourself internally, rather than in heated confrontations.

Many families operate under the assumption that members have the right to know all about each other's business, and that privacy is not only taboo, but is a direct challenge to the family's very existence. Family members are repeatedly asking each other to explain themselves, to come up with answers when confronted by domineering relatives, etc. Families also tend to "take attendance" on ceremonial occasions like weddings, funerals, graduations, bar mitzvahs, parties, and holiday gatherings, and if you were not present, your preference in the matter is considered no excuse. Similarly, family members tend to question your dress, or generally your personal appearance. They are equally good at demanding explanations for why you didn't get a haircut or why you disappointed this or that relative. They are super at monitoring any behavior which they or "society" label "deviant," as harmless as it may be. They are the toughest people in the world to deal with when it comes to your not expecting them to understand you all the time, because these are the folks who often *insist* on having an "understanding," and will work at accomplishing it, even though it seldom happens. While family ties can be very close and beautiful, you must be alert for the big victimization that may tie you up.

I am always intrigued by the number of people who, on the verge of divorce, will say things like, "Yes, I'm going to get my freedom pretty soon." Why do so many think of divorce as achieving freedom, even though they may say such things facetiously? Is marriage so widely thought of as the opposite of freedom, which is slavery?

In many, many cases, it is—and with good reason. People in marriages, or in families, do not feel free, mostly because they live with the constant expectation of having to prove themselves, or the fear of not being understood all the time. Take away these two features, and most marriages which end in divorce could be rejuvenated.

A friendship, on the other hand, one that lasts for a lifetime, is a relationship in which neither party has to prove himself. A friend has no expectations except that you will be yourself, and honesty is the cornerstone of the whole affair. Whenever I talk with parent groups, I suggest that they look hard at their own friendships, and begin treating their children and other family members as they do their friends. For example, if a friend spilled a glass of milk on your table, you would probably say, "That's all right, let me help you clean it up." But to your child you might say, "Dummy, watch what you're doing! Why do you always have to be so clumsy?" Be like a friend to your spouse, your children, and the other members of your family. Primary families are where many of the seeds of mental distress are sown, partly because few families realize that if members are not respected, with guarantees of privacy and the right *not* to have to prove or explain themselves every moment, the bonds of love get pulled too tight and become the strings of stress. I think these poignant words from Emerson's beautiful essay on *Friendship* sum this crucial point up so well that I used some of them in the dedication of this book:

A friend is a person with whom I may be sincere. Before him, I may think aloud.

In my experience with family and marriage counseling I have encountered very few families which use the criteria of friendship in their everyday relationships. If they were consistently applied in families, however, there would be far fewer victims in the world. But you can teach your family members that you want and are prepared to give respect, by behaving in ways which do not call for you to be their victim, and by giving up the ghost of having to explain yourself.

PEOPLE WHO WANT YOU TO JOIN THEM IN THEIR MISERY

Listen to Lydia Sigourney, an American author of the early nineteenth century, on dealing with gloomy people:

Keep aloof from sadness, says an Icelandic writer, for sadness is a sickness of the soul. Life has, indeed, many ills, but the mind that views every object in its most cheering aspect, and every doubtful dispensation as replete with latent good, bears within itself a powerful and perpetual antidote. The gloomy soul aggravates misfortune, while a cheerful smile often dispels those mists that portend a storm.

The simplest and usually the most reasonable way to deal with grumpy people who are not willing to change is to stay away from them. This may sound harsh, but it is a very useful strategy. Grouchy people, like all others with "erroneous zones" dominating their lives, get something from their despondency—and usually their dividend is your attention, or even worse, the satisfaction of dragging you down there to join them in their misery.

You have no responsibility to join gloomy people or even be around them. Surround yourself with happy faces—people who are interested in growing and enjoying—rather than with complainers and people who love to carp about how the world is treating them. You can certainly offer your comfort and assistance to the chronically unhappy, but beyond that, particularly when your outreaching is repeatedly rejected, you have a responsibility to yourself to avoid being around people who may well drag you down.

Others will often scowl or glower at you out of their misery to get your attention, and if you respond, you only reinforce the very habits you want to extinguish. By hanging around with these sourpusses and feeling irritable, you are teaching them to continue their behavior. You will be doing you both a favor by abandoning those who want to be grim whenever their distasteful behavior surfaces. Not only will they learn to stop complaining, and get up and do something productive, but you will be able to use your present moments more propitiously for yourself.

People whose debilitating brand of melancholy you have to look out for spend their lives disasterizing and fault-finding. They seldom have anything pleasant to say and look forward to the worst rather than facing the future with delight or optimism. They feel done in, and with their tales of woe will resist all your efforts to be pleasant. They victimize others by claiming that no one understands them, at the same time adamantly refusing ever to be understood. They are by definition impossible to please, and always unwilling to begin to work on themselves. Some folks in this category spend their entire lives, from youth to old age, with this self-destructive mind-set. You will be the world's biggest fool if you stick around people like this, whether you are related to them or not, because all you can expect are their interminable stories of disaster: this mugging over there, the death report over here, the accident just yesterday, my gas pains, my sciatica, the lousy weather, the cold winter, the crooked politicians, the lousy economy—and on and on. For them, there is never a nice day. The best you can ever get out of them is, "It'll probably rain."

Virtually all this behavior persists because it has been suffered gladly by fools and reinforced down through the years. But you don't have to be one of those fools. You can stay away, you can blatantly ignore it, or you can come right back with statements like, "For someone who had such a rotten childhood, you sure talk about it a lot," or, "You must like those gas pains—you keep having them and talking about them." Don't be sarcastic. Just let people know that you will not go along with endless *kvetching* or complaining. Be good-natured, but if the croaking continues, leave, and say why very bluntly. You enjoy life, and are not interested in being brought down.

The best way for chronic complainers to get out of their misery is to get involved in projects they care about and can invest themselves in. Be willing to help them, but if your honest offers to help are rejected, refuse to feel guilty or to sit around and listen to excuses about why the "victims" can't do this or that.

Be an "accepting confronter," but not a victim's victim. When despondent people find out that you really don't want to join them, they almost always stop trying to victimize you, and ironically, their despondency begins to disappear as well.

SENTENCES COMMONLY USED TO VICTIMIZE PEOPLE BY NOT UNDERSTANDING THEM

Here are some clever little variations on the themes of not being understood and not accepting quiet effectiveness which you will observe yourself and others using regularly in victimizing ways.

- *I don't understand why you do those things.* You are being told that you have a responsibility to make yourself understood, and until you do, you're bad.

- *How could you do such a thing?* Not only is the speaker upset about what you dared to do, but he is trying to make you believe that your doing anything he doesn't understand is unforgivable.

- *I've never heard of such a thing.* The dimension of incredulity is here added to the above tactic. Your victimizer pretends total shock at what you have done, said, etc., implying that everyone (or "they") would frown on it, and therefore you were and are wrong—and consequently you should do what the victimizer says.

• *How could someone with your brains and your background do such a thing?* Sentences like this take the above tactics one step further, and add the ingredient of guilt, seasoned with concealed flattery. "I am not only shocked and scandalized, but disappointed because you, of *all* people . . ."

• *I'm stumped, you really have me perplexed.* This kind of confession conveys the unwritten message that "you have a responsibility to unperplex me." The victimizer will use this if he knows that you cannot tolerate people not understanding you. So he gets stumped, and you feel an obligation to unstump him, and off you go to the dumping grounds.

• *Please go over it one more time so I'll understand.* If you heed this call to repeat your story endlessly, you can be victimized endlessly.

• *You should know how I'm suffering.* Here you are asked to feel bad because you don't understand how bad somebody else chooses to feel. This reverses the victimizer's non-understanding of you, and puts the blame for not understanding on you.

• *I can't believe you're going to do that now, when . . .* This kind of ploy can keep you from jogging, reading, napping, or whatever you happen to want to do, because of a schedule which the victimizer has made up or is now making up. Your doing whatever it is wouldn't be so bad, but the victimizer has got an option on what is to be done now. So the speaker will be confused and hurt if you do whatever it is you want to do—which is the victimizing game. The request here is often accompanied with, "You could wait until tomorrow and skip it this once." Of course, the fact that you are on a jogging program and don't want to skip it, is of little consequence, because the victimizer simply doesn't understand your intransigence in this matter.

• *I don't understand how one little piece of cake is going to hurt you.* With this tack, you are supposed to give up your firm conviction to diet, because someone else doesn't understand your resolve. This device is also used to keep you in the same self-defeating patterns that your victimizer finds it difficult to break. The message is that you should do things that you don't want to do (be a victim) because someone else either wants you to, or doesn't understand why you aren't thinking the same as he or she is at that moment. This can also be used in reverse, to say, "I don't understand how you can eat that cake—look at me, I'm not doing it." Same logic, only it's used for different purposes.

● *You never tell me what you're thinking.* This may be an attempt to get you to reveal yourself and abandon your "neurotic" needs for privacy. Once you have said what you are thinking, the other person can pounce on you by insisting that you have no right to think that way.

● *Do it for me.* When your victimizers can't get you to conform by pleading that they don't understand you, they fall back on some personal plea like this, and you are asked to do what you don't want to do because it will please them.

● *You've offended me.* Watch out for people who take offense just so they can give you "good reasons" to feel awful and change your behavior to suit them.

● *I demand an apology.* This device can control your behavior by pressuring you into saying something you don't mean, or by backing you into a corner: You are in the position of not being able to apologize even if you want to without also yielding to the power of the demander. But keep in mind, and be prepared to point out, that such a "conceded" apology is worth nothing, since it does not carry the sincerity of the apologizer.

These are some of the most common forms of victimization-through-not-understanding in our culture. These examples have been gleaned from thousands of counseling sessions in which people have told their tales of being pushed around and disparaged by victimizers masquerading as friends, colleagues, neighbors and relatives. Below are some specific tactics you can use to counterattack and defuse the "I don't understand" artillery.

STRATEGIES AGAINST THE "I DON'T UNDERSTAND" GAME AND FOR BEING QUIETLY EFFECTIVE

● Stop explaining yourself whenever you realize that you resent doing so. Remind yourself and others that you are not obliged to explain your own personal behavior to anyone, and that any explaining you do will be done because you choose to do it, rather than to fulfill someone else's expectations of you. Once you have taught people *not* to expect you to explain yourself on their every request, they will stop making such foolish demands. Feel *free* to explain yourself if you enjoy doing so, but if you feel compelled, your strings are being pulled by the unreasonable demands of others.

• Stop telling yourself that you are responsible for making people understand you, and tell others outright that you expect to be misunderstood sometimes, but that is only natural among human beings, and not an indication of any pathology in you or your relationships. When people tell you they don't understand you, try a shrug, a smile, and the famous Emerson quote from *Self-Reliance*, "To be great is to be misunderstood."

• Practice ignoring demands by total strangers that you make yourself clearer. Say to yourself that demanding strangers are very unlikely ever to understand you, even if you emblazoned your message on your T-shirt, so you are free to go about being misunderstood without feeling any guilt or sense of failure as a person. You are perfectly capable of tuning the verbal assaults of strangers out of your consciousness completely. You accomplish this in precisely the same way that you tune out a radio which is playing within earshot of you and you don't care to listen. Become a quietly effective "tuner-outer" when it is called for. If you practice "tuning out" the *self*-sentences mentioned above, ignoring the demands of strangers will become easier.

• When you suspect that you could never satisfy a person's demand that you explain yourself, simply ask, "Do you think you *could* ever understand?" If the answer is yes, then ask the person to give his own interpretation of your behavior, and agree with the parts he is correct about. In this way you put the responsibility for understanding on the person demanding it, rather than on your own shoulders.

• In the same vein, when you believe someone is not understanding you as a ploy to victimize you, try having him repeat back precisely what you have said, before permitting him to go on "making his own points." The key to this technique is that your potential victimizer must agree to the ground rules, which are that:

You will give your point of view, and he will listen without interrupting. Then he will repeat back what you've said to *your* satisfaction. When you agree that he has actually heard you, he may give his point of view, and *you* must listen and repeat it back to *his* satisfaction. Any time either of you says, "No, you didn't hear it right," he restates what he actually said.

With these simple guidelines, you can avoid being victimized and also significantly improve participants' listening skills. You are far more likely to be understood when you complete several interchanges of this type.

• Practice being *quietly* effective by postponing announcements about your achievements. Time yourself on one-, two-, or three-hour delays, and then ask yourself if you still have to tell someone. This is particularly useful for handling news that will make you appear superior to the person you are informing. The delay system works because after waiting for several hours, or even days, you no longer feel the urgency to portray yourself as a winner, and once the news does come out (if it does), you will seem like what you are becoming—a person who takes achievements calmly and modestly in stride.

• When you are in the company of boorish people who you feel are abusing you with their stories, bragging, or pushiness, practice excusing yourself, getting right up, and leaving. Even in such places as restaurants, you can fight the habit of just sitting there and "taking it." Just go for a little walk. You will not only feel better at having exercised some control, but you will also have taught your troublesome companions to stop using these tactics around you, since they just send you off without an explanation.

• Label up front the attempts of companions to drag you down. When you feel someone trying to get you to join in his misery, say, "I think your misery is demanding my company." Any sentence like this, stated in a non-hostile way, will demonstrate to your potential victimizer that you are wise to the games and command respect for your intelligence and your honesty, even though the person may deny this at first.

Next you can tell the complainer that for the next hour you are not interested in hearing anything about how awful things are. Time the conversation, and the moment a bad-news droplet leaks out, stop it with, "We agreed to go for an hour." This will gently remind your groaner of a habit he may not even have realized he was so carried away with, and perhaps encourage him to work on breaking it. At the least, it will free you from having to hear the same tiresome stuff for an hour, or a day, or however long a respite you want to insist on.

● Teach people, with your behavior, that you are going to insist on your privacy. Don't spend endless hours *demanding* to be left alone. Just take what time you feel you want for yourself. Do it firmly but gently, but DO IT. Take your walk, your nap, your reading time in your room, or whatever, and don't be seduced into giving up your privacy because someone else doesn't understand you or labels you a recluse.

● Learn to accept it as natural that other people label you, rather than as something to be upset about. If you are called a freak, a weirdo, a loner, a rebel, and you show that labels don't bother you, then the labeling will be useless, and will ultimately cease. But as always, if you feel guilty about those labels, or argue about their inapplicability to you, or get upset by them, then you are merely reinforcing the labeling behavior.

● Use the strategy of identifying the feelings of someone else when that person begins to get upset with you or attempts to bring you down. "You really feel bad about this, and you are retelling me so that I will feel bad also," or, "You don't understand me at this minute, and you're upset because I've disappointed you." Show people that you are aware of their feelings, and that you are unafraid to bring them out into the open.

● When someone insists on having you "eat this" or in acting incredulous when you are about to complete your own exercise regimen, state firmly and without hesitation, "I am dieting and I don't want to eat anything," or, "I am going to run now." Forget all the excuses such as, "I hope you don't mind," or, "Please forgive me," or, "I hope I'm not hurting your feelings," simply because those are invitations for you to have the matter discussed further, and ultimately you will end up eating so as not to hurt the person's feelings or whatever. Be firm and full of conviction, and your wishes will be respected.

● Use sentences like, "You've offended yourself," or, "You're hurting yourself." These are the kinds of verbal statements which preclude your feeling guilty, and which place the responsibility for someone being offended where it belongs, that is, on the person who has decided to be hurt or offended.

● Get rid of the foolish idea that you should feel bad if some of your friends don't like others. Obviously there are many people in the world you would not choose for friends, so why expect that those you do choose for your own unique reasons will all automatically choose each other? Yet people often find themselves worried or upset because their "matchmaking" efforts fail, rather than simply accepting the naturally selective laws of "friendship chemistry."

Similarly, avoid upsetting yourself when friends of yours desperately want you to like their fond acquaintances. You are not obligated to share the feelings of your friends' friends, or your relatives' friends, and if you don't, it is no reflection on your original friendship. At the same time, catch your own or others' expressions of sentiments like, "How could she like him? I find him distasteful." People shouldn't have to account to others for their taste in friends, or be subjected to pressures to reject some of their friends in favor of others. If you feel this kind of string-pulling used on you, as always don't be afraid to point it out, or to stick to your point by using the most "quietly effective" strategies you can muster.

• Whenever you find yourself in danger of being wheedled into an argument you would rather not be victimized by, try announcing, "I just decided I'd rather not argue over this. If you insist on arguing, you'll have to do it alone. We either talk with respect to each other, or I won't participate." Your arguer-partner may be stunned by the brazen honesty of this brand of psychological shock therapy, but you must carry it through by resolutely refusing to argue, even if it forces you to walk out.

• When you are being as logical as you can, and it is getting you nowhere with an "adversary," learn to abandon logic and search elsewhere for strategies.

A friend of mine named Jim once had to deal with a meter maid who was about to ticket his car. He told her the meter was faulty, and she could plainly see that it was. But she argued that parking was not allowed in spaces with broken meters, and so he should have parked elsewhere.

Jim responded logically, saying that parking places are for serving people, who shouldn't be deprived of perfectly legal spaces just because the meters happen to be jammed. He explained his logic very carefully three times, but each time her answers conveyed that she just wasn't hearing him.

Finally, Jim abandoned logic and pleaded with her just to be nice and not give him a ticket, even if he *was* wrong. This she liked. She needed to hear Jim admit that he was wrong so she could establish some power over him. Once he asked her to ignore his "mistake" she agreed, and he drove away.

Jim could have continued with his "defense," which he still believed in, but he would have ended up a "logical victim," forced to take a day off from work and go to court to fight a $10.00 fine. In court he would have been even further victimized by the entire bureaucratic machinery, which he has learned to avoid. His practical solution, which involved abandoning logic and doing a little acting, obviously served best.

• Stop trying to prove yourself as a winner with supervisors, authority figures, people with titles, and so on. Give them the feelings of power they need, let them think *they've* won encounters with you, and keep it quiet that you know otherwise.

Bosses don't like to be proven wrong, and you can use this knowledge to avoid a lot of trouble with them. Even if you believe from your soul that you are right about this procedure, that promotion, etc., don't confront the boss with, "I think you're really wrong about this," and put him in a position where he *has* to fight you to defend his own ego. The oldest trick in the book is working things out so that the boss thinks *he* suggested what you want—especially if it's something like *your* raise or promotion. This doesn't mean being a weakling at all; it simply means strategizing effectively in your own best interests, which calls for knowing when to be quiet about your own views and when to express them aloud.

• Stop doing little things you don't enjoy just because *they* wouldn't understand if you didn't: for example, kissing relatives or acquaintances you'd rather not kiss. Just don't do it the next time. If they want to discuss it, you can use any of the strategies listed above for dealing with folks who don't understand you, but before it gets to that, just stop. *Just don't go* one time to that deadly tea party at Aunt Miriam's, and see what happens. If others insist on trying to coerce you, again use the strategies outlined above, but first begin to assert yourself in deciding where your body ends up. It is your body, after all, and you are not obligated to put it in places where it doesn't want or have to be.

• Stop apologizing for yourself and your behavior. You don't have to be sorry when you do something you or others don't like; you can simply learn from it, announce to whoever may have been hurt that you are going to work at not repeating the behavior, and then get on with living. Also, remember that it is not your responsibility to be sorry when other people don't understand you. By apologizing to them, you take on their responsibilities and teach them to continue not understanding you or your motives.

Saying "I'm sorry" all the time can become a horrible victim-habit, a reflex of "taking all the blame." I once saw a woman sitting on the subway who said; "I'm sorry!" when a stranger stepped on *her* feet.

• If you are caught up in the constant analysis of everything in your relationships, make a commitment to stop. Just "let it be" for a while, free from the compulsive need to interpret all motives, behaviors, and so on. The analyzing itself can become a disease, rather than a useful tool to overcome problems, and more than one beautiful relationship has been analyzed to death. Don't get so carried away with "working on your relationships" that they become all work and no play, because at that point there's nothing left to work on.

• If *not* revealing something is more effective for everyone concerned, and to reveal it would violate your own personal sense of privacy, then don't reveal it. If you can't refuse, then cover it up the best way you know how, and don't label your behavior as lying. Remind yourself that you have a right to hide personal information, particularly when you feel that someone has no right to be asking about it in the first place.

IN CONCLUSION

You will never be a prophet in your own land. You will never be understood by everyone, and you will almost always become a victim if you feel you have to prove yourself to other people. Being quietly effective involves being able to wink at the world, with the sly understanding that you are making things happen for you and that you are free enough within yourself that you don't have to tell anyone else about it. To be completely appreciated for what you are, you have to be long gone from this planet—and if you understand this, then you'll stop *needing* to be appreciated and make your life work far better while you are still here to enjoy it. Dostoyevsky understood this. As he wrote in *The Brothers Karamazov*,

> Men reject their prophets and slay them, but they love their martyrs and honour those whom they have slain.

So why should you allow yourself to be slain, even if it is done psychologically? And even more important, why should you wait until after you're gone to be honored? Decide to live now, and accept not being understood by everyone all the time. The choice is really up to you.

6

Teaching Others How You Want to Be Treated

Most people are nicer to total strangers than they are to their loved ones and to themselves.

How are you treated by people? Are you repeatedly used and abused? Do you find others taking advantage of you, or not respecting you as a person? Do people make plans without asking you and just assume you will go along? Do you find yourself in roles you dislike because everyone else in your life expects you to behave as you do?

These are some of the common laments I have heard from clients and friends who feel victimized in multitudinous ways. My response is generally the same: "You get treated the way you teach people to treat you."

If you feel abused by others' treatment of you, then look at your own thinking and behavior, and ask why you have permitted or even encouraged the abuse you complain of. If you don't make yourself responsible for how you are treated, you will continue to be powerless to do anything about it.

The Roman philosopher Epictetus summed up these same ideas over two thousand years ago:

It is not he who gives abuse that affronts, but the view that we take of it as insulting; so that when one provokes you it is your own opinion which is provoking.

This chapter updates those ancient words, containing one of the most important lessons of life, as they apply to our present culture, but in essence, the truth still holds. Your hurts come not from what others do to you, but from what you choose to do with their actions. If you change your attitudes and expectations about being hurt, then you'll soon find the abuse terminating, and your victim status eliminated.

THE "TEACHING OTHERS" PROCESS

You teach others how to treat you on the basis of what you will tolerate. If you simply "take it," and you have been for a long time, then you have sent out the message that you will not resist abuse.

This is not a very complicated theory. If you send out the message that you simply won't tolerate abuse, and back it up with effective behavior, your abusers will not receive the payoff they are looking for, which is to see you immobilized so they can manipulate you. But if you just take their string-pulling, or register mild objections and then go right on being controlled, you are teaching them to continue using you as a dumping ground.

Gayle was a client who came to me because she felt mercilessly controlled by her dominant husband. She complained of being a doormat for all his abusive language and tactics of manipulation. She was the mother of three children, none of whom showed her much respect, and she was at her rope's end with depression and hopelessness.

As she told me about her past, I heard a classic case of someone who had permitted herself to be victimized since childhood. Her parents had always spoken for her, and insisted that she answer to them for everything she did. Her father was exceedingly dominant, and had monitored her behavior throughout her formative years right up until her marriage. When she had sought out a marriage partner, he had "accidentally" turned out to be exactly like her father, so marriage had just put her in the same victim pigeonhole again. All she had ever known was being spoken for, being told what to do, and suffering in silence when no one would listen to her.

I pointed out to Gayle that she had carefully taught people to treat her that way, that it was not "their" fault at all, even though she was very fond of blaming them and everyone else for her misery. She soon learned that she had been victimizing herself by taking all that abuse for all those years and never looking for effective counterstrategies. Once Gayle had gained the insight that it really was her responsibility to look inward rather than outward for answers to her problems, counseling helped her learn new ways of teaching people to treat her differently. I first relayed my "karate chop" theory to her. It goes something like this.

THE "KARATE CHOP" THEORY

Think back to the very first time your spouse abused you, by raising his voice, getting angry, hitting you, or whatever. What he did was help you to become upset.

It is very likely that the incident you have in mind occurred before you were married, had children, etc. Imagine yourself back in that situation. Your future husband's abusive behavior comes as a total surprise, since this is the first time he has tried it.

Suppose that instead of being shocked, stunned, afraid or tearful, you had showed your partner your hand, told him that it was a registered weapon, and given him a solid karate chop to the stomach, followed up with, "I don't intend to take that kind of abuse from you. I think of myself as a person with dignity, and I'm not ever going to be shoved around by you or anyone else. Please give yourself a heavy dose of second thoughts before you try something like that again. That's all I have to say about it." And then you proceeded to carry on an intelligent conversation.

While this may seem an absurd thing to imagine, it illustrates the point: Had you reacted from strength and firm intolerance for abusive behavior right from the very beginning, you would once and for all have taught your partner something very important—that you will not indulge such nasty behavior for one second.

But your reaction was probably disastrously different. Whether you cried, acted hurt or insulted, or showed fear, you sent out a fatal signal that you would not necessarily like the way he was treating you, but that you would take it, and even more significantly, that you would let yourself be manipulated emotionally by it.

When I told Gayle this theory she said, "I could never have reacted anything like the way you say I might have!" At first she wanted to defend her entrenched position that her husband and her children were totally at fault for her victim status, and she wanted me to feel sorry for her and become an ally in her misery. When I persisted in stating that the "karate chop" doesn't need violence, physical or any other kind, to have its psychological impact, and that she might have left the room, refused to talk with him, or even called the police, to illustrate her intolerance, she began to get the message. She soon accepted the fact that she had indeed taught almost everyone that she was willing to be a "dumpee," and she resolved to work at changing from then on.

Gayle's new behaviors were geared toward teaching her husband and her children that she wouldn't be taken for granted. It took some time for her to get the message across, since victimizers hate to give up their power without a fight, but she was determined, and she won most of her battles. When the children showed disrespect, she reacted with a very loud voice and a firm demand that they do their required chores, or whatever it was they'd been shirking off onto her. This was a total shock to the children, who had never heard their mommy so much as raise her voice. She refused to chauffeur on given days, and let the children fend for themselves. If they couldn't walk, ride their bikes, or find someone else to drive them, they'd have to give up the activity.

Gayle's children soon learned that Mom was not going to be the sweet little victim any more—not because she cried and yelled a lot, but because she taught them with new behaviors and a determination to make them stick, as guilty as they might try to make her feel.

With her husband, Gayle developed a new approach to how she was going to be treated. One of her husband's favorite tactics was to get angry and disgusted with her, particularly when other adults, or the children, were around to hear him. She had always shriveled at this; *she* didn't want to create a scene, and so became embarrassed, quiet and obedient. Her first assignment was to stand right up to her husband in an equally loud voice, and then to leave the room.

On her very first try, her husband and everyone else present went into shock. Little meek Gayle was giving it back in spades. They couldn't believe it. Her husband reacted with a classic guilt line: "What will the children think, hearing their mother talk like that?"

After several months of practicing more effective behavior, Gayle was happy to report that everyone in her family was indeed treating her quite differently. They had tried to stop her by labeling her self-ish, "not nice," and phrases like, "You're not supposed to say that, Mommy," and, "If you loved us, you wouldn't be so mean." But Gayle had been alerted to these ploys, and when she ignored them, they soon disappeared.

Gayle learned firsthand that you do indeed get treated the way you teach people to treat you. Now, three years later, she rarely receives disrespect or abuse from anyone, particularly her immediate family.

YOU TEACH PEOPLE WITH BEHAVIOR, NOT WORDS

"We should believe only in deeds; words go for nothing everywhere." So spoke Fernando Rojas, a Spanish author, almost five hundred years ago. If you attempt to get your important messages of non-victimization across through lengthy discussions, your only payoffs will be in the words that pass between you and your victimizers. And long discussions are very often the tools that victimizers use. "All right, we've had our little talk, and I see your point, and you don't want me to do that to you any more." But the next time the problem crops up, your entire discussion is forgotten, and you end up with the same old treatment. If you then have another talk and agree that things will be straightened out, you get yourself all the more deeply into the word trap. There may be lots of "communication" between you and every-one else, but until you learn to behave in effective ways, you will still get pushed around, and you will still talk about it a lot. Many people do all this talking to their therapists, who in turn listen to endless stories about all the horrible victimizers in their clients' lives—and that is all that ever gets accomplished, just a lot of talk.

Therapy ought to be an experience which teaches new *behaviors*, and discourages meaningless talk. If you just tell *anyone* else how bad you feel, and that person gives you nothing more than a lot of empathy and support, then you are a double victim. You get it on one hand from the victimizers of the world, and on the other hand from the person you are paying to feel sorry for you.

The most effective teacher in the world is behavior. Action which demonstrates your resolve is worth a million well-intended words. Watch young children and how they deal with bullies. A bully will intimidate nine out of ten smaller children, and each of the victims will plead, cry, yell or complain to a big person, but still, the bullying goes on and on. Then a tenth child, even though he may be smaller, will haul off and let the bully have it. The bully now has an internal reminder: "He's the one who hits back, and even if I'm bigger, I don't want to be kicked again, have to chase him and lose face. . . . I'll leave him alone next time and pick on someone who'll take it."

Behavior is the only way to teach others not to bully you. By standing up and taking that risk, even though you might get "hit back," you send out a message that you aren't interested in being bullied, and that you simply won't take it. Forget all of those fancy words and promises when it comes to people that push you around in any way.

Carlyle put it this way:

If you do not wish a man to do a thing, you had better get him to talk about it; for the more men talk, the more likely they are to do nothing else.

Whenever you are trying to explain to someone how you want to be treated, ask yourself if your explanation is really accomplishing anything. Are you using up your energy talking to a salesperson who really doesn't care what you are saying? Are your words to your children going in one ear and out the other? Does your spouse quietly listen, and then go right on doing the same things you object to again and again? Here are three examples of situations in which words are useless, but through the creative application of behavior, people begin to receive the treatment they desire.

1. CHILDREN AND PARENTS   Corinne has three small children by whom she feels victimized a great deal of the time. She spends virtually her whole life talking to them, but nothing seems to sink in.

On vacation, Corinne and her family are at the beach. Her husband is enjoying himself, but Mommy has taught the children that she will referee their every dispute, so this is what you hear:

"Billy threw sand on me, Mommy."

"Billy, stop that this minute."

Three minutes later, "Billy was splashing me, Mommy. Tell him to stop doing that."

"Tell your father."

"I already did. He said he didn't care, but to take it up with you." Dialogues like this can go on forever. Each child reports to Corinne and gets her attention. Corinne reacts just as she has taught the children that she would, scolding or complaining, but never getting through.

In the supermarket, the youngest child asks for some bubble gum from a machine. Corinne says no. The child throws a tantrum until Corinne can't stand it any more and gives in. The message: "If you want something, don't listen to me, just have a fit, and you'll get it." Corinne spends virtually all her time talking to the children, but they never hear what she says, because the words are not connected to reality.

Corinne can teach her children with behavior rather than words, or she can use words followed up by action. When the children ask her to be a referee, she can simply disappear. Yes, I mean physically leave and allow them to work out their own disputes. She can go to the bathroom and lock herself in, go for a short walk (if the children aren't too young to be left alone in the house), and so on. Or she can just say, "You settle it yourselves this time," and ignore their complaints about it.

She can let her youngest child go ahead and throw her tantrum in the store, teaching her that Mommy is not going to be manipulated because she fears embarrassment.

When left alone, children are sensational at resolving their own problems, and they seldom ask for referees when they know it isn't going to get them attention or an advantage in settling their dispute. When you don't step in and referee all the time, you really teach children to think for themselves, to consult their own strength, and not to manipulate others. Most of her children's behaviors that Corinne complains about are the results of her having used words exclusively rather than behavior to try to communicate with them.

2. SPOUSE CONFLICTS   George has a terrible sexual relationship with his wife. He has talked to her about it until he is blue in the face, but to no avail. She simply does not behave in the ways he would like.

Whenever they are finished making love, George typically complains or tells his wife how he feels, but she doesn't seem to get the message. Her goal is to have the sex act completed as soon as possible. George would like her to be more aggressively excitable and do different things, instead of just going through the motions. But she hasn't really learned how he wants to be treated.

George can teach his spouse new ways of behaving without ever saying a word. He can put her hands where he would like them to be, he can slow the whole experience down by slowing his actions down, and he can demonstrate techniques rather than talking about them.

If you don't like the way you are treated sexually, it may be fine to talk about your dissatisfaction, but these expressions of dissent will very likely cause more problems than they will resolve. It is far better to go after what you want. If your lovemaking is always too fast, slow it down with behavior that shows that more time can be better for both of you. If you aren't having orgasms, work at helping your partner to know what you want, through the intelligent channel of behavior, rather than discussion.

This is not an indictment of oral communication by couples, but a look at how to get treated the way you want to be treated after words have failed to get the message across effectively.

3. THE BATTERED WIFE   Physical abuse of wives is far too common in our culture, as any therapist who has spent much time in family therapy can attest. It would be far less common if women learned to react to such tactics with behavior rather than words.

Marie was a target of her husband's physical attacks for three years. She had sustained bruises, welts, and even a few broken bones. After each incident her husband apologized profusely and vowed never to do it again. And Marie, after complaining, crying and praying a lot, did no more than hope for the best. But when his volatile temper erupted in rage again, she would take another beating.

Marie was finally convinced, after he'd given her a particularly nasty black eye, that she should not return home for three days. She did not call and explain where she was, nor did she even let her husband know where she was staying. She simply took the two children and checked into a motel. Her goal was to teach her husband that she would not tolerate physical abuse any more, and wouldn't be around any more if it occurred again.

During the three days she and the children were gone her husband was frantic. When they returned he complained a lot, but he had started to learn an invaluable lesson—hit Marie and she disappears.

Marie's husband did beat her one more time—after which she left for a week. If necessary, she was prepared to disappear from his life forever, even though she didn't bother to have a long conversation with him about it; she just told him in so many words. But by this time her husband sensed she had determined that being alive was much more important to her than being married to a man who beat her regularly, even though she loved him very much, and he "decided" he had to control his temper. By adopting radical reactions to his abusive behavior, Marie successfully taught him how she would be treated, and has not been a battered wife since.

These very typical experiences, which you might meet in your own life, illustrate that you need not do anything immoral or against your own personal values when you need to teach and words have proved to be empty air. Indeed, as Ibsen said, "A thousand words will not leave so deep an impression as one deed." So begin to take constructive steps toward teaching people how to treat you, by dismissing the words when they simply don't work, and developing instead an arsenal of effective behaviors that put your whole self where your mouth is.

WHAT DO YOU EXPECT FROM A DRUNK?

One of the more illogical victimizing games people play on themselves is to expect totally unrealistic things of others, and when others do not live up to their expectations, they are shocked, scandalized, offended, distraught. This game involves wishing others would learn what cannot be taught, or what it is not your business to teach. A classic example of this kind of self-victimizing thinking lies in the way many people react to drunks.

Here is a drunk. You have spotted and labeled him as a drunk, and you know very well what a drunk is. Now if you find yourself upset when this drunk acts drunk, are you in tune with the world and the way it works? And who is the loony person? The drunk who acts in drunken ways, or you who expect him to act sober? If you expect many drunks to be unruly, overly talkative, uncoordinated, or whatever, you should hardly be surprised when tonight's drunk displays this behavior, and you should act accordingly: Ignore him, get away from him, or whatever strategy works. You thereby avoid allowing him to pull your strings in any way.

Here are some examples of the general "expecting sober behavior from a drunk" mentality that victimizes so many people:

• "My wife is a quiet person. It really upsets me that she doesn't talk to me more."

What do you expect from a quiet person, noise? If your spouse is quiet, being upset when he or she does exactly what you'd predict is pretty absurd.

• "My kid doesn't care about playing ball. It really upsets me that he's so unathletic."

But why would you expect someone who doesn't want to throw a ball around to be good at it? So who's crazy? The kid, who is doing just what you'd expect, or you, who expect an unathletic kid to be athletic?

• "That son-in-law of mine is always late. It really upsets me when he isn't on time."

This kind of list could obviously go on forever, and it does. The point is that whether or not you begin to teach people to eliminate habits which impose on you, you teach them that you will not allow yourself to be hurt or immobilized by them when they are only behaving just as you would have predicted.

ON BEING EFFECTIVELY ASSERTIVE

Many people assume that being assertive means being unpleasant or deliberately offensive, but it doesn't. It means making bold, confident declarations in defense of your rights, or your non-victim position.

You can learn the art of disagreeing without being disagreeable, and you can stand up for yourself without being cantankerous. If you get treated the way you teach others to treat you, then without assertiveness you are most unlikely ever to be treated as anything but a victim.

People who achieve their goals by pulling their own strings are unafraid to risk standing up and insisting upon their rights when they are threatened. They have learned how to fight their internal fears. They may not be "brave," but they are firm and unwilling to back off in the face of potential victimizers. And the other side of the coin is that the more you avoid assertive behaviors, the more you teach others that you are willing to be their victim.

Below are some examples of "assertive successes" reported by clients who were specifically working on their assertive behavior when these incidents occurred.

• Lois brings her five-year-old son with her to the bank. Suddenly he has to go to the bathroom. She approaches the bank teller and asks, "Can I use your bathroom, please? My son has an emergency." She is told, "I'm sorry, the bathroom is for employees only." What can Lois do? Take it and have her little boy wet his pants, rush around looking for a restroom in a gas station, or any of several alternatives that would victimize Lois and her little boy? No indeed, she marches right up to the manager and asserts herself: "My son is having an emergency and I would like to use your bathroom right now. I've been refused by the teller and if you refuse me I will never do business with this bank again." Lois is instantly granted admission to the bathroom with apologies for the teller's insensitivity. Conclusion: You get treated the way you teach people to treat you—be assertive and you won't be a victim.

• Charlie walks into a store, asking the clerk for change of a quarter to feed the empty parking meter. The clerk responds in an irascible tone, "What do you think we run here, a changing service? We're in business to make money, not to give change." Charlie instantly stands up to the clerk and responds, "You're obviously ticked off about something, and my asking for change has really set you off. I'd appreciate it if you'd make an exception and give me change and I hope your day improves as well." Charlie was shocked at the response of the clerk. He not only received his change, but an apology, "I'm really sorry to have yelled at you, things haven't been going so well. Don't take it personally." Had Charlie just skulked out he would have been upset, a victim and without his change. A simple act of assertiveness turned the whole thing around for him, and as he reported it in a counseling session, he was ecstatic over his new-found skill.

• Patti's husband brought a puppy home and informed her that "they" now had two dogs. But he expected *her* to clean up its paper-training mess, feed it, discipline it, put up with it teething on her kitchen set, cabinets and moldings, etc. Patti had taught her husband by her past behavior that she would accept such unpleasant chores whenever he forced them on her.

Her solution was calmly to tell her husband that he was welcome to have another dog in the house, but that it was his decision alone, and so the responsibility for the dog was his. She then refused to change the puppy's papers, to allow it into the kitchen, or to walk it. After two days her husband returned the puppy to the pet shop, and he had learned how she was going to be treated from her assertive behavior.

• Murray had decided to quit drinking. Signs of impending alcoholism had been pointed out to him in counseling sessions, and he had decided to tighten up his own strings. But he wasn't getting much help from his friends, as illustrated by this dialogue he encountered in a nightclub.

"Murray, have a beer."

"I don't want to drink."

"Come on, don't be a spoiler, have a drink."

"No, thanks."

To the bartender, "Give him a beer."

"No, *thanks!*"

To the bartender again, "Give my friend Murray just one beer. There, Murray, you have to drink it! I already bought it for you!"

"You can buy all you want, but I still won't have a drink."

By refusing to engage in self-destructive drinking, Murray used his new assertiveness to teach his friends how he was going to be treated, despite their use of several maneuvers to try and victimize him.

• Adele had always cooked a Thanksgiving dinner for her entire family's gathering, and never received any help with it from anyone. She had never enjoyed it, but somehow it had evolved into a huge event. She had to put her time and energy into preparing a menu, cleaning her house from top to bottom, spending more money than she could afford, serving the meal, and cleaning up afterward, without even minimal recognition. She always felt victimized during the holiday, and after every Thanksgiving she would spend a week in a fit of depression, vowing to never let it happen to her again. Yet after twenty-two years, she still did it just because it was expected of her.

But one year Adele sent out a letter to the entire clan on October 10, informing them of a new tradition. Thanksgiving dinner would be in a beautiful downtown restaurant. Each family would be responsible for making its own reservations. Afterward they could all attend a concert. Everyone thought the idea was delightful. For the past three years Adele has avoided the Thanksgiving doldrums and actually enjoyed the holiday which had once been such a sore spot in her life. Assertive behavior won out not only for Adele, but for everyone concerned.

• Irene and Harold found themselves victimized by an acquaintance who had adopted them and their home as a place of refuge. Sam had arrived unannounced and consumed hours telling them about his broken marriage, along with any other sordid stories they would absorb.

At first Irene and Harold didn't want to hurt Sam's feelings by telling him how they really felt. They thought it better to be dishonest and victimized by their friends than to offend a guest, cause a scene, etc. But after two months Irene couldn't stand it any more, and finally told Sam she didn't *want* to listen to the sad details of his life, and that she didn't want him to invade her home whenever he got the urge to have an audience.

From that moment on, Sam didn't abuse their friendship. He began to call and ask before he came over, and he visited less frequently. Irene's assertive behavior taught Sam how she wanted to be treated, just as her timid behavior taught him that it was okay to victimize her and her husband.

• Tony had always been meek in dealing with salespeople. He

often found himself buying things he didn't want because he was afraid of hurting clerks' feelings. While working on becoming more assertive, Tony went to buy some shoes. He was shown a pair he liked, and told the salesman he would take them. But as the salesman was putting them in a box, Tony noticed a small scratch on one of them. He suppressed his immediate urge to "forget it" and said, "Please bring me another pair. One of those is scratched."

To his astonishment, the salesman responded, "Yes, sir, right away." Tony walked away from the experience with a perfect pair of shoes, and the knowledge of how easy it is to avoid being victimized, even in small ways, if you assert yourself.

This particular incident was a turning point for Tony. He began to practice assertive behavior in all areas of his life, where the payoffs were far greater than getting an unscratched pair of shoes. His boss, his wife, his children and his friends all talk about a new Tony, who is not just "taking it." Tony not only gets what he wants more often, but he has gained immeasurable respect from others and from himself.

SOME COMMON CATEGORIES OF PEOPLE YOU HAVE TAUGHT TO VICTIMIZE YOU

Below are some common categories of potential victimizers and a little bit about how you might size them up if you are to teach such people how you want to be treated. You will undoubtedly recognize yourself as having been victimized by many of these types in the past, and if you are candid with yourself, you will also note that you have fallen into some of these categories in victimizing others.

- *Drunks and people who are high.* Although you may not want or be able to teach someone who is "out of it" anything he will remember for long, in the short run you can teach him that he gets nothing out of using abusive tactics on you. Drunks and "highs" who want to talk forever, slobber or stumble all over you, etc., will usually stumble elsewhere if they get no response. If they can hardly tell you from the furniture when they try to "corner you," they will go elsewhere in search of a "live one." And if they don't, you do.
- *Bores.* If you sit politely listening to a bore, nodding your head but gritting your teeth in annoyance at his conversational selfishness

and insensitivity, you are teaching him to do just what you resent. But bores are usually aware on some level that they are pinning you down, and they will often relent if you show that you know how to break their hold, perhaps with some firm but good-natured remark like, "Hey, do you realize you've been talking for fifteen minutes straight without noticing that I'm not interested?" It's better to loosen up than to lose your ear altogether.

● *Whiners and complainers*. People who abuse you as a big ear for their complaining and whining can also be made to appreciate that without victims they are out of business, and you can teach them a lot by showing them just how non-existent their "holds" on you really are.

● *Bullies*. People who shove others around, "playfully" or otherwise, will seldom respond to subtleties; teaching them that you just won't take it usually requires some very assertive behavior.

● *Victimizing hosts and hostesses*. If you are people's guest they can try to make it very hard for you to avoid playing games you don't enjoy, eating foods you don't like, or any of a number of things that may be demanded of a "polite guest." But the right "quietly effective" strategies can rapidly teach them that politeness has to work both ways.

● *Arguers*. To avoid arguments you don't enjoy, you usually have to refuse completely to stick to the game plan. Argumentative people thrive on their victims' inclinations to be seduced into conversations first and then let themselves be trapped into vituperation. The secret with them is to stay emotionally detached so you can implement the strategies mentioned earlier.

● *Braggers and storytellers*. Don't "brag back" or get caught in a contest to see who can tell the longest-winded story of the least interest to anyone else. If you don't participate yourself, you can teach others what they need to know by viewing them as bores.

● *Admonishers*. People who love to tell you why you shouldn't have behaved as you did, or who willingly give you morality lectures based on their conviction that you should think, feel and behave as they do, will continue forever unless you teach them that they are simply in no position to manipulate you in such a condescending way.

● *Interrupters*. People who just can't wait for conversational openings before jumping in with *their* points have to be taught a little patience. If you then interrupt them, you endorse the rule that "the loudest and most persistent voice gets the floor." But if you react with sudden, "shocked silence" the instant they cut you off, you make them realize what they've done, and often they'll apologize. If they miss the hint, the next time you may have to say, "You just interrupted me for the tenth time! Can't you remember what you want to say until I'm finished?" Unless the person just wants to browbeat you (and you know what to do then), he will usually make an effort to curtail his habit, although he may continue to need good-natured reminders from you.

● *Shockers.* If you can be shocked by language, sexual images, jokes, weirdo stories or anything, then shockers will use them to victimize you. Teach them that it doesn't work by refusing to be offended for their benefit or entertainment, and if necessary by showing that you consider such behavior childish.

● *Con artists and fast-talkers.* The cold shoulder is usually the only effective teaching tool for people who don't care about you at all (though they will pretend to) except for what they can do you out of.

● *Resenters.* People who try to use their resentment at something you have done, to manipulate and victimize you, will only desist when you teach them that you refuse to let their resentment influence your future decisions. Try telling them this, and if that doesn't work, go to strategies for dealing with people who just won't understand you.

● *Reporters and squealers.* You can only be blackmailed if you believe someone else's opinion of what you've done is more important than your own, or if you harbor paralyzing fears about "what will happen if . . ." Many times a shrug and a brief "so what?" will teach a "reporter" that you are not intimidated. Remember that threats may be useful to these people, but actually squealing is almost always useless.

● *Headstrong insisters.* People who are persevering and adamant in their attempts to get you to do things their way will by definition seldom be swayed by talk. The only way to combat their pleading, begging, cajoling and demanding is to develop a deaf ear and a refusal to be moved.

● *Guilt merchants.* People who want to sell you guilt for their own price, which is usually your manipulation, will learn not to peddle their wares on you as soon as they register a few resounding "no sales." Try to tell them why you think their deals are rotten if you want, but don't expect talk alone to make them stop offering.

• *Moody people*. If someone else's shift into a blue funk, or any "contrary" mood, can take you with it, your independence (not to mention your happiness) can be undermined, and you can then be a good little victim. Persist in the mood you prefer, tell people their misery doesn't need your company and vice versa, ask if they think two people wallowing in sadness are better than one—but in the end, of course, be prepared to ignore such moody behaviors.

• *Greedy people*. Greed may very well be the world's original victimizer. If someone close to you is greedy and you place loyalty to him above your own principles and independence, you can virtually be taken for all you're worth, whether it's in terms of your time, your money, or your freedom, etc.

It is quite possible to love people and still not be seduced by their illegal or immoral greed. In fact, if you just tag along and take it, you are not doing a very good job of loving. Greed is just wanting more than your share of something at someone else's expense, and rip-off artists are never happy people. Greed in people you don't know or care about is to be expected and dealt with through whatever antivictimization strategies that will teach them to leave you alone. But greed in someone you do care about has to be knocked back with every principle and behavioral strategy at the non-victim's command.

The above seventeen categories of common victimizers will pull your strings unmercifully unless you teach them not to. You always have a great deal more control over your reactions and their habits than you might think.

SOME TYPICAL VICTIM TARGETS

No one is immune from the victimizing efforts of other people. Rich or poor, black or white, young or old, each of us has our own peculiar battles to fight. No matter who you are, the victim stamp can come out of the blue at any time without warning and smack you right on the head—unless you have your antivictimization umbrella with you and a keen eye for predatory weather. There are, however, always some people who must fight even harder than most to avoid victimization. The philosophy and strategies of pulling your own strings still apply to them, but their battles are tougher and longer, and their tolls of unavoidable failure are far greater. Sometimes the struggle to teach people that they won't be victimized is so costly that it seems the victories could not possibly be worth it. But for those who have persevered and won, there has been no such thing as compromise. As John Gardner stated, "There are no easy victories."

The greatest leaders of mankind have known all too well that people teach and learn how others are to be treated from behavior. Departing a moment from the highly personalized approach to non-victimization that dominates this book, and shifting for a moment to a larger social context, let's compare the philosophy of non-victimization, as it's unfolded so far, with the attitudes of some "great people" who have fought against mass victimization—victimization of oppressed groups—down through history. We'll find that they anticipated the philosophy of non-victimization in their own times.

Abraham Lincoln knew slavery would never be abolished if people just talked about it. He understood that slaveowners had to be taught with behavior, adamant behavior that showed that this "institution" would not be tolerated.

Martin Luther King knew that people had to get out there and make noise, march, stir things up, enact legislation, if his dream was to come true.

Lincoln and King both knew that the civil rights of minorities were being violated because not enough people were standing up and saying, "Hold it right there! We won't tolerate slavery in *our* society for another *minute!*" Words, words, words . . . and finally *action,* to teach people how you will be treated.

Churchill understood that you didn't *bargain* with Nazis, as Chamberlain had so painfully learned. All the world would have been conquered by Nazis if people hadn't stood up with their behavior, risked their lives and often lost them, to halt the madness of total victimization that Nazism spawned.

Jefferson and Franklin knew the American colonies had taught the British they were willing to be treated as "subjects," and that if things were going to change, the colonists would have to stop talking and act on their desire for independence.

Similarly, women in contemporary America have learned that they must claim their rights with their behavior, rather than asking for them with meaningless words and pet phrases. Women have been victimized largely because they have taught men they would endure their subjugation. When that tolerance disappears, amazingly enough, equalization begins. The American Indians have learned that treaties and powwows are meaningless, and they are being listened to now, because they won't continue being victims.

The examples in social history are endless. Ralph Nader typifies this concept in contemporary America. He has convinced people, through his behavior and the behavior of his "raiders," that he will not just sit back and let abuse continue to be visited on consumers. He is an activist who is making a difference by being visible and demonstrating his moxie with effective behavior where it counts. And Ralph Nader is getting results. Whether you agree with him or not, he is getting the big businesses of the world (including the U.S. government) to take note of his antivictimization stance. This is the way all social change experts have operated—with behavior and a clear understanding that you will always get treated as you teach others to treat you.

The major categories of people who have been victimized in recent history are patently obvious. *Older people* who have gone into retirement and let the younger generations take over have more to offer the world than any single group, but they have been relegated to second-class citizens whom society tolerates at best, because they have taught younger people to treat them that way. Anyone over sixty-five who doesn't wish to be viewed as inferior or washed up generally isn't, but as a group older people have allowed themselves to become relatively impotent in the western world. (But watch out for the activist *Gray Panthers*.)

Religious minority groups in the United States have also been widely abused, including at different times Jewish people, Catholics, and members of virtually every Protestant sect. Those groups which have insisted on their rights to their beliefs and stood up for them, generally emerged with respect. Yes, the cost has often been very dear, but nevertheless, the logic holds true: if you allow yourself to be persecuted and don't offer resistance, then you'll never be able to pull your own strings.

Obviously, the story of racial minority groups in this country has been one of struggle every inch of the way. Black Americans, Native Americans, Asian Americans, Puerto Ricans, Chicanos, and whatever others you can think of, have all had to stand up and demand their rights, or go on being victimized. The great leaders of these minority groups were risk-takers who stood up to be counted. While racial discrimination certainly continues today, the remedy is truly not going to reside in words, but in action that teaches the victimizers just how minority groups must be treated.

Many students in universities and high schools also learned the hard way that the road to a voice in their affairs did not rest in the toy student-governments that administrations offered, but in demanding that they be heard on the real issues. What is at stake in all these struggles by victimized groups is independence, people's rights to pull their own strings. Thomas Jefferson wrote in the Declaration of Independence about the right of a whole nation burdened with a victimizing government, to "alter or to abolish it and institute new Government."

The analogies to individual victimization are painfully obvious when we talk about altering social conditions so that groups of people are not victimized by other groups who happen to have positions of power. You can apply the lessons of effective liberation of groups to your own life. Anyone who attempts to force you in a direction you don't choose for yourself is no less irresponsible or out of line than a slaveowner, a Tory or a dictator. You must have your independence to be you, and you will only get it by teaching others the limits of what you'll put up with.

STRATEGIES FOR TEACHING OTHERS HOW YOU WANT TO BE TREATED

Here are some attitudes and behaviors you can implement when you want to teach other people new, non-victimizing ways of treating you.

• Stop expecting to be abused. Accept that you have a history of being maltreated not primarily because others have taken advantage of you, but because you have taught them to do so. The attitude that you are responsible for most of your treatment by others transforms what you expect to suffer from them into what you expect of yourself. Virtually all human change begins with attitude.

• Adopt a non-victim code of ethics for yourself which you can work on in quietly effective ways, and about which you refuse to compromise. For example:

1. I will not be taken advantage of by drunks. I will not talk to them for more than five minutes, nor will I ever get into a car to be driven home by a drunk.

2. I will refuse to explain myself to anyone who is obviously not interested in hearing what I have to say. The moment I become aware that I am talking to a stone wall, I will cease attempting to explain myself further.

3. I will not pick up after anyone.

These kinds of rules of conduct are important, but unless your resolutions contain practical changes you have to let others know about—such as, you refuse to drive your husband and all his friends to the golf course every Sunday, so they'd better look for another ride—they need never be discussed with others and usually shouldn't be. You might create useless arguments and end up feeling as if that's "doing something."

• Practice reacting as much as possible with behavior instead of words. React drastically to being abused. Try out new behaviors which will shock your victimizers. If you are intimidated by someone's swearing, give it back in spades just for the shock value and to teach that you are capable of being assertive. Walk out of situations where someone is assaulting you verbally. If you need to, you can always take a cab home. Be firm with behavior at the beginning of your new teaching process, so the message that you are not going to take any more abuse comes through loud and clear.

• If someone in your house shirks his responsibilities and your usual tendency is to complain but do the job yourself, remember that you have taught the person to act that way. Next time, teach him something different. If your son is supposed to empty the garbage and doesn't, remind him once. If he ignores you, give him a deadline. If he ignores the deadline, calmly empty the garbage on his bed. One bed-emptying exercise will do more to teach him that you mean business than all the meaningless words that have got you nothing but upset.

• Eliminate complaining words and phrases from your vocabulary. Stop blaming everyone else for your foul treatment. Stop yourself from saying things like, "It's his fault," "She's to blame," "I can't help it," "They did it to me," "They don't respect me," and the like. Instead, think to yourself, "I taught them to do this to me," or, "It's my fault for allowing this to happen." These are reminders to work at changing your victim status, rather than reinforcing it.

• Stop waiting for things to get better. If you are waiting for people to stop abusing you, you'll end up waiting forever. Become that effective teacher *now*, and don't stand around anticipating that passing time will bring you better treatment.

• Vow to take active risks when dealing with potential victimizers. Build up the courage to strike back at the bully just once, and take a good look at the results. Talk back to an overbearing person. Speak up when group-doings victimize you. Walk out of situations that you see are hopeless or not worth a hassle. Kick yourself in the rear end just once and *do it*, and you'll find assertiveness getting much easier. Every march of a thousand miles begins with one step, but you must be willing to take that first step by overcoming your fear and inertia for just one tiny second.

• Practice assertive sentences, even in places where it may seem silly. View these exercises as rehearsals for the big events. Talk up to waiters, salespeople, strangers, bellboys, desk clerks, reservationists, cab drivers, milkmen, or whomever. Tell them what you would like from them and see if you don't get your respect and service from your "practicing." The more rehearsal you try, the better equipped you'll be to assert yourself when it really counts.

• Stop using sentences that permit or invite people to victimize you. Such put-downs as, "I'm not very important," "I'm not really that smart," "I'm no good at figures," "I never understand legal matters," or, "I'm not too coordinated," are really licenses for others to take advantage of you. If you tell a waiter you're no good at figures while he's adding up your check, you're teaching him that you won't catch a "mistake."

• Refuse to do chores which you absolutely hate and which are not "necessarily" your responsibility. If you hate mowing the lawn or doing the laundry, then stop it for two weeks and see what happens. Hire someone to do some of the work if you can afford it, or teach others in the family to begin to take care of themselves. If you've always done the laundry for the grown-up members of your family who are perfectly capable of doing it for themselves, then you have taught them to use you as a victim and a slave. The only way out of the trap is to stop doing it, and when they want clean underwear, they can wash it. Not only will you be doing them a favor by teaching them some self-reliance, but you'll be freeing yourself from the drudgery of always having to wait on others. This can also apply to things like getting the coffee at the office, taking the minutes at meetings, etc. Generally you are the doer of menial tasks only because you've taught others that you'll do it without complaining.

• Don't be seduced by the initial efforts of victimizers to reject what you're trying to teach them. The reactions may be extreme in either direction. You may find people getting very angry and loud, or you might be indulged with a few bribes, such as gifts and extra doses of consideration, when you become more assertive. View all initial reactions as tests, and let time determine their persistence. Be firm in your resolve regardless of the reactions, which many times you may be able to predict. Before very long, others will see that you are serious, and they will treat you as you teach them to treat you—that is, with respect.

• Don't let others make you feel guilty about your new assertive behaviors. Resist the temptation to feel bad when someone gives you a hurt look, or a plea, or a gift (bribe), or an angry response. Generally the people whom you've taught to victimize you won't quite know how to react to the new you. Try to be lovingly firm at these times. You can be willing to explain why you are being assertive, as long as they are willing to hear you. But if they start with, "Yes, buts," or whining, "It's not fair," or, "You never did that before, why are you doing it now?" then you revert to behavior which says that you are determined to carry out your convictions. Be alert for genuine feelings of exasperation, which you can talk about, as opposed to attempts to manipulate you into being the good old victim that you've always been, which you simply refuse to acknowledge.

• Teach others that you have a right to reserve time to do the things you enjoy. Be adamant about taking breaks from a busy office, a hot stove, etc. Go poke around in the world. Count your relaxation and "enjoying" time as of paramount importance, which it is, and be religious about not allowing others to encroach on it. If you are constantly being interrupted, try the same strategies recommended earlier for dealing with people who interrupt you in conversations.

• Refuse automatically to become a middleman in resolving other people's disputes, especially those of little children. Teach people that you value yourself too much to be a referee (or to take sides) in their battles unless *you* want to, and can clearly do some good.

• Keep a log of how others victimize you with their words. If you're a beleaguered mother, chronicle how many times a day you hear, "Mommy, Mommy, what should I do?" or, "Do it for me," or, "That's okay, she'll do it." When you see how often others use their language to reaffirm you as a victim, you'll be better equipped to combat it with new behavior, and a log or a diary will help you see.

• Practice not being angry with others you've taught to manipulate you into anger. If you have traditionally got bent out of shape by anger and ended up saying and doing things that you've later regretted, win back your self-control. Children are expert at helping parents become angry, even if it means spankings or being sent to their rooms. What they have won is a certain mastery of the situation. By being firm rather than outrageously angry, you maintain control, and only then can you avoid being immobilized by others and begin to teach them anything. When your angry outbursts cease, that alone will often stop the victimizing behavior of others.

• Get an ally to discuss your new teaching strategies with you. Develop a confidential relationship with someone who can think with you about your victories and defeats. Be candid. Sharing your feelings about your new efforts with a sympathetic listener and friend will give you strength—and perhaps a supporter in certain encounters.

• Remember always to consider your alternatives in teaching others not to victimize you. Even if some alternatives seem impossible at a given moment, list them all. You can share these ideas with your confidant and brainstorm about which are the best. By detailing them in writing, you'll soon see in black and white that your rigid tunnel-vision approach to most circumstances could be shifted toward numerous viable options.

• Say NO! This is one of the world's best teaching words. Forget the maybes, the hemming and hawing that gives others room not to understand what you mean. You'll see that all your fears of this simple, basic word are inside you. People respect a firm NO more than a lot of herky-jerky fence-walking that conceals your real feelings, and you'll respect yourself more too if you use the word whenever you need it. Stand in front of a mirror and practice, No! No! No! You have the power if you'll just take the risk and do it—NOW!

• When you encounter whiners, interrupters, arguers, braggarts, con artists, bores, or similar victimizers, you can label their behavior calmly with statements such as, "You just interrupted me." "You said that already." "You are complaining about things that will never change." "You spend a lot of time bragging." While such tactics may sound cruel, in essence they are terrific teaching-devices to inform people that you aren't just one more person who is going to be victimized by their alienating behavior. The calmer you are, and the more candidly on target you are with your observations, the less time you'll spend in the victim seat.

IN CLOSING

You get treated the way you teach people to treat you. If you adopt this as a guiding principle of your life, you'll be on your way to always pulling your own strings. While teaching some people is more difficult than teaching others, don't compromise on the basic idea—because to believe otherwise is to give up control of yourself to all those who would gladly take over the reins if you are willing to loosen your hold.

7

Never Place Loyalty to Institutions and Things Above Loyalty to Yourself

If you are what you do, then when you don't, you aren't.

TWELVE-ITEM TEST

Here are twelve questions about you and your behavior toward institutions and things. Take this little quiz as your personal introduction to this chapter on how institutions and personal attitudes can victimize anyone who is willing to let it happen.

Yes *No*

_____ _____ 1. Do you take your job responsibilities more seriously than your personal or family responsibilities?

_____ _____ 2. Do you find it difficult to relax and clear your mind of job-related matters?

_____ _____ 3. Do you find yourself sacrificing your time for the sake of making money or acquiring material objects?

_____ _____ 4. Are you devoting your life to the pursuit of such things as pensions or retirement plans?

_____ _____ 5. Do you place a higher priority on acquiring things and prestige than you do on enjoying people?

_____ _____ 6. Are you easily befuddled by red tape and barriers erected by bureaucrats?

_____ _____ 7. Do you believe it is terrible to fail at a task, or that you should always do your best?

_____ _____ 8. Do you think the team or the company is more important than the individual?

_____ _____ 9. Do you find yourself upset about sitting on committees, or participating in meaningless job-related rituals?

_____ _____ 10. Do you find it difficult to take days off from work without feeling guilty?

_____ _____ 11. Do you always move and speak quickly?

_____ _____ 12. Are you impatient with people who don't do things the way you believe they should?

If you answered yes to any of these questions, you are very likely in that category of victims who have placed loyalty to an institution above loyalty to themselves and their personal fulfillment. Once again, the importance of you as a living, breathing human being must be stressed. Nothing is worth devoting your life to at the expense of your own happiness. The doctrine of loyalty to things and institutions is a victimizing one which you can challenge and banish from your view of your world.

Freedom, as discussed in the opening chapter, is not limited to being free from the domination of other people. Being independent of domination by things, jobs, companies, and other manmade institutions, is just as important. Some people fight vehemently for their personal freedom in their relationships with family and friends. They demand to be respected as individuals and refuse to be told how to run their lives. But ironically, they are complete slaves to their jobs, to the institutions they are paid to serve. They often find themselves unable to regulate their own time, and so have almost no say in how their daily lives are conducted. They are seldom at peace with themselves. Their minds are always racing. They never have any energy to devote to anything but their employment duties. Yet these people claim to have attained their independence from being owned.

Take a hard look at yourself as you read this chapter. If you are a slave to any institution, be it a job, an organization, a hobby, a school, your studies, or whatever, and leave no time for yourself, if you make your tasks bigger and more important than your own happiness, then you have allowed yourself to be victimized, or victimized yourself, by the institutions of your life.

THE MISUSE OF LOYALTY

Loyalty does not mean slavery. You can be faithful to any organization and devote yourself to its tasks with honesty and integrity without having to become its servant. The most important person in the world, to whom you should be unswervingly loyal, is yourself. You only have one life, and to let some business, or other institution, control it is particularly foolish, when you consider that so many more alternatives are available. Loyalty is misused when people are given less importance than profits, and when the human spirit is sacrificed for the name of good old "Anything, Inc."

How you use your loyalty is totally up to you. You can make your own happiness and responsibilities to help and love others in your family the most important things in your life. You don't have to explain it to anyone, but you can begin to make your life work around the concept of loyalty to yourself. Very likely you'll discover that it makes you even more productive on the job, and a lot more pleasant to be around.

Any executive who can't leave his desk doesn't belong behind the desk at all. But you are the executive of your own life, and you can actively plan to use your own time in ways that are loyal to your chosen institutions, but which also lead to your happiness, health, and most important, fulfillment.

The misuse of loyalty is literally a killer. It will fill your life on this planet with stress, tension, anxiety and worry, and put you in your grave long before your time. The things that really matter to you will always be pushed aside in favor of some task which "must" be accomplished yesterday, and all this push-pull, wear and tear, endless "trial and tribulation," will be defended in the name of your duty. But in the end, the very thing you've devoted your life to will be your murderer. And you will have defended it with the rationalization of all the fools who have lived before you, who have claimed that the glory of "Anything, Inc." is more important than the people who serve it.

Go ahead and buy that nonsense if you must, but do understand that you are the biggest victim of all when you misplace your loyalty in the name of a task, profits, or your duty. Rudyard Kipling once wrote, "More men are killed by overwork than the importance of the world justifies."

Indeed, institutions ought to be built to serve man, rather than the other way around. In fact, companies do not exist at all in the *real* world, the world of man. Take the people away from General Motors and what do you have? A lot of rusting machinery, empty factories and offices, file cabinets filled with reports—useless equipment. People are what make institutions work, and since you are one of those people, all your institutional involvement ought to be directed at improving the life of people—and most important among them, yourself and your loved ones.

COMPETITION VS. COOPERATION

People who are victimized by institutions are very often devotees of *competition at all costs*. They have learned to deify the sacred "competitive spirit," and they attempt to impose the holy neurosis of competition on everyone they encounter.

Take another look at competition. Ask yourself if you are not being victimized by the very thing you so strongly endorse.

Institutions thrive on competition. They are in the business of "outdoing the other guy," and so they work very hard to addict everyone in their power to the competitive mind-set. Institutions set up specific machinery to infuse the correct spirit of competitiveness in their duty-bound devotees. Reward systems are built in to ensure that people will sacrifice themselves to outdo each other for promotions and "status." Individuals are taught to look over their shoulders for "the other guy who wants to take over."

Running an institution requires a great deal of competitiveness in a capitalistic culture. And yes, it is a competitive world out there. But you as an individual can compete effectively within the institutional framework without mistakenly carrying that heavy emphasis on competition to extremes, and most destructively, into your own personal life. If you get carried away with competition, you can put terrific pressures on your family to be the way you are, and to compete with everyone else in their lives. While the results of heavy competition are everywhere evident in our modern buildings, our superhighways, our sophisticated electronics, and so on, take a hard look at what they have cost in human terms.

Executives in our country are generally loaded with tension and stress. Heart attacks, ulcers and hypertension are considered "normal" in the high-powered institutional levels of business, where employees have very little time for their families and "normally" become heavy drinkers, smokers, pill-poppers, or insomniacs, with no time left over for loving or making love.

This little excerpt from *The Gospel According to the Harvard Business School*, by Peter Cohen, illustrates how competitive pressures are infiltrating our schools and universities.

April 8: The scene was all too familiar. First the police and then the dean and then, a couple of hours later—when people were having dinner—the little black wagon came. There were two men in the wagon with a two wheeled cart— they took the cart into one of the wings of the dorm, and when they came out, there was this thing strapped to the cart . . . That's how James Hinman left his first year at the Harvard Business School—dead of poison.

This is the third guy now, leaving like that. God knows how many times you have been told that competition is the American way and the only way, how you have heard it from lecterns and pulpits, and how you have almost come to believe it. And then you see a little cart wheel away what could have been a lifetime of laughter and tenderness and bright ideas. Suddenly you see the problems of it, the cost, and you wonder whether there really is no other way. Because when you come down to it, all competition is, is behavior. A piece of behavior that builds on the need of individuals to be faster, cleverer, richer than the next guy. Everybody forgets that despite its undeniable advantages competition is a wasteful process. That every winner comes at the cost of a hundred, a thousand, a hundred thousand losers. And this is where the American society is at: it talks of *competition* as if it had never heard the word *cooperation*. It refuses to see that too much pressure doesn't move people, it kills them.

I believe Cohen's essay conveys a very telling message. You can truly victimize yourself, your spouse and your children, by giving excessive competitiveness top priority in your philosophy or behavior. Schools which demand all "*A*'s" from students, and force them into sometimes vicious competition with each other, may produce a few shining lights—but are those shining lights of heat and pressure what you want for yourself? So what if everyone else looks up to you as the very best? If you need that recognition for your own ego strength, then you are being fulfilled by the plaudits of others rather than from within, and this is one of the surest signs of insecurity and low self-esteem. But even worse, if your worth as a human being is dependent upon your doing things well, being on top, outdoing everyone else, then what will you do when the cheers stop and you are no longer on top? You will collapse because you no longer have a reason to feel worthy.

Competition is one of the major causes of suicide in this country. Its primary victims are people who had always felt worthy because they were outdoing the other guy. When they "failed" at that, they lost any sense of their own worth, and decided that their miserable lives were not worth living.

The suicide rate among children between the ages of eight and twelve has risen four hundred per cent since 1967. Imagine—young children killing themselves, finding *their* individual lives are not worth living, many because they believe they must do things better than each other to be worthy. Pressures to get on Little League teams, to get top grades, to fulfill their parents' goals and please everyone else—these are not the values of life a healthy person will risk his life for, let alone purposely die for.

All human beings are worthy of life, and can be happy and fulfilled, without having to look over their shoulders at other people for their self-worth. In fact, fully functioning people are not interested in doing things better than everyone else; they look inward for their life goals, and know that competition will only dwindle their efforts to accomplish what they uniquely desire. Remember, in order to be in a state called "competition" you must have someone else in the picture for comparison. And when you have to look outside yourself to assess your own position or worth, then you are not in control of your own life. Look inward rather than at how you measure up to the other guy.

THE RESULTS OF TOO MUCH COMPETITION

While competition may indeed build better mousetraps, and improving the quality of life is certainly an admirable ambition, there is also the other side of the coin. Cooperation is a much more efficient way to upgrade the quality of your own life and the lives of others. When people join in to help each other, it benefits all concerned.

In schools, if students are competing for a few "A's" that are doled out by unthinking teachers or professors, the total result is quite wasteful. Students become paranoid, and they begin to cheat, lie, and go to any lengths to get "the reward." Cooperative classrooms, on the other hand, produce healthy children who want to share their joy instead of keeping it all for themselves.

We have over twelve million alcoholics in our country. More than 100 million prescriptions a year are given out for antidepressant and tranquilizing drugs, and an additional twenty-five million for amphetamines for losing weight. Over-the-counter drugs for sleeping, staying awake, relieving tension, aches, cramps and the like, are consumed in untold quantities. We have become a whole nation of pill-poppers and psychological addicts. Insomnia, impotence, and episodes of depression are reaching astronomical proportions, and people are seeking therapy in record numbers. Young children are being carted off wholesale to social workers, psychological counselors and psychiatrists. Teenage alcoholism is a major problem and suicide particularly for people under twenty-one is all too frequent.

These facts are the direct products of a culture which institutionalizes competition at the expense of cooperation. Alvin Toffler detailed the problems in *Future Shock,* and predicted some horrendous results if we don't take stock of ourselves now. But you do not have to be a victim of this rat-race mentality if you choose otherwise. It is possible for you to function very effectively in any pressure-cooker situation and refuse to get steamed up about it. You have the capacity to undo any tensions that are a part of your life. But as with all other problems mentioned in this book, you will have to become alert to your own victimization routines, take some risks, and work on your behavior, if you plan to free yourself of this category of abuse.

ONE OVERLY COMPETITIVE EXECUTIVE

Alex was in his mid-forties. He came to me for counseling after suffering a mild heart attack and two bleeding ulcers. He was a perfect example of the business executive who has achieved towering success at the expense of his mental, physical and social health. His marriage was over because his wife had refused to tolerate being married in absentia; his health was in serious jeopardy, and still he was pushing himself beyond tolerable limits. He had become a chronic "social" drinker (alcoholic), and was having two or three equally empty affairs with younger women.

Alex was a striver who had pursued academic excellence with a fury in his college days. He was one of the youngest presidents of a major corporation. And yet if you talked very long with him, you would clearly see that he was a loser. He had been weaned on competition, and it had driven him perilously close to suicide, whether he committed it directly—with pills, a gun, or whatever—or indirectly, by his death-defying life style.

The tone of our counseling together was firm and direct. I pointed out to Alex that he was killing himself because he had placed achievement in the business world above everything else, including his own life. He had systematically ignored everything that he *said* was of value to him. He talked a good game, but as good an "executive" as he was supposed to be, he was unwilling or afraid to administer his own life for the sake of his own happiness. He said he wanted love, but he ignored those who loved him. He said he wanted peace of mind, but he consumed all his present moments with helter-skelter activity. He said he wanted to be a good father, but he never spent more than a few minutes of the day with his children. He said he wanted health and security, but besides his heart attack and two ulcers, he had driven his blood pressure abnormally high. In fact, everything Alex said was in direct contradiction to his behavior.

I began by encouraging Alex to set up daily goals for himself, rather than make an immediate long-term rearrangement of his life. He would leave the office at a given time of the day, regardless of how important the meeting. This soon taught him that the business would go on without his presence at every meeting. He would mutually arrange to spend an afternoon with his two children, and view the agreement as a legally binding contract.

Before long, Alex developed new, non-competitive, non-flustering behaviors. He learned to slow down, to stop demanding things from himself that required superhuman effort, and to stop insisting that his family be the way he wanted them to be. He was able to effect a trial reconciliation with his wife, and they came to family counseling together. Alex gradually learned to take it easy through the hard work of acquiring new thinking and behavior to slow down his pace, to stop his overcommitment to his job, and to live out what he stated as his life goals.

Some two years later, long after Alex and his family discontinued counseling sessions, he actually quit his job and left the hustle-bustle of New York City to raise farm animals in Montana. He took the active risks of giving up a huge income for a far greater payoff, that is, a far more tranquil life style and a personally rewarding life.

This is not a mythological story. Alex is a real person who made an about face that saved his life. But first he had to rethink what was once the unthinkable, and learn that competition was not the essence of life. He learned a fundamental truth expounded by philosophers over the centuries. Sometimes *more is less*.

PEOPLE ARE MORE IMPORTANT THAN THINGS

Occasionally it takes a hard kick in the pants like Alex had received to understand that people are more important than things. You will be a top-level victim if you place a higher priority on the acquisition of goods than you do on human life, particularly your own life. If you devote yourself to things, events, and money, you'll very likely end up demoralized.

Things-oriented people have a great deal of difficulty relating to others. They find talking *with* people a chore, and so they often talk *at* them, order them around, and use them in the acquisition of things. The people who are ordered around resent others attempting to turn them into emotional slaves, so they choose to stay away from these things-oriented people, who then turn even more toward things, and the cycle endlessly repeats itself. Finally the things-oriented person is left with only his things for comfort. But things cannot give comfort, they are sterile, dead and without affection. Things cannot be loved in a mutual way, so loneliness and frustration are the ultimate rewards of overemphasis on achievement and acquisition.

People and living things are all that matter. Without life around you to bounce off of and to share, you have no possibility for joy. If you took away all life, there would be nothing left in the world to have or give meaning. Life is all that counts.

When you find yourself sacrificing human relationships daily for material wealth, money and status, ask yourself what having these things would really provide. If you have no people to love and who give love in return, if you have lost your feelings for life, then all your things shrink to insignificance.

Challenge the idea that you need more and more things to improve the quality of your life. Most wealthy people really do often talk longingly of the leaner, hungrier days, when they appreciated the simple things, when love could freely be trusted not to come with a dollar sign attached.

It does not take much material wealth to be happy. Look at little unspoiled children. They don't really need money, or toys, or anything. Let them alone and they can take joy in just being alive. So can you, provided you are willing to rearrange your priority list and place the emphasis on what really matters—life itself.

Louise was in her mid-forties and going through a divorce. Her husband was making things difficult by trying to keep her from getting a just property-settlement. She complained to me about the injustice of it all, and how she was driving herself crazy with depression and worry over the property—a house, some furniture, a car, several thousand dollars, and some jewelry.

In counseling Louise soon admitted that she was consumed with the idea of the "great value" of these things, and that she had placed far more importance on acquiring them than she had on her own personal happiness. She had been willing to sacrifice her happiness, and indeed her sanity, for a few things.

Louise had always been a things-oriented person, as had her husband. Their divorce was to be a battleground in which she felt she had to prove herself the most tenacious warrior by getting as many things as she could. Louise had learned as a little girl that having more toys than other kids somehow mattered. She had placed dollar values on everything. Her language patterns all revolved around costs, assets and liabilities, and she always discussed items in terms of their monetary worth. She had a dollars-oriented personality, and it was becoming the master of her life.

Louise soon learned to place her values where they would serve rather than enslave her, to put her own fulfillment at the top of her list. I pointed out that she was sacrificing her own happiness to constantly worry about "winning" in her divorce settlement, when there were so many more viable alternatives, including ignoring her husband's efforts and letting her attorney handle the entire matter. She agreed that her lack of inner peace was motivated by her need to win things-battles, and so she agreed to work at new ways of thinking and behavior. As a result she told her attorney to do what he legally could for her, but that she didn't want to know about every little detail of the case. She also agreed to stop discussing the matter with her ex-husband, and not to let him victimize her in regular confrontations about it. She turned the work of getting her estate in order over to a professional, and turned her own mind toward other, more rewarding activities, like going back to school, taking a vacation from the divorce battleground, getting back into dating, and mostly, having fun and enjoying life.

In one session I had asked Louise, "What will you have if you win the settlement skirmish and get everything you want? Will you then have happiness for yourself?" She knew the answer before she spoke, and it was at this point that our counseling took the focus of helping her to change around that self-defeating attitude which will victimize a person every time. Remember, people are more important than things.

ON WINNING AND LOSING

If you lose a tennis match, what have you really lost? Well, nothing. You just have not hit a ball over a net and stayed within given boundaries as well as somebody else has. But it is truly amazing how many Americans seem to feel that games aren't worthwhile if they're "lost."

The tremendous emphasis in our culture on winning at games and sports produces just as many victims of would-be "recreation" as the emphasis on competition from which it springs produces in business and elsewhere. But what is winning in this context? Running faster, hitting a ball farther, getting more tricks in a game of cards. So what? Of course winning can be *fun,* and even more fun than losing. But if you need to win to prove yourself, you have lost all healthy perspective. If the game becomes bigger than life, instead of a pleasant part of it called *play,* and you find yourself immobilized, enraged, depressed or whatever, then you have victimized yourself. And ironically, the less emphasis you place on winning, the more likely you are to win.

But the absurd attitude that "beating" others makes playing worthwhile is a disease that is systematically being spread throughout our culture. I have seen coaches feeding young athletes pep pills called greenies on game days for the sake of winning. I have seen young people exposed to the most outrageous, bombastic ridicule because they "missed a play," or because a little slip-up had "cost them the game." I have observed scandalous behavior on the part of recruiters, offering to bribe athletes, provide them with prostitutes, illegal payments, and anything else, in the name of winning.

If those are the prices one must pay to be a winner, I'll take non-winners any time. You do not need victories over other human beings to control yourself from within and be fulfilled. Only losers need to win, since needing to win implies that you can't be happy unless you defeat someone else out there. If you can't be happy without someone else out there whom you must defeat, then you are being controlled by that person, which makes you the ultimate loser, since people who are controlled by others are psychological slaves.

No, coach. winning isn't everything *or* the only thing; it is *only a thing*. It may be fun, and even wonderful to pursue, but never at the cost of human life, which is the most precious commodity of all. If you have to take drugs, involve yourself in crass behavior, berate other human beings, in order to win, then winning isn't worth your victory-stand appearance. The true man of knowledge pursues victory as if it matters to him—but when the game is over, he doesn't look back on his victory as worth remembering. He knows that what is over cannot be relived, and so he chooses another experience and acts it out with vigor.

When we teach ourselves that we must have victory at all costs, we become victims of our own ridiculous belief systems. We won't allow ourselves to fail, even though failure is a natural and necessary part of the learning process. Failure is often met with self-disparagement and anger toward ourselves and others. You can surely look at winning as something terrific to achieve, but you should be even more certain that your essence as a person does not depend upon the achievement.

CHARACTERISTICS OF VICTIMS WHO ARE LOYAL TO THINGS AND INSTITUTIONS BEYOND LOYALTY TO THEMSELVES

As described earlier in the chapter, people who have placed loyalty to their jobs and to things above loyalty to themselves have typically victimized themselves and their loved ones in many ways. Meyer Friedman, M.D., and Ray H. Rosenman, M.D., have devoted an entire book to the effects of "striving personalities" on heart attacks. Their book is called *Type A Behavior and Your Heart*.

People with Type A behavior display habits such as placing explosive emphasis on key words when there is no need for accentuation, needing always to get in the last word in conversations, and always moving, walking and eating rapidly. They are impatient, constantly urging others (and themselves) to speed up and "get on with it." They are likely to become unduly enraged at things like traffic jams, and to find it exceedingly difficult to stand in lines without jumping around or complaining a lot. They are almost incapable of doing one thing at a time, such as listening to someone else without doodling or excusing themselves for phone calls. They find it almost impossible to listen to others' interests without interjecting their own points of view and shifting conversations around to themselves. They feel guilty about relaxing or "doing nothing." They cannot observe natural things for their own beauty because they are constantly preoccupied. They live their lives by schedules and calendars. They allow almost no time for unforeseen contingencies. They feel compelled to challenge other Type A people, rather than have compassion for them. They often have clenched fists, nervous laughs, tightness about their bodies and use much hand-pounding and emphatic nonverbal behavior.

These people, according to a great deal of hard medical research, are primary candidates for heart disease, hypertension, and other physical ailments. Imagine that! Your own choices and behavior patterns as the cause of heart attacks and other physical maladies, perhaps even more significant than smoking, overeating, or improper diet. Friedman and Rosenman have shown beyond a doubt that more than ninety per cent of the males under the age of sixty who suffer heart attacks are of the Type A variety. And much of these people's self-destructive behavior comes as the result of victim choices they make, by misplacing loyalties onto institutions and by valuing things and money over people.

The six categories elaborated below constitute the most general kinds of victim behaviors that will ultimately "do you in" if you practice them as regular parts of your life.

1. *Intense striving.* This is the kind of non-relaxing behavior that was outlined in the novel *What Makes Sammy Run*—constantly pushing yourself, wanting more, and never being satisfied in a present moment. The striving is not necessarily goal-directed; it is more striving just for the sake of striving, and it is a killer both physically and mentally.

2. *Competitiveness.* Always attempting to "one-up" others leads to never looking inward for satisfaction, but judging your worth on the basis of how you performed in comparison with other people.

3. *Deadline urgency.* Ruling your life on the basis of a timepiece and a calendar and always rushing to meet self-imposed deadlines,

leads to intense pressure and nervousness when the deadlines approach and the tasks aren't completed. Constantly referring to a watch, hurrying to meet scheduled appointments, and compulsively running your life on a "tight" schedule leave you no time to enjoy yourself or your family.

4. *Impatience.* Here you constantly demand that other people speed things up, impose standards for yourself which you can't always meet, and then persecute yourself for not having lived up to your "bargain," and find yourself constantly irritated with things like traffic jams, slow talkers, "unruly" children, "unambitious" neighbors, and "inefficient" colleagues.

5. *Abrupt speech and gestures.* Harsh speech patterns which include a lot of yes, yes, yes, uhm, uhm, uhm, you-knows, and other fast talking activities that demonstrate a hurry-up attitude toward communicating, which also surfaces in gestures to get people to speed up. Also using unnecessary emphasis to get points across.

6. *Excessive drive and overcommitment to the job.* This is the behavior described in the earlier sections of this chapter, in which a person places more emphasis on tasks, jobs, things and dollars, than on relationships with people.

If you recognize characteristics of your own behavior in these deadly six categories, you are quite likely victimizing yourself by ruining your personal relationships, putting extreme emotional pressures on yourself, and most neurotically, destroying your own body.

HOW INSTITUTIONS WORK

Business institutions exist for one reason: to make profits. They seek only to perpetuate themselves so as to return dollars to the people who have taken the risks of financing them and manufacturing the products or delivering the services. They are not in business for charity, and they don't pretend to be. Therefore, any victimizing you experience as a result of your connection to an institution has probably come about because you allowed it to happen.

If you believe a business institution owes you some kind of loyalty and ought to reward your long service with a lot of benefits to you as a person, then you are carrying around groundless illusions. The institution will attempt to deal with you in as utilitarian a fashion as possible. It will pay you for your services until you can no longer deliver the services it needs, and then you will be dismissed in as inexpensive a manner as possible.

This is not a sour view of business in western culture; it is simply the way things are. Whenever you become an employee of an institution, this is the implied agreement. Even if it has such things as pension plans, profit sharing, incentive programs, or any other devices designed to hold on to employees, the fact remains that when it doesn't need you any more, you will be replaced, and every effort will be made to get rid of you as cheaply as possible.

Institutions simply do what they are designed to do, and there is no complaining about them being written in these pages. But you are not an institution. You are a human being who breathes and feels and experiences life. You do not have to be upset about the way businesses operate, nor do you have to commit yourself slavishly to institutions just because you are encouraged to do so by institutional spokesmen who stand to gain by your self-victimizing loyalty. The man who retires after devoting fifty years of unflagging service to a company, and receives a gold watch and a small pension for his lifetime of devotion, has not been victimized by the institution. It owes him nothing, so he should feel grateful for the watch. He did his job and received his paychecks, and the company received his services. That is the way it is supposed to be. But the retiree has been victimized if he has devoted himself beyond normal requirements and sacrificed his own personal goals and his family activities, because institutions do nothing but continue on, whether you kill yourself for them or simply see them as ways for you to make your living.

SOME COMMON INSTITUTIONAL VICTIM GAMES

1. Making the Institution a Person   Perhaps the most significant way to victimize yourself through your work or association with an institution is to conceive of it as somehow human and treat it as you might a lover or a friend.

When you think of the company as another person who needs you, or even who can't function without you, then you are in trouble.

Institutional representatives would love for you to think this way, because they know you will then deliver your services on twenty-four-hour call and deny yourself any private life of your own. If you really believe the institution is a human thing, ask yourself, "Would the institution continue if I left it?" "Would it die tomorrow?" "Would it be upset or break down?" "Would it cry?" You already know the answers to these questions, so why not put the company or other institution into proper perspective and begin to treat it as *at best* a mechanism through which you are paid a fair price for a pleasant, stimulating, productive and satisfying use of your talents? Because there *is* no fair price for your sacrifice of the most important commodity you have—your life.

2. SWEARING YOUR ALLEGIANCE FOREVER   Another way you can victimize yourself is to swear undying allegiance to "your" company and proceed to make this obligation, which you have invented, more important than your obligations to yourself and your family. This kind of devotion is absurd in many ways, because nine times out of ten you would gladly move on if you received a better offer elsewhere, and if you wouldn't, the worst reason in the world would be that you felt you were betraying some kind of unwritten law of loyalty. In big-league sports, where "team spirit" and loyalty can actually be vital to success, you seldom see such confusions. Athletes are playing their hearts out for one team one day at the same time they are negotiating for bigger contracts. If they can do better for themselves elsewhere, they go to another team and instantly become loyal to the team they swore to wipe off the field, the court, the ice, or whatever. Managers of professional teams switch around on a regular basis, and they always understand that their loyalty lasts as long as their contracts. You are in a similar position with your job. If a better offer comes along, you would be a fool to pass it up. If you find yourself unable to swerve from your allegiance to your employer, remember that the institution itself has no such problems with you.

3. ADHERING TO RULES AND COMMITTEE PROCEDURES AS IF THEY WERE SACRED   Going along with the policies of your institution and acting as if they are rules to live your life by can also victim-

ize you. Rather, look at rules and procedures as contrivances of people who have very little else to do.

Take a look at the way colleges and universities are run. Make no mistake about it; these institutions are big business, and they are in business to make money and to perpetuate themselves. They are run by administrators who suffer from the "committee neurosis," who appoint committees to study everything vaguely connected with the university. There are committees to study the curriculum, to redo the curriculum, to undo the curriculum, to study the feasibility of inaugurating a new curriculum, ad nauseam.

If a camel is really a horse put together by committee, the daily running of universities is like an endless caravan of camels parading solemnly in circles. Grown men and women gather together week after week to sit around tables and discuss feasibilities, "prioritizing," rearranging, promotional and tenure decisions, building improvements, language requirements, grading procedures, evaluations, alternate procedures, and on and on. Rarely is anything substantial accomplished. The professors, deans and vice presidents continue to meet religiously week after week. When they talk with each other privately, they admit how foolish the entire game is, and that all the decisions that take twenty weeks to make in the committees could easily be accomplished by one intelligent, fair-minded person in twenty minutes.

But as so often happens with institutions, the procedures become bigger than the people they are designed to serve. And for the most part, the people who are trapped in the maze of the committee neurosis ironically seem to love it. After all, if they didn't have their petty committee meetings to attend, their minutes to read and reread, their points of order, and their Roberts Rules of Order, they'd have very little else to do.

People who sit around and talk for a living rarely are doers. They become administrators worked up in their own words, and they personify the Peter Principle—that is, *cream rises until it sours.* People who want to get things done refuse to sit around and talk about what *could* be accomplished if people would get off their rear ends instead of endlessly spinning out the possible ramifications of what is proposed.

Gail Thain Parker, a former college president, writing in the *At-*

lantic Monthly, described her first faculty meetings at Harvard in 1969 this way:

> It was like watching a basketball game in which the object was to take time-outs rather than to complete plays. The most active man on the floor was the parliamentarian who repeatedly leapt to the stage to confer with the president, while the president in turn sat quietly in front of a huge red flag emblazoned VERITAS.

Having paid my dues by spending six years as a college professor, I can personally attest to the veracity of her remarks. Professors sit around in caucus demanding to be heard on an issue of no consequence. A debate ensues for thirty minutes, with the result that an *ad hoc* committee is formed to come up with a feasibility study, which will take at least two years to get to the floor. When it does, it will be debated for more wasted hours, chewed up, and spit back to another committee. Anything to keep the issue from being resolved and acted upon, even if it is so inconsequential as to require nothing more than a sensible clerical decision.

Non-doers gain their self-worth in these meaningless ways, maintain the status quo by instituting evasive gimmicks, and tend to label the entire process democratic participatory decision-making. The following words of a North Dakota state senator illustrate how the endless, meaningless tripe that spews out of so-called decision-making bodies sometimes attains the heights of the sublimely ludicrous.

> What we ought to do now, obviously, is suspend all activity until we can hold a plebiscite to select a panel that will appoint a commission authorized to hire a new team of experts to restudy the feasibility of compiling an index of all the committees that have in the past inventoried and cataloged the various studies aimed at finding out what happened to all of the policies that were scrapped when new policies were decided on by someone else.

If you participate in this kind of activity, or find yourself even mildly upset by it, you are victimizing yourself. This kind of evasive talk has been going on as long as man has had councils, commissions, governments, etc. It will always continue, no matter who stands up and talks about how to eliminate it. Your only escape is to refuse to participate by being quietly effective and simply shrugging at the inanities that rage around you. You can refuse as many committee assignments as possible, and when you can't avoid them, be a mute member who is a voice of reason whenever you have to break your silence.

You can stop being upset by the workings of the committees and go about performing your own tasks, actively minimizing your participation in the nonsense that so occupies many people. Be you a mechanic, a teacher, a dentist, a cab driver, a florist, or whatever, you are never immune from the victimizing efforts that collectives will attempt to impose on you in the name of progress, democracy, or improved efficiency. But when you see the committee neurosis surfacing, you can opt for a quietly effective choice that will not victimize you.

4. BEING SEDUCED BY THE BUREAUCRATIC MAZE UPON WHICH INSTITUTIONS THRIVE   Institutional bigness creates distance between organizations and the people they are designed to serve. The larger the organization, the more bureaucratic machinery must be oiled to keep it operating. The U.S. government is a classic example. It is run by an endless list of committees, departments, agencies, divisions, and other subgroups. Each group has departmental chairmen, agency heads and other bureaucrats who want to hold on to their jobs and their power positions. Furthermore, the entire bureaucracy employs thousands of people who do not want to rock the boat and perhaps lose their jobs. And so you find yourself confronted with fearful functionaries who are loath to give you straight answers because they are being faithful to higher-ups who might chastise them.

You become the victim when you attempt to get service. Just try to get straight answers from politicians who have been lifelong bureaucrats. They talk with fuzzballs in their mouths, and respond to simple yes or no questions with answers like, "I considered the alternatives and I've committed myself to further study." "I hate to give a firm yes, but on the other hand I would not rule out the possibility of a negative response if other contingencies arise of which I have heretofore not been apprised."

Bureaucrats are paper shufflers who usually send their victims from one office to another with never a firm answer. I have seen people shuffled around for an entire day when they simply wanted to register their car in a new state. You know what it's like to deal with unemployment-office personnel, or clinics run by the government. The forms are endless, and the clerks have a very special way of attempting to victimize anyone who wants to be treated with dignity and expeditious service.

5. FALLING INTO THE JARGON TRAP The jargon of bureaucracies is indeed something to ponder. Bureaucrats have invented a language of their own, which is a technique to keep action at bay and to perpetuate the evasiveness upon which their entire institutions function.

Psychological workers talk about human beings in frightening terms. They are quick to pigeonhole people with psychological terminology and forget that they are talking about human beings. People get labeled manic-depressive, psychopathic, sociopathic, schizophrenic, brain-damaged (or cerebrally dysfunctional), or the like. These labels may serve the therapists, but are dangerous in that they often victimize human beings, who are no longer viewed as people, but as mere collections of symptoms.

Once a person is labeled, he is for all purposes negated as a human being. If you call a child "autistic," and you believe that autism is incurable, then you have given up hope for a human being. *Son Rise*, by Barry Kaufman, tells the story of two caring parents who refused to accept the diagnostic label of autism for their young son and invested themselves totally in him, eventually bringing him out of his mysterious walking coma. When they took him back to the many doctors who had labeled him "autistic," they were told that he had been misdiagnosed, because autism was incurable. There is the Catch-22 logic that labelers use over and over again in protecting their theories and neglecting human lives. While few professionals do it, nevertheless it is far more functional to *label behavior* rather than people—for example, "He has staying-in-bed behavior, or non-talking behavior," instead of labeling him a depressive or a mute.

Legal language is another prime example. Lawyers have made sure that our laws are written in such a way that the average Joe doesn't stand a chance of unraveling the terms of a contract, and so must hire specially trained decipherers to interpret documents like contracts, leases, deeds and insurance policies. All efforts to simplify our laws are met with keen resistance by legal lobbyists. Citizens' lobbies attempting to simplify divorce proceedings or bring about no-fault-insurance provisions find the legalists blocking the way with the very kinds of arcane obscurities the citizens are trying to weed out, protecting the "interests" of the people who make their livings out of being the only ones who can do such things, and who will do whatever is necessary to keep "untrained" hands out of their pie.

Government agencies are experts at using language to obscure meaning, and ultimately to victimize people who are looking for service. The military is a classic example. The Pentagon, one of the largest bureaucracies within the government, has created its own impenetrable semantic subjungle, with its regulations in quadruplicate for every available contingency, spelled out in such immensely complicated and convoluted language that the average person cannot possibly make any sense out of them.

After years of hacking through bureaucratic semantic thickets at the U.S. Public Health Service, a sixty-three-year-old official named Philip Broughton finally hit upon a sure-fire method for converting frustration into fulfillment—jargonwise. Euphemistically called the Systematic Buzz Phrase Projector, Broughton's system employs a lexicon of thirty carefully chosen "buzzwords" and is reported directly from the *Times* magazine, February 9, 1976, page 27, a supplement to *Army Times/Navy Times/Air Force Times*.

Column 1	Column 2	Column 3
0. Integrated	0. Management	0. Options
1. Total	1. Organizational	1. Flexibility
2. Systematized	2. Monitored	2. Capability
3. Parallel	3. Reciprocal	3. Mobility
4. Functional	4. Digital	4. Programming
5. Responsive	5. Logistical	5. Concept
6. Optional	6. Transitional	6. Time-phase
7. Synchronized	7. Incremental	7. Projection
8. Compatible	8. Third-generation	8. Hardware
9. Balanced	9. Policy	9. Contingency

W. J. Farquharson, writing in the *Times* magazine, explains the procedure, whereby bureaucrats may simplify their jobs of obscuring the facts. "Think of any three-digit number, then select the corresponding buzzword from each column. For instance, number 736 produces 'synchronized reciprocal time-phase,' a phrase that can be dropped into virtually any report with that ring of decisive authority. No one will have the remotest idea of what you're talking about, but the important thing is that no one is about to admit it."

This kind of language game can be played with virtually any institution that has its own jargon—big business, medicine, the law, psychiatry, insurance, accounting, public-service agencies, etc. The way to escape the bureaucratic victimizing game is largely to avoid it whenever possible; otherwise go into it with a complete understanding of how it functions. You can avoid being upset by anything you encounter, and you can refuse to deal with bureaucratic clerks whenever possible. You must ignore the language and other bureaucratic roadblocks, and never allow yourself to be sucked into the same kinds of absurd behaviors.

6. FAILING TO UNDERSTAND THE INSANITY OF BUREAUCRATIC LOGIC Besides using direct language as seldom as possible, bureaucrats do not operate on logic; they simply follow the rules and the established precedents, even when they make no sense at all. Here are two telling examples, both of which are true stories.

• *The milk truck.* Joe was a milkman who owned his own truck. One day to his dismay the truck was stolen. It was recovered by the police, however, and Joe went to claim it at the local station. He had no other source of income, so he was desperate. But he was informed that the truck was being held as evidence for the trial, which might come around in three months.

Joe got the same story from all sides of the bureaucracy. He could not have his own milk truck back, despite the fact that he needed it to make a living—unless he was willing to drop charges against the thief! If he pressed charges, he had to be victimized by losing his truck for three months.

Joe refused to be a double victim, so he simply dropped charges, and the thief was released. This is how the bureaucracies of the world often function at the expense of the people they are supposed to serve. Each person Joe dealt with said he was powerless to do anything, and Joe was shuffled around until he finally had had it, and decided to get the hell out of there before he joined them in their insanity.

● *The widow.* Nancy's husband died suddenly. As so often happens in such cases, Nancy was forbidden to touch any of their funds, including her very own money, because it was all tied up in estate proceedings.

Nancy waited four long years before the estate was settled. All the bureaucrats who victimized her explained that they were sorry, but that was how things worked. Her very own bank account was frozen, as well as all joint holdings, simply because the mindless bureaucrats in their gray flannel suits wanted to spend four years debating how Nancy's income should be handled. Because of the long delays and the multiple lawyers who had their greedy fingers in the estate, to the tune of claiming sixty per cent of it in legal and handling fees, Nancy had to go out and scrounge up another job to pay her bills.

The only way to beat these kinds of victimizing occurrences is to be dishonest and not report a death, or to obscure your funds from estate-hungry bureaucrats. The law, which is supposed to serve people, ironically encourages them to circumvent it in order to survive.

Honoré de Balzac once said, "Bureaucracy is a giant mechanism operated by pygmies." If you are not alert, persevering, and determined not to be victimized with a hatful of strategies, then you may find yourself done in by bureaucrats with institutional, man-eating tentacles that will gobble you up in a moment. Below are some typical ways in which institutions and their representatives attempt to victimize you, along with some very specific suggestions you can implement to keep yourself free from their clutches.

STRATEGIES FOR ELIMINATING INSTITUTIONAL VICTIMIZATION

● Most importantly, you must shift your belief system around to get rid of all ideas that you don't count as much as the company, or that the institutions of the world are more significant than its individuals. Every time you find yourself behaving in a self-sacrificing way wherein your time is being given up for an institution, you should assess if that is really what you want for yourself. You will entail some risks in eliminating any slave status you may have earned, but first you must accomplish the crucial attitudinal shift whereby you as a person come out on the top of your list of things which command your loyalty.

• Assess your life priorities with the people that count the most to you. Talk with your family about your conduct and what you are seeking. Ask their opinions about your own job responsibilities, and whether they are feeling neglected. Make a list of the things you really want to achieve, and why. Then look at your own behavior. Are you moving toward the personal fulfillment that you covet, or are you digging yourself into a deeper hole? You can only shift things around when you put the whole thing into perspective, and begin living your life a day at a time, in the pursuit of happiness rather than neurosis.

• Gradually increase your quiet time, privacy, and chances to do things that are really important to you. You may have to force yourself, at first, to schedule breaks away from the job and take time to be with your children or your spouse, take a nap, go out to dinner with a loved one, or talk with someone you've been neglecting. But if you give yourself minimal times like this at the beginning, they will ultimately grow into regular, healthy, fulfilling habits.

• Practice being quietly effective in relieving your mind of the tensions of institutional slavery. Don't tell anyone about your new attitude or program; simply make your mind work in self-enhancing ways. Knock off excessive time you spend in committees, or on trips, or just overseeing the business. Practice leaving your work behind when you leave the office or the plant. Stop rethinking everything that happened during the day, and stop being preoccupied with tomorrow's or next year's business. Instead of harping constantly on your own business problems, learn to talk about family members' feelings, their accomplishments, *their* ambitions. Quiet your mind by just allowing it to go blank for a few minutes. Push out work-related thoughts when you find yourself thinking about pressure and the job. On vacations, practice enjoying the entire respite from your working world that you've worked hard to earn, rather than wasting the time by worrying about the future or reliving the past. One of the healthiest techniques for career success is learning to forget about it regularly, which also brings you back to it refreshed, more efficient, and able to view your work in new and better perspectives.

• Get the word *retirement* out of your vocabulary. Make up your mind that you are never going to retire, that when you leave your current job, you will still be productive and useful, and life will be full of enjoyment. Stop thinking about your future years, and get on with making your present years worthwhile. Regardless of your age, if you believe that you will someday retire and just sit around watching birds and sunsets, you are fooling yourself. That kind of activity will make you feel useless, though retirement communities thrive on advertising it. You can live every moment you are allotted on this planet fully and freely, and your age will never be an inhibiting factor unless you let it be. If you live now, in every now, there will never *be* a time when you're "retired." So get the concept out of your head. And if you now have a job you hate, and are just staying in it to fulfill pension requirements, reassess if you really want your life to be used up in such a fruitless way. Stop postponing your gratification. Remember, the future is promised to no one. You could drop dead the moment after you've finished sacrificing your entire life for your retirement.

- If you dislike an institutional assignment, and you resent working where you do, leave. Don't be afraid of the risks. If you are a dedicated person who wants to fulfill your responsibilities in a job that fulfills you, then you'll never tolerate anything else, and you will soon find a new position. You don't have to stay where you are forever, simply because you happen to be there today and it is easier to stay than to move on. Risk-taking is at the heart of not being victimized by institutions and bureaucracies.

- Live your life as though you only had six months of it left. When you really think about time and its infinite thousands and millions of years, your own life span suddenly becomes breathlessly short. Six months can look like six minutes. If you knew that you only had six months to live, what would you do differently? Then ask yourself the very realistic question, "Why in the hell aren't I doing it?" Now . . . Do it!

- Stop using the excuse "I have a responsibility to . . ." to tell yourself why you can't be fulfilled in your own life. And when victimizers try to make you feel as though you owe it to the institution to sacrifice yourself beyond the time or trouble you're being paid for, because you must prove your loyalty to the institution, remember, consciously or not, they are just doing what *they* are getting paid for, which is to get the most they can out of you. You can almost always discharge your legitimate responsibilities *and* have a life of happiness, especially when you stop rationalizing your unhappiness and get on with doing things differently.

• Go through each of the characteristics of Type A behavior detailed earlier. Give yourself some exercises to do that will eliminate the deadline urgency, the fast talking, etc. Slow yourself down and enjoy life a moment at a time.

• Don't be seduced by props of power, such as titles that will be bestowed upon you if you work hard, promotions, decals for your helmet, ribbons, a bigger desk, your name on the washroom door, or whatever. All these prestige symbols are dangled before you to make you believe that you will be more worthy when they are bestowed on you. If you remember that your worth comes from within, then you won't be foiled by the need to collect more and more props of power, which ultimately amount to more and more "instant approval" from everyone you meet. If you aren't at peace with yourself, then none of the props in the world will mean anything, because your life will be wasted and you will know it.

• Simply refuse to participate in committee assignments which you feel are worthless. Politely decline to be a member, or if you are assigned, just attend without being an active participant. You will be surprised how much fun it is to avoid being placed on silly committees and work-study groups, and how creatively you can eliminate these little nuisances from your life.

• Take away your foolish self-demands for excellence in everything you do, and your demands for the same from your loved ones. Allow yourself the pleasure of just doing. Paint a picture, just for fun. Don't worry about "not being a painter"—just enjoy doing it. Take a similarly relaxed, non-competitive approach to as many of your life activities as you can, rather than pressuring yourself to be perfect at everything you do. Ask yourself why you've put such pressures on yourself, and probably on your family too. You'll find that your competitive edge will be even sharper in the areas where it's useful or necessary when you stop competing in all the areas where it's needless and destructive.

• Try throwing away your watch and calendar occasionally. See if you can handle not running your life on a schedule for a day. Let go of the compulsion to run your life against the clock by just doing things like eating, sleeping, talking, etc., when you feel like it, rather than when you are "supposed to."

CONCLUDING REMARKS

Your job can be a source of great delight, but also a fatal source of victimization. Few drop dead from purely physical overwork nowadays, as countless slaves used to do a century ago in some parts of the world, but many Americans now die from overworry and overanxiety. If you are in any way a victim of institutions, whether your slavery is self-inflicted by your excessive loyalty, or comes from institutionally imposed policies which you treat like laws of the land, you can do something about it by vowing to change your attitudes and your behaviors. You only live once, so why should you live at the mercy of manmade institutions? Obviously you shouldn't, and you won't any longer when you decide to stop being a victim.

8

Distinguishing Between Judgments and Reality

Everything that exists in the world, does so independently of your opinion about it.

JUDGMENTS VS. REALITY

As strange as it may sound at first, many people victimize themselves by placing more stock in their beliefs about or attitudes toward what is real than in reality itself.

Before you deny any allegation that you might be one of those people, consider the evidence—that almost everyone uses words, sentences and phrases every day which are *judgments* on reality, as though they were reflections of reality itself. For example, people often say, "It's really a lousy [or nice] day today." While this may seem like a harmless little sentence, it in fact is not "reality-based." The day is only "lousy" or "nice" depending upon the judgments you decide to attach to it. If you've come to accept that rainy is lousy, then you'll make that judgment on every rainy day, and most of the people in the world (except farmers, etc.) will agree with you. But in reality, the day just *is* and whether you choose to label it lousy or not is of no consequence to the day itself, because the day is going to be precisely what it is regardless of how you label it.

Now all this talk about judgments and reality may seem far-fetched in relation to the practical problems of your victimization, and nit-picky when we talk about such harmless-sounding utterances as, "It's a lousy day." But it becomes absolutely vital when applied to areas of your life in which confusions about judgments and reality can victimize you—and consider for a moment the implications of letting a little bit of rain cast a shadow over a whole day of your life for no good reason. If you conduct your life according to the belief that judgments and reality are the same thing, you are in for a ware-house full of self-imposed woes. The conflict originates when you ex-pect the world to be the way you want it to be and you find yourself upset because things aren't going the way you want them to go, or as they used to go, or even worse, as you insist that they go. And the conflict resolves itself when you see reality for precisely what it is and stop hurting yourself just because the world revolves the way it does.

Here is a little excerpt from "War Is Kind," a poem written by Stephen Crane back in 1899:

> A Man said to the universe:
> "Sir, I exist."
> "However," replied the universe,
> "The fact has not created in me
> A sense of obligation."

This is the essence of reality. The world does not owe you a living *or* a happy life, and the more you think it does, the harder you make it for yourself to get these things. Reality just is, independent of what you demand or insist upon, or how you are otherwise immobilized by your judgments about the way it ought to be.

This is not to imply that you shouldn't work at changing injus-tices, the parts of the world which you find unwholesome, for change is at the heart of progress and growth. But you can accept things which have already happened as simply over, and therefore worth learning from, but not worth upsetting yourself about. And things which are now happening and which you cannot change are not worth hurting yourself over either—so you need not judge them as good or bad, but can simply see them as existing. Things which you predict might happen, and which you might be able to influence, you set about to improve—but you don't *demand* that they be otherwise and get frustrated when they are not.

People who are constantly cursing reality doom themselves to lives of needless anger and frustration. They are apt to victimize themselves by saying things like the following.

• *"This shouldn't be happening right now."* By saying that something which *is* happening shouldn't be happening, you may become victimized because you become upset. The more upset you become because of your demands that reality be different than it is, the more tightly the chains of neurosis are bound around your world. Say instead, "This is happening right now, and I am going to do what I can to stop it, or to see that it doesn't happen again."

• *"The world is a cruel place."* People who judge the world to be cruel, rather than accepting it, ignore the fact that the world itself isn't cruel; again, it simply is. "Cruel" is a manmade label used here to blame the world for not always being the way we would like it to be. You can call the world anything you want, and then be upset about it, but it will just go right on being whatever it is. A more reality-based way for you to think of it would be, "There are things in the world I want to change, and I'm going to work on them. Those things I can't change, and which I dislike, I will stop expecting to be different, since my expectations will always end up being disconfirmed, and therefore upset me."

• *"People are vicious and uncaring."* Once again, "vicious" and "uncaring" are words we use to disapprove of some ways people behave.

The fact is that people often do things which you would not choose to do yourself, and which in some cases you might find reprehensible (or worse) on principle.

So just don't make choices like that yourself; work at not letting such behavior encroach on your rights or the rights of others. If it does, do whatever you have to do to stop it, but don't waste energy merely labeling the people and allowing yourself to be upset and immobilized just because they exist. And above all, don't throw up your hands and say that *people in general* are vicious and uncaring, because that is to give up hope for everyone—*yourself included*—and therefore to give up your own life. This is an illustration of why it is much more helpful to label behaviors rather than people. People change and don't always fit neatly into any single compartment. "They are participating in stealing and slapping-around behavior, and I'm not going to tolerate it," may sound odd, but is a much more effective way to look at *people* whose *behavior* you find objectionable.

• *"What a horrible thing that was."* Things are not horrible except in men's minds. "Horrible" is not a thing in the world; it only expresses a person's judgment about something. While you don't have to like what happened, it is futile to label it as horrible and then fasten your mind to the horror as though *it* had happened. You can recognize the incident you dislike, such as a mugging, a bankruptcy, an accident, as having occurred, and you can learn from it. But remember that the world doesn't assess events, it simply has them. Any label you use to assess events is fine, *as long as the labeling process doesn't victimize you,* but calling things horrible will generally keep you immobilized in the present moment by encouraging you to recall "the horror" and, if the event happened to you, get a lot of sympathy which further victimizes you.

Judgments are only victimizing when they keep us from enjoying present moments, or when they furnish us with built-in excuses for behaving in self-destructive ways. Any judgments about reality which do not victimize us, and which we enjoy, are certainly worth keeping, as long as we know that they are judgments and not reality itself. For example, the word *beautiful* is used for judgments about reality, and to label a flower beautiful, or pleasantly aromatic, and then proceed to enjoy it, is sensational. Similarly, to label behavior as good, exciting, sterling, fabulous, stately, exquisite, loving, thrilling, or any of a thousand other such things, is not at all victimizing. But those judgments which keep us immobilized, which are confused with reality or which tend to place blame for what we are on others, or on God, or the world, must be challenged and eradicated.

NEVER VICTIMIZE YOURSELF BY REALITY

Take a hard look at the world and the people in it. Note how the world operates, observe carefully all the elements that constitute what we are calling reality. Whatever it is that you see, practice not allowing yourself to be victimized by it. Our planet functions in some pretty predictable ways, as do the people who reside here. True non-victims are those who don't engage in a lot of useless fighting, who flow with the currents instead of bucking them, and who are peacefully loving and enjoying their sojourn here.

The reality you see looks very exciting when you pause to enjoy it. When you are in the desert, it will be hot and sandy. Now you can fight this mentally if you like, and you can complain about it, and the desert will just go on being hot. But you also have the option of looking around with new eyes, and beginning to enjoy the desert for what it is. You can feel its heat and let it sink into your pores. You can see and hear little lizards scurrying everywhere, appreciate a cactus flower, watch a hawk soaring overhead. There are hundreds of ways to appreciate the desert, if you don't choose to call it boring, complain about the heat, wish you weren't there, and all the foolishness that comes from being victimized by reality.

You can experience a thunderstorm in a multitude of ways. You can fear it, hide from it, condemn it, curse it, and each of these choices will deprive you of the chance to experience that moment of your life in a fulfilled exciting fashion. But you can also loosen up during a storm, feel it on your body, listen to it, smell it, caress it, and delight in the uniqueness of all that a storm can be. When the storm clears, you can tune in to the clearing when new clouds form, you can watch them, observe how the winds move them, check out their changing formations, and endlessly appreciate the reality of each moment.

Similarly, you can opt for being fulfilled by the reality of a party, a committee meeting, an evening alone, a ballet, a football game, or eating a meal.

Whatever reality is there—and you can see most of your realities as the result of your choices—you can make it a glorious experience, or you can be victimized by not tuning in, and by judging it in unreal terms. Think of the logic here. How foolish ever to allow yourself to be upset or immobilized over things when your upset will do nothing. You could have exactly the same reaction from reality by not being upset. The conclusion for a sane person seems inescapable. If you can be either upset or not upset about reality, and neither will influence it, then choosing to be upset is simply crazy.

Henry David Thoreau, at Walden Pond, wrote, "I never assisted the sun materially in his rising, but, doubt not, it was of the last importance only to be present at it." That is the attitude of the non-victim. Be present and enjoy. Slow yourself down. Recognize the folly of being upset about things that just are. Stop believing that there are such things as bad days. Don't kid yourself. Days just are. Wednesday doesn't care if you like it or not, it will just go on being Wednesday. Your opinions make it bad for *you only*.

HOW BELIEFS WORK AGAINST YOU

It is my belief, Watson, founded upon my experience, that the lowest and vilest alleys of London do not present a more dreadful record of sin than does the smiling and beautiful countryside.

Sir Arthur Conan Doyle
The Adventures of Sherlock Holmes

The famed private eye is stating some very fundamental truth in that little quote above. Things that come under the rubric of beliefs, such as "sin," are where *you* find them. You are sinning only if you believe you are, and each person in the world can judge "sin" in any way he chooses.

Your beliefs will only victimize you if they somehow keep you from functioning effectively in your present moments. While most of your beliefs about reality are accurate and helpful in keeping you as a fully functioning person, many of them are misleading and can be destructive. Here are three of the most typical and general kinds of beliefs about reality which can prove to be victimizing, largely because they do not reflect reality as it is.

1. GOOD VS. BAD If you believe that reality contains things which are good and bad the same way in which it contains things which are red and green, and spend your time judging or trying to guess which is which, you have signed up for needless frustration, or worse. Good and bad are judgments about things in the world, generally based on your own personal preferences. Those things you like or agree with, you call good, and the rest are bad. Consequently, when you encounter someone who is different than you, rather than simply

labeling him different, you just might label him bad, and therefore justify hating, fighting or being upset by him. When you encounter obstacles in your path, defects in human products, holes in the road, etc., you can label them as bad, think of little pockets of "badness" everywhere, and justify your pessimism and gloom. You also can become victimized by other people's opinions of good and bad, when they are applied to you. If someone thinks your behavior is just plain bad and pressures you to change it for that reason alone, you have to be alert for a cheap and groundless victimizing shot.

People are always labeling things good and bad, almost as a way of judging and forgetting them, instead of experiencing them fully. "That has a bad smell." Let's think about the concept of a bad smell. You may not like a given smell, and it may be because your body is warning you, for instance, that what you smell would be no good for you to eat. But in reality, the odor itself is never bad. Similarly, people say their cats are bad because they hunt birds. But cats don't know how to be anything other than cats. Bad is not a word that applies to animals, since they only do what they know how to do. Cats hunt instinctively, and if you label them bad for hunting, it won't change a thing, except to help you victimize yourself with expectations for a reality which will never be, regardless of how you label it. If you are being victimized by the *good/bad* routine, think instead in terms of *healthy/unhealthy, legal/illegal, effective/ineffective, works/doesn't work*, which are reality-based dichotomics that can have real meaning in your life.

2. RIGHT VS. WRONG Once again, man invents terms that say this behavior is right, and that is wrong, this event is right, that wrong. But reality has no use for such judgments. If someone convinces you that you are wrong, be it morally or otherwise, he can push you around until you are behaving right, which is often just the way most people behave, but which is never determined by any magic "rightness" or "wrongness" of your position. Any objective observer would soon see that one person's "right" behavior is another's "wrong," and vice versa. It is purely a judgment.

Many people have been sent off to die in stupid wars because it was "the right thing to do," even though both sides end up shaking hands when the whole thing is over. People often believe that allegiance to a country, a team, a school, or whatever, is always right, and that having a contrary opinion is definitely wrong. People victimize each other by saying that loyalty to family members is *always* right, or that one must always tell the truth because it is the right thing to do. Similarly, swearing is wrong, as is yawning, sneezing, twitching, or picking your nose. Why? Because people have decided to discourage such behavior, not because there is anything innately or always wrong in any of these activities. You must decide for yourself not whether your behavior is right or wrong, but whether it is effective or ineffective in the pursuit of legitimate goals. One way to see through victimization-by-calling-you-wrong is to demand that your accuser substitute for "wrong" some description of your behavior which proves you are victimizing someone else. If he can't, he is either just plain misguided by "right" and "wrong," or trying to victimize you.

3. BEAUTIFUL VS. UGLY When applied to people, these judgments are pure unreality at its most vicious. People are not prettier or uglier than other people in reality; they are just different. A large nose is not ugly unless you choose to evaluate it that way. Hairy is not unattractive, nor are short, tall, fat, skinny, black or white. When beautiful becomes something that everyone either is or isn't, it can be used by those who can get most people to agree they are beautiful to put down and victimize the rest. But you don't have to agree to anything if you don't want to, and least of all to the use of terms that do little but set one class of people over another on the basis of "beauty" and "ugliness." If you are victimizing yourself with erroneous beliefs about your looks which are actually the beliefs of others, get rid of these labels, and you'll be ousting a major "unreal" outlook on the world which is almost always destructive to you.

Mark Twain once wrote, "Man is the only animal that blushes, or needs to." Do you suppose he knew that a blush was a reaction to a judgment on reality, and that since animals only know how to accept reality as it is without judging it, they are incapable of being embarrassed about anything? While we don't want to be reduced to the limitations that animals face, we might want to look more closely at their behavior and learn what we can about not victimizing ourselves by our beliefs about reality.

A LIST OF THINGS THAT DON'T EXIST IN REALITY

Just for fun, take a look at the following list of words and phrases. They all represent judgments that simply don't exist in reality, but without which most people would find their own existence impossible. Do you really need these beliefs?

disasters	a perfect person
luck	a dumb bird
the "people demand"	a normal attitude
mistakes	a guarantee
almost	a dreadful dress
a bad odor	a gorgeous hairdo
the best wine	you shouldn't have
forever	terrible language
a nice day	improper grammar
a successful career	a magnificent human being
a beautiful woman	excessive taste
an awful sight	bad manners
the right way	a little bit pregnant
a good boy	a depressing game
a stupid person	an inferior bread
an undeserved death	a shallow personality
a bad accident	a disgusting display

Remember, I am not judging the use of these concepts, I am merely challenging that they can exist in reality. Each represents a judgment about reality, and if that judgment is not self-defeating, then I say go ahead and judge, but if it does victimize you in any small way, then be aware of the need for you to challenge your beliefs, and to subscribe to new beliefs that are not only reality-based, but are self-enhancing as well.

DEVELOPING A QUIET MIND AS A MEANS FOR ACHIEVING A REALITY PERSPECTIVE

Just as your body needs a judicious alternation of exercise and rest to be healthy and fully functioning, so does your mind. Learning how to quiet your mind and allow it to be totally free from thinking, analyzing, figuring, and constantly replaying the past, is a most important skill to cultivate as you work at minimizing your self-depreciating judgments about reality.

Thinking can be a disease when it is overdone. Many clients I've known have suffered from the "restless-mind syndrome," in which they analyzed the world to death, and never allowed themselves the freedom of a peaceful, non-thinking moment. Reality is best enjoyed in the absence of thinking, through simply being and experiencing.

Recall the most beautiful experience you've ever had. As you examine it, what was it that made it so special? That you were so into the experience itself that you weren't even conscious of what you might be thinking about it *while it was happening.* What was the greatest sexual encounter of your life? Whatever the occasion, during the actual experience, you were so involved in the doing, the loving, that your mind was not focused on having a good time, but instead was blank to all analyses and reflections. You were letting your body do what it knew how to do, that is, to have a beautiful, loving experience—without mulling over what, how come, why, or any other "loud mind" activity.

The heavy emphasis in our culture on meditation in recent years is an expression of our natural desire to learn how to rest the mind in the face of the modern world's frenetic activities and still be able to function. Meditation is not an esoteric discipline which involves having to spend time (and money) with a specialized guru who will give you the secrets of the ancient masters. Meditation is a very simple process which allows you to relieve the tensions, the stress anxieties, of your overworked mind, by simply making it relax and be silent. To accomplish this you can concentrate on a color, total blankness, or repeating a single sound slowly to the exclusion of all other thoughts. Whenever you feel your mind-field being invaded by one of your domineering thoughts, refuse to let it enter—literally push it out by telling it that it can wait for the designated period of your meditation. That period can be fifteen seconds for beginners, and up to twenty minutes after you've practiced for a while. This kind of mind-relaxing is just as important to you as relaxing your body on a regular basis, and you have the power to do it whenever you choose.

BEING VS. THINKING ABOUT BEING

Learning to be is really the process of learning how to *not* think. "Being" means simply allowing yourself to take part in an activity, and to do whatever is natural for you, without any prodding or persecution from your reviewing, analyzing, planning mind. For instance, once you have taught your body how to accomplish a task, your mind will inhibit it in the performance of that task if you are constantly thinking about it.

Consider everyday activities like driving a car. After you have learned how to do it through thinking and training, you no longer think about what your body is doing while you are driving. You simply let it do what it knows how to do. To make a turn, your foot moves from the gas to the brake to slow you down, and your hands spin the wheel in such a way that the car moves smoothly around a corner, staying in its lane, missing the curb, etc. Then you let the wheel spin back by changing your grip, accelerate again, etc. If you started thinking and worrying about every little move you made, you would probably break the stream of your actions, lose your coordination, and foul it up. It would be like going back to the halting, uncertain stages of learning. You have undoubtedly seen drivers who are always thinking about their driving, who seem never quite to have left the hesitant, awkward act of "putting it all together." They seem to be aiming their cars, nervously "oversteering," as though the car would jump off the road if given half a chance. They get concerned about every turn, about staying in their lanes, about their speed; in short, they are not proficient at driving because they haven't learned how to do it without having to think about doing it.

This same point applies to playing any sport, such as tennis, basketball, or Ping-Pong. You perform your greatest shots in tennis when you are not thinking about them. If you just quiet your mind and let your body do what it knows how to do, then it will hit great backhands, outstanding volleys, and so on. You know tennis is always called a mental game, and that coaches are always referring to mental attitudes. The most proficient players are those who are relaxed enough in their heads not to be nervous about performing, and are able to let their bodies do what they've trained them to do.

I have observed many tennis matches between challengers and

champions in which the challengers take early leads, largely because they just go out to hit the ball. In their own minds, they don't even consider winning, and so don't worry about it. They whale away at the ball, just letting their bodies perform. Then, after building up sizable leads, they begin to think. They might really win. They have something to protect now. So they start pressing, pushing; their minds take over; they ease up on their strokes, try to "steer" the ball, and before long they are losing. Had they been able to relax with quiet minds and just let their bodies play tennis, they probably would have held onto the leads they'd built up by doing just that. As we've said before, it's almost as though you can't think about winning if you're going to win.

Great champions in every sport do things naturally, without thinking, because they have drilled their bodies to respond immediately to the precise needs of the game at a given moment, without distraction. Concentration is said to be the way, but if it is, it is the opposite of dwelling on, analyzing, drawing out all aspects of a problem, and it is more like meditation than like thinking or theorizing. Rick Barry can hit on better than ninety per cent of his free throws in the pressure-packed arena of professional basketball not because he thinks about every movement he has to make each time, but just because he doesn't *have* to think about the pressure on him or anything else. Johnny Unitas didn't think about what to do with his arm, his legs, his fingers, etc., every time he threw a pass. Great athletes don't allow time for "looking out" for all the ways they might fail, any more than you do when you casually flip a wad of paper into a wastebasket.

Well, you can develop the same kind of quiet-mind approach to the sports you play, and in fact, to all life's games, large and small. If you have a terrible backhand in tennis, but every now and then you hit an "unconscious" shot which sails neatly over the net and into your opponent's corner for a winner, then you know that is something your body knows how to do, if only you will stop interrupting it all the time. By being "unconscious," you will let your real, natural proficiency show. "Unconscious" really translates to not thinking while you are playing, and just letting your body play.

Sexual activities are another field in which a quiet mind is needed to let you break through to simple, unjudging participation in reality.

Have you ever heard of having to teach a fourteen-year-old boy how to have an erection? Of course not. But you very likely have heard of having to teach forty-year-old executives how to remember how to have erections. Impotence, like other "put-offs" of natural behavior, is generally caused by preoccupations, distractions, anxieties, conflicts—having a mind which will not let go of other things, such as troubles on the job, and so will not allow the body to do what it knows better than anything how to do. The irony of most sex therapy is that it focuses on teaching people to stop thinking and worrying about their sexual performance, and so to take away the pressures they've put on their bodies through their loud, active minds, which in turn can easily block their bodies' functioning. By just being with your partner and enjoying sex, rather than letting your mind go in all directions, you will have the greatest sexual experiences of all.

It is well known that not dwelling on the symptoms of many physical maladies will actually diminish the symptoms—as long as you don't do anything else to aggravate them. Meditation is increasingly used, along with judicious exercise, instead of drugs to break the pain-tension-more-pain-more-tension cycles of chronic backaches. And consider the common cold. By thinking about a cold, talking about it, "indulging it," you will very likely reinforce the cold symptoms, which your own body will naturally suppress if it has more pressing business.

Howard was going to make his very first parachute jump. He left the house with a serious cold—runny nose, coughing, and blocked sinuses. He arrived at the airport and suddenly became totally occupied with the prospect of jumping. He had to listen to the jumpmaster and review all his instructions, get into the airplane, adjust his chute, count out the seconds, get out onto the jump platform, position his body correctly, and so on. He spent two hours totally involved in the excitement and stimulation of the jumping process. When he finally returned to his car for the long drive home, the challenge and activity past, he suddenly found his nose running again for the first time in two hours. During his total involvement in the activity of parachuting, his mind had not been focused on the cold, and his body, while it was still "fighting" the cold, was also naturally "medicating" its symptoms, in the same ways which manmade medications imitate.

I once had a client who had a problem with the "runs." She knew that her particular case was psychosomatic, because her attacks only occurred when she had unpleasant things to do. But she literally had to plan her days around bathrooms, and was terrified of driving her car too great a distance for fear of not being near one. After several months of learning to quiet her mind, to stop focusing on and trying to fight the diarrhea, which only increased her tension and aggravated her condition, she overcame the problem.

This kind of antithinking strategy, when the thinking is self-defeating, can be very helpful in eliminating many infirmities. While it is obviously not a substitute for adequate medical care, when the cause of the problem is purely in the head, or when the head can aggravate the symptoms of a physical problem out of all proportion to its real seriousness, then learning to relax, to stop thinking and just be, can be a very powerful antidote to physical maladies.

Overeating and dieting of course furnish more prime examples of how overthinking can victimize you. Your body knows how to find its normal weight. If you are overweight, it is almost certainly because of your mind, not because of any bodily deficiencies. If you stop idolizing food, and make up your mind just to stop eating when your body is no longer hungry, you don't even have to think in terms of dieting. Your *body* will usually be satisfied with only a few bites of food. The physical pangs of hunger dissipate. But you keep on eating because you have an active, food-oriented mind. You may tell yourself you're "supposed" to eat everything on your plate, that it is meal time, that if you don't eat a ton of food now, you'll get hungry again in twenty minutes, that the roast is exquisite, the chocolate sundae is divine, and so on. You expect to be ravenous; you have an irrational fear of hunger; even when your hunger expectations are fulfilled, you are "starving to death." But in reality, your body is being overstuffed and abused, and you know it.

One of the most helpful ways of losing weight is to put just one spoonful of food on your plate at a time. After each bite, ask your *body* whether *it* is still hungry. If not, then stop right there, and don't eat another bite until your *body* wants to. Feed it only enough to satisfy it. Bodies dislike being stuffed, paunchy and bloated; it is painful to overeat, and if you quiet your gluttonous mind and tune in to the many signals your body sends out to try and stop your overeating behavior, you will come to a truce with it, and it will reward you by adjusting to its optimal weight. All of those tight, crampy feelings, that heavy breathing when you walk up stairs, those gas pains, etc., are signals from your body that it wants to be left alone to eat just what it needs in order to function. Quiet your mind about your food intake, and you'll soon be the physically fit specimen that you really are inside that fat-minded, self-defeating exterior.

Stammering and stuttering behavior provides a sterling example of what the quiet-mind technique can do. This type of disruption of normal physical functioning is a mental rather than a physical problem in virtually all cases. Stuttering comes from talking to yourself in certain ways that lead to unnatural means of communicating.

Sheldon had been a chronic stutterer all his life. Like many serious stutterers, he had a *fear of speaking improperly* that dated back to his youth. His judgmental, "perfectionist" parents had tolerated no "mistakes" or "nonsense" from him. As a child he had constantly been corrected, and so he punished his parents in return by developing a stammer. The one thing they *wouldn't* be allowed to control was his speech.

The habit of stuttering had stayed with Sheldon until he was forty-two years old. He was a classically loud-mind person when it came to his stuttering. He would always think before he spoke, and consequently didn't allow his body to do what it absolutely knew how to do, which was talk normally, without hesitation or impairment. His first project was therefore to stop thinking before speaking, and to allow himself the luxury of stuttering if his body wanted to do it, without being concerned in his mind about what other people would say. His goal was to give himself the mental gift of being able to stutter without evaluating himself as having failed or done something wrong. He had to learn that talking in *any* fashion was just talking, and that the idea that it had to be done "right" was a judgment about how to talk.

As soon as Sheldon started to quiet his mind and allow anything at all to come out of his mouth, he made astounding progress. When it no longer mattered to him how he spoke, ironically he began to eliminate his stuttering. Quieting his mind also freed him from the self-deprecation that had been his life style since he was three years old.

In almost every life situation, once you have taught your body how to behave through the process of thinking, rethinking, drilling and correcting, then it is time to ease up and let your body do what you've taught it to do, without the interference of the pressures that come from persistent thinking. Easing up on yourself, ironically, will improve your performance rather than allow it to deteriorate. All great teachers understand that human beings must be able to do things naturally if they are to do them proficiently. Whenever stress is placed on an organism, be it from without or within, the mind is working against the very things it wants to achieve. "Stress" is the organism's own "house divided against itself." The English novelist Charles Kingsley once wrote these fitting words about thinking as a destructive cause and symptom of human misery:

> If you wish to be miserable, think about yourself; about what you want, what you like, what respect people ought to pay you, what people think of you; and then to you nothing will be pure. You will spoil everything you touch; you will make sin and misery for yourself out of everything God sends you; you will be as wretched as you choose.

There is that word "choose" again. You have the capacity to stop choosing a mind that is actively working to keep you from enjoying reality.

SOME REALITY-BASED TECHNIQUES FOR ELIMINATING SELF-DEFEATING JUDGMENTS

Whether you decide to do something about your beliefs or not, reality will still go on being exactly as it is. If you can become more aware of what constitutes a belief about reality, and if you find that your beliefs are hurtful to you in any way, then you can change your beliefs, and accept and appreciate what is out there, rather than wasting your life evaluating, judging, and being upset by it. Here are some specific things which you can do to become your own "reality expert."

• Begin by believing that you have the power to control your own attitudes toward anything. If your attitudes are uniquely your own, then you are in charge of them, and you do not have to hold on to any self-canceling ones. If you hang onto the idea that you cannot help what you think and feel, and that these are ways you have been programmed, then you are just plain stuck where you are right now. Resolve to decide upon your attitudes rather than be a slave to them.

• Give yourself reality-appreciation assignments on given days. Try studying everything in your perceptual field, rather than simply letting it pass you by. Log as much of your world as you can into your consciousness. Don't feel you have to *do* anything with it, other than experience it. If you're in a car, note the traffic patterns, who is in front of you, the inside of your car, the land formations you are passing, etc. Check out the guard rails, the cloud patterns, the architecture, the wind direction, and everything there is to observe. Give yourself these kinds of exercises and you'll not only eliminate boredom, but you'll also develop habits which will serve you in ultimately making every moment of your life something to appreciate.

• Reassess your own vocabulary and ways of talking about reality. Check out how many times in an hour you use phrases which reflect beliefs instead of reality. How many times do you say things are awful, that it's a bad day, that he or she is worthless, ugly? Work for moments at a time at correcting yourself when you become destructively judgmental. By changing your speech behavior, you'll be changing your attitudes in the direction of accepting reality for what it is, and you will find yourself eliminating much needless upset from your life.

• When you hear someone saying things with which you violently disagree, eliminate the violence from your internal reaction. Why be upset about the fact that he doesn't see the world as you do? Reality is such that everyone is different, and the less time you spend upset about the fact, the healthier you'll be, and the more you'll be pulling your own strings. If you have upset yourself over something and you know you'll get over it, work at getting over it a bit faster. The "time reduction" technique will help you reprogram yourself not to let what is really already over immobilize you. Eventually you'll get into the habit of not being upset at all over things you can't change, and you'll learn to take action, rather than sulk.

• Be personal about your reality. Practice seeing things in ways that others *don't*. If others want to be upset because of what you've chosen to appreciate, then so be it. Let them wallow in their misery if that is their choice, but you can make the conscious choice (which will eventually become an unconscious choice) to enjoy every moment of your life. Remember Walt Whitman's famous line, "To me every hour of the light and dark is a miracle. Every cubic inch of space is a miracle."

• Reduce your tendency to evaluate, assess, analyze and interpret the world, and replace this futile activity with doing, enjoying, being and loving. Do this a minute at a time by catching yourself in the evaluative process, and at that moment announce to yourself that you don't have to figure it out, that you can just enjoy the delight of this minute.

A long time ago you learned to put a premium on grades and the grading process. As a young student you were taught that things had value only if teachers graded them high, otherwise, they were worthless. But in reality, the grading process is foolish, since things don't occur in better or worse terms out there. You will be forever hung up on the grading of performance or activity if you end up measuring life in "school terms" like, "I'd give that day a B+," unconsciously or otherwise. Forget that neurotic preoccupation with grading that you learned as a little child, and get on with just doing. If you keep "grading" as part of you, among other things you'll develop the avoidance pattern of staying away from everything in which you can't "get an A" and consequently you'll miss out on practically everything enjoyable in life. You may once have been convinced that A's in all subjects gave those subjects their value. If so, you were seduced then, and probably upset when the A wasn't there—but you don't have to be seduced today.

• Assess all your relationships, not as permanent entities, but as moment-to-moment decisions to renew what has been up until now. In essence, forget about the word *relationship*. Recognize that you can only live with a person in this moment, and that because you want this moment to be fulfilling, you are going to make that happen now. All your talk about permanence can go for nothing in one second with the death of one partner, or with a decision by either person not to continue on with the other. But why be distraught because there is no "ideal" permanence, when you can get it on happily in this moment?

• Accept that there will always be snobs, kooks, weirdos, crimi-nals, prejudiced people, and all kinds of folks that you don't like. In-stead of evaluating them as bad and cursing the world for tolerating such "badness," remember that they probably see you as bad too, and if they had their druthers (which they don't), they probably would like to see you and your kind eliminated from this planet. Just grant them their separate reality, and stop letting the very existence of these people control your emotional strings.

• Stop owning others in your mind. Get rid of the illusion that your children, spouse, friends, or others, owe you something simply because they live with you, work with or for you, etc. You can never own them, and hopefully you can never get them to think the way you do just because you browbeat them. Armed with this knowledge, you can free yourself of a lot of headaches and self-imposed vic-timization by just letting *them* be. You can offer guidance to young-sters, and offer to help those who would like it, but you can never, ever own them, and no amount of your upsetting yourself is going to alter that reality.

• Refuse to allow yourself to be corrected, and eliminate any ten-dency you may have to correct others—to make them do things "right" as you may define "right." The business of constantly correct-ing people's language, for instance, or monitoring people's stories and correcting every tiny exaggeration or inaccuracy is a most rude vic-timizing habit. When you correct others all the time, you send out signals that you know how they ought to behave and they should always check with you before doing anything. When someone con-stantly corrects your speech, stop him with, "You just corrected me again for no good reason. I guess you just know how I ought to talk?" Or try, "Did you understand what I was conveying? If so, then what do you think language is for? To communicate, or to play right-and-wrong games with each other all the time?" This kind of stance will show that you are not interested in having your life monitored by others, and that you don't need someone else to evaluate your own re-ality. As we saw with the stuttering example, children who are con-stantly corrected tend to clam up in one way or another, because they resent such victimizing intrusions into their lives. I have seen many well-intentioned parents who believe that their continual correcting behavior with their young children shows their concern for communication—but in fact, it is nothing but persistent harassment, and teaches children not to think *or* speak for themselves.

• Practice quiet-mind exercises like meditation, especially during your busiest days. Push out all thoughts and simply allow your entire body and mind to slow down and relax. You become a true appreciator of life, a connoisseur, when you aren't so preoccupied with analyzing it that you no longer experience it.

CONCLUSION

Reality just is. This philosophical maxim and the attitude toward life that goes with it are as important to your quest for freedom from victimization as any of the more concrete lessons of the earlier chapters. In fact, it is what they add up to, in a way. Just learning to appreciate life without cursing reality all the time, and so destroying your one chance for happiness now, can be both the first and last step in your own pursuit of complete fulfillment.

9

Being Creatively Alive in Every Situation

*There is no way to happiness;
happiness is the way.*

You always have options. In every situation, you can choose how you are going to deal with it and how you are going to feel about it. The word *option* is most important in this chapter, since you will be encouraged to have an open mind about attitudes which may well have kept you closed to being creatively alive. Wherever you find yourself in your life, whatever the circumstances, you can make the situation into a learning or growing experience, and you can choose not to be emotionally immobilized. Whether you are in a hospital bed, a prison, a routine job, in Hogwart Junction, the New York City slums, Wide-Spot-in-the-Road, Missouri, or on a long trip—the setting is irrelevant. You can be alive enough to get something out of the experience, and you can either like where you are, or if you prefer, work at moving to another, more fulfilling place.

THE CONCEPT OF CREATIVE ALIVENESS

By "creative" I don't mean having a specialized skill in the arts, or being able to create culturally. "Creative" here has nothing to do with music, literature, art, science, or any of the typical definitions attached to it. When it comes to *aliveness,* "creative" refers to the individual's capacity to apply himself to any undertaking in the world. If you consult yourself rather than a manual or somebody else's idea of how things should be done, you can be creative in doing anything. The non-victim creatively applies himself in every life situation, and refuses to be victimized by the circumstances into which he, after all, chooses to put himself.

Creative aliveness means looking around any setting where you find yourself and asking, "How can I make this into a terrific experience? What can I say, think, feel or do that will bring about learning and fulfillment for me?" This kind of an attitude is yours to have if you decide to want it, and to stop allowing yourself to be victimized by yourself or those around you.

A lifeless party furnishes a typical situation in which people victimize themselves because they lack creative aliveness. The conversation is dragging, and focused on some inane topic like the color of the drapes or the dog do-do on the lawn. *Most* people are victims who sit there complaining to themselves about how dull everyone is, upset and maybe even furious inside. But the non-victim has his mind going, thinking about how he is going to change things around or at least not be victimized by the current state of affairs. He knows he has hundreds of options, and begins to conjure up some delightful alternatives.

Perhaps he will stand up and stay standing while everyone else sits, until they become puzzled by or curious about his "standing behavior." Maybe he'll ask, "How close to the ceiling does a fly get before turning upside down, since it can't fly upside down?" Or maybe he'll ask someone interesting to go for a walk, even in the middle of the night. He might ask someone to dance to radio music, or take a poll on people's favorite aromas. He might let his mind wander off on its own creative odyssey. He might begin work on a novel right there. There are thousands of alternatives to talking about the drapes—for a creatively alive person who will not be a slave to circumstance.

LIKING WHERE YOU ARE

How many times have you heard people talk about boring cities, dull events, horrible places to be? The creatively alive person likes it everyplace, since his attitude is, "This is where I am right now. I might as well like it as opposed to disliking it and being victimized by my upset."

People are always asking things such as, "Do you like it in New York?" Of course you can like it there, particularly when you are in New York. If you go to Bismarck, Birmingham or Bethesda, you can like it there. Geographic locations are simply places, pieces of land with certain distinguishing characteristics—and of course, you remember from Chapter Eight that places are not distasteful, but are only judged to be so by people.

You can like the street you live on, your home, the party you are attending, the company you are keeping—especially once you recognize that the places where you find yourself are ninety-nine per cent your choice and one per cent purely circumstantial. You are virtually always *deciding* to be where you are. So what is the payoff in ever going to places you are not going to like? If you do find yourself in a place where you'd rather not be, but which you can't practically get out of, such as a prison, or a committee meeting, then what is the point of not liking it, if you don't have the choice to go somewhere else?

Work hard at breaking the self-victimizing habit of not liking the places you choose to be in. Infuse yourself with opportunities to be creatively alive, instead of hurting yourself by complaining, which will get you nowhere but into further dislike of your setting.

LIFE IS A CONTINUING SERIES OF EXPERIENCES RATHER THAN ONE SINGLE EXPERIENCE

Many people victimize themselves by seeing life as one experience to be judged as a whole, which is either good or bad. If such a person has had a series of bad experiences, he views his life as bad.

But life is not a single experience. Life is always changing, and every day of your life—every moment of every day—represents something totally new, which has never existed before, and which can be used in uncountable new ways if you decide to view it that way.

Single-experience exponents are seldom happy, because consciously or unconsciously, they are constantly reviewing and judging their lives, which already sets them against reality and wastes their present moments. They typically think some other people are lucky enough to have happy lives, while they themselves have inherited unhappy lives. They get stuck because they believe they have no control over their own destinies.

But the continuing-experience exponents are in a different ballgame. They view life as ever changeable, and therefore as something over which they can exercise a great deal of control. They tend to look for new ways of living, instead of hanging on to old ways. Change doesn't frighten them. In fact, they welcome it with open arms.

One of the biggest turning points in my life came many years ago when I happened to spend forty-five minutes supervising a study hall as a substitute teacher. On the back bulletin board of that room were written the words, "Success is a journey, not a destination."

I studied these words for the full forty-five minutes, and let them sink into my very soul. Up until that day, I had in fact viewed life as a series of destinations; events, if you will. Graduations, diplomas, degrees, marriage, childbirths, promotions and other similar events were all destinations, and I was going from stop to stop, rather than seeing myself as on a journey.

I vowed right there in that room that I was going to stop evaluating happiness on the basis of arriving at destinations, and instead see the whole of my life as a continuing journey, each moment of which was there for me to enjoy. That key study hall assignment gave this former teacher one of life's most important lessons: Don't evaluate your life in terms of achievements, trivial or monumental, along the way. If you do, you will be destined to the frustration of always seeking out other destinations, and never allowing yourself actually to be fulfilled. Whatever you achieve, you will immediately have to plan your next achievement, so that you will have a new gauge of how successful and happy you are.

Instead, wake up and appreciate everything you encounter along your path. Enjoy the flowers that are there for your pleasure. Tune in to the sunrise, the little children, the laughter, the rain and the birds. Drink it all in, rather than waiting to get to some always future point where it will be all right for you to relax. Indeed, success—even life itself—is nothing more than moments to enjoy, one at a time. When you understand this principle, you will reduce your victim stance immeasurably. You'll stop evaluating your happiness on the basis of achievements, and instead look upon the whole trip of life as something to be happy about. Or to sum it up, *there is no way to happiness; happiness is the way.*

TURNING ADVERSITY AROUND

Your capacity to be creatively alive in virtually all life circumstances will depend in large part upon the kind of attitude you choose for yourself. The most crucial test of your attitude development will be in the face of adversity, rather than while things are running smoothly.

You may find it much easier, albeit far more self destructive, to give in to adversity and become a victim of your sour feelings. But if you are effective enough at not having victim expectations, you can also work at turning misfortune around and even making it work in your favor. The cornerstone of your attitude must be *alertness for taking advantage of your situations,* making your expectations revolve around wanting to emerge as a non-victim, and looking hard for the right kind of opportunity. Even if the opportunity does not surface, you can keep your attitude positive so that your glumness does not blind you to potential advantage.

As a young child you had no idea that life might be one big misdeal for you, so you were expert at turning adversity around and making it work for you. Even if a big snowstorm canceled something you had looked forward to, you did not waste your day looking on it as something terrible. Instead it became an opportunity for you to play, build forts and snowmen, have snowball fights, make money by shoveling snow, or whatever. You simply didn't have *time* to be grouchy; you got on with being creatively alive.

At one time you knew how to make a dull classroom into something you could tolerate by inventing impromptu diversions. You could have fun doing just about anything, because you had the natural propensity for being creatively alive in every situation.

You may by this time have lost a bit of that inclination by becoming victimized with a give-up attitude when things aren't going as you would prefer. And consequently you may find yourself being done in because you don't have that quick-to-recover attitude and behavior that you had as a child.

Turning adversity around involves being alert for the special put-offs that others use regularly to make people think they are trapped, so they might just as well give in and take their punishment for being alive. If a victim can be convinced that nothing can be done in the face of adversity, he can be made to wait forever to get on with his own life. A few examples of such common put-offs are:

1. *"We'll get to you in due time."* This is perhaps the purest of the put-off devices. It just plain tells you to hang back and wait, and it is tantamount to, "Go away and be a good little victim." You must, of course, combat such put-offs by refusing to accept them and by quietly devising your own strategies for attaining your goals. Whether this involves going to supervisors, writing letters, etc., or sneaking around and getting your way with no one but you the wiser, you simply refuse to be put off in your own mind, no matter how many others are willing to take it.

2. *"The check is in the mail."* This proverbial put-off promises that what is coming to you is on the way—but of course, if you don't get it, the mail's fouled up, and that's something for which the people who owe you can't be responsible. And you have no way of proving that "the check" was ever really sent. The ultimate strategy is to keep you at bay, and hope that you'll just give up. If it's literally a check you've got coming, you fight this by insisting that another one be issued (payment on the one "in the mail" can always be stopped), demanding proof from the treasurer or whomever that it really was issued, asking to talk to a superior, or whatever. But you don't allow this put-off to keep you in this adverse situation.

3. *"It's not my fault, what do you expect from me?"* By putting you on the defensive in adverse circumstances and exonerating himself, the victimizer hopes to make you go away. But you can keep this kind of put-off from even slowing you down if you make it clear that you are not fault-finding, but only looking for results.

4. *"It's the computer."* People have always been willing to "get to you in good time"; some checks have been "in the mail" since the beginning of history; and it was undoubtedly some cave man who discovered that if it "wasn't his fault," he could get out of doing anything about it. But the computer has become, literally and figuratively, the twentieth century's own contribution to mankind's stock of automatic scapegoats for all kinds of bungling and victimizing human behavior.

People tend to forget that you can always bypass a computer by going to the people who feed it, as much as victimizers might want you to believe, for their own purposes, that they too are at the mercy of their heartless and headstrong mechanical monsters. "Garbage in, garbage out," as the computer proverb goes, so if a computer deluges you with garbage, seek out the people who put the garbage in. Remind them that it's as true as it ever was that if someone's hitting you with a hammer, it's not the hammer's fault.

These are four common types of put-offs, and of course a variety of themes can and will be played on each of them. But when things appear to be adverse to you, if you are alert, ready, and most important, creatively alive and willing to take corrective action, you don't have to buy any of them.

THERE IS NO ONE WAY TO DO ANYTHING

The art of being creatively alive requires suspending as much of your rigidity as possible. If you believe there is one right way to do everything, and that you must perform in some specific manner in every situation, then you lack spontaneity as well as creativity. If you "fixate" on always doing things in certain ways, and you impose this one-way standard on others, you'll become a victim every time circumstances change and alternate behaviors are warranted. But if you have an open mind, and allow for many possible ways of accomplishing the same task, you may retain your preference for doing things in certain ways, but you will not be blinded by turning them into mandates or absolutes.

Stuart is only twenty-six years old, and yet he has already developed the "one way" attitude. While he is exceptionally competent as an accountant, he finds it increasingly difficult to get along with his wife and many of his co-workers.

Stuart confided to me in a counseling session that he firmly believed there was never any excuse for doing things "improperly." In fact, he used the words "proper," "correct," "right," "precise," etc., a great deal in his everyday vocabulary, and he was determined to prove that his wife and children constantly did things the wrong way. He complained to me that he would spend hours teaching his young son how to do simple tasks, and then be infuriated when the boy would go at them in totally different ways, seemingly "on purpose." Similarly, his wife seemed almost defiant in her unwillingness to live by his rules as to how their home should be run. Yet Stuart insisted on having her do things his way, the *right* way. He even went so far as to tell her how she had to balance her very own check book, and would become enraged when she would make out a check incorrectly, or date it improperly, or do any of hundreds of typical things that Stuart allowed to drive him mad.

Our counseling together took the form of having Stuart examine his own rigidity instead of blaming his wife for being obstinate. Stuart soon discovered that he ran his entire life on the one-way principle, and he realized that very few people really enjoyed being around him because of his boorish insistence that everything be done his way. He was the one who always read the rules when they played fun games like croquet, Monopoly, or even Cootie, and he insisted on slavish adherence to the rules, to the extent of spoiling the kids' fun. In fact, he once admitted that fun was okay, as long as it was done properly, and by the rules, but he couldn't admit that it might be fun not to follow the rules, or even make up your own rules, now and then.

Stuart began to work on new assignments to rid him of his paralyzing rigidity. He was slow to come around, as many very rigid people not surprisingly are, but after several months he was on the way to loosening himself up and allowing himself and his family more spontaneity and more options. His inelastic attitudes eventually were turned around on the job, as he admitted the possibility that accounting didn't always have to be done his way—although when he left counseling after five months, he was not willing to consider changing his own accountant behaviors.

Friedrich Nietzsche once said,

This is *my* way . . .
What is your way?
The way doesn't exist.

This is a fitting motto for people who want to improve their creative aliveness and eliminate some of the self-defeating rigidity in their lives.

If you are involved professionally with anyone who victimizes you with a one-way mentality, you would be a fool not to consider your own options to end that relationship. Imagine for a second the dangers of having a lawyer who is unwilling to shift his strategies with the discovery of new data, or a surgeon who despite new evidence will not give up his insistence that your problem is with your appendix, and proceeds to operate "as planned." An obdurate personality is never truly professional, and is a potential disaster which you can eliminate from your life.

Let us consider rigidity, which might also be called "uncreative deadness," at a little more length in connection with the crucial field of medicine. Much has been written recently about the appalling amount of unnecessary surgery habitually performed in this country. Many women especially are victimized every year by unnecessary hysterectomies, ovarian and other gynecological surgical procedures, which might have been avoided. If you don't believe this is a serious problem, consider the following advertisement by Blue Cross/Blue Shield of Greater New York, which appeared in *Newsday*, November 10, 1976. The title of the ad is, UNSURGERY. THE CURE WITH NOTH-ING TO SHOW FOR IT. The ad then goes on to say, "Unsurgery. The scar that didn't happen because you didn't go under the knife. Unsurgery. The opinion of a second surgeon you saw, who said the operation wasn't necessary. Unsurgery. The surgical opinion you didn't pay for, because it's the latest benefit from Blue Cross and Blue Shield." The ad goes on to describe how to get a second free surgical opinion, and then the kicker—the absolute evidence that many doctors are so determined to do things only their way that they abhor second and third opinions: *And your first surgeon need never know.*

Why in the world is it necessary for a medical-insurance company to advertise that it will pay for second surgical opinions and keep that information from people's first doctor? Simply because so many doctors are so rigid in their thinking that they are unwilling even to entertain second opinions. They see with tunnel vision, even when *their* restricted vision may lead to *your* unnecessarily losing a few organs.

Obviously, many surgeons want and routinely seek out second, third, and even fourth opinions, and it seems logical that any able doctor willing to admit he was human would want to have his diagnosis for surgery rechecked by as many competent people as possible. But people do desperately need protection from medicine's "one way" minds, and after reviewing the literature on surgical development in the United States in *The Will to Live,* Dr. Arnold A. Hutschnecker concluded, "Today we recognize that the victims of a surgeon's rash diagnosis are legion."

No non-victim would hesitate to get as many opinions as necessary for *his* satisfaction before consenting to surgery. And if his doctor even intimated disapproval, the non-victim patient would look elsewhere for a doctor who would put the patient's life and welfare above his own vanity and personal rigidity. Rigidity is also rampant in education, with examples ranging from teachers who believe there is only one way to do arithmetic, science labs, book reports and themes, to college professors who rigidly apply manuals of style for research papers. You have undoubtedly been exposed to it for as many years as you have spent in schools, and for the most part you bought the logic or still buy it, because to be contrary is to be victimized by poor grades, by being "held back"; in a word, by "failing." But you don't have to buy it today, and you likewise don't have to impose the "one way" mentality of learning on your children.

Whenever people are taught that there is only one way to do anything, they are lined up for victimization. No creative writer consults a grammar text to decide how he is going to use his own natural language. Similarly, no great artist believes there is only one way to paint, sculpt or compose. Greatness in any endeavor is always unique; it reminds you of no one else, and can be imposed by no one else, although it can be cultivated by others. So encourage yourself and others to be flexible and open about doing any task in a myriad of ways, and selecting the method which is most propitious for the moment, with the full recognition that another tack might be more appropriate tomorrow.

W. Somerset Maugham included this tiny description of a "rigid" character in his novel *Of Human Bondage:* "Like all weak men he laid an exaggerated stress on not changing one's mind."

Victims and victimizers alike take this narrow approach to living, which keeps them from growing or allowing growth in others.

THE IMPORTANCE OF PERSEVERANCE

Victims give up, mostly to emotional paralysis, whether it comes from fear, anger, or frustration. Non-victims persevere without such emotional immobilization. If you want to be a non-victim, you will have to give up your giving up, and replace it with some dogged perseverance.

As we have implied above, a great many victimizers operate from the premise that if you just put a protesting victim off long enough, he will give up his battle. Many lawsuits are conducted on precisely this strategy. Lawyers for victimizers know that if the "little" person challenging them cannot see winning this year or even next, he may well just say, "To hell with it." And one of the prime bases of our legal system seems to be to discourage most people from seeking "everyday justice" by making it seldom worth its price. Hence you must always make your own decisions about whether persevering is worth the effort, in the legal arena or anywhere else, or if the actual act of following up will victimize you even more. But if you are imaginative enough, you can quite often devise ways to persevere without a lot of heavy involvement, or if you have the resources, you can simply hire other people to do your persevering for you.

Demonstrating that you will not be victimized generally involves choosing which battles you want to fight, instead of avoiding, and then sending out signals that you are willing to go as far as you have to in order to win. It will seldom profit you, and often hurt you, to say you're going to fight something in some particular way if you aren't prepared to back it up. In life as in poker, a bluff is no good unless you have a reputation for not bluffing. Ralph Charell, in his book, *How I Turn Ordinary Complaints into Thousands of Dollars: The Diary of a Tough Customer,* presents what is primarily a chronicle of how perseverance pays off, how his determination and willingness to fight all the way paid off for him against would-be consumer victimizers, usually thought of as some of the hardest in the world to beat. This is something that is entirely possible for you if you really want to avoid being a victim.

Perhaps the most important key to perseverance as a non-victim is to take on your tasks without becoming upset, without any malice or other destructive emotions that waste your time and tear down your patience and resolve. View your encounters as games in which you can use your imagination in setting your own rules for reaching your objective, rather than feeling obliged to follow someone else's. Ralph Charell talks about his involved conflicts with Ma Bell, with landlords, theater managers, bankers, and many others. His message is clear: If you persevere and follow up tirelessly, never even entertaining the idea of being put off, then you will almost always emerge not only having reached your goals, but often having far exceeded your initial expectations.

The fact is that the companies and individuals who habitually victimize are not well equipped to deal with persevering folks, mainly because they encounter so few, and when they do—since they are by nature types of bullies—they usually find it easier and wiser to give up on them and move on to more willing victims. Most people act like sheep when it comes to standing up for themselves. They victimize themselves before they start by their own attitudes of not being able to win against bigness, or against "the man," or "city hall." But you now know that these are myths the creatively alive person pays no attention to. It is not only possible, but very likely that you will win, if only you'll jump the first few hurdles that crop up in your path and stay with your program. Those initial hurdles are there just because most people are defeated by them. But once you get over them, you'll often be surprised how few real obstacles remain in your way.

It is not necessary to be mulish to persevere. Your determination can take on the flavor of a simple and straightforward resolve not to be victimized. You will just do what is necessary to get the results that you seek, rather than victimizing yourself with all sorts of anguish and turmoil. Henry Ward Beecher once wrote:

The difference between perseverance and obstinacy is that one often comes from a strong will, and the other from a strong won't.

Young children who have adopted nagging behavior know it as the most effective way to reach their objectives with their particular parents. "If I persevere long enough, and nag Mommy for the bubble gum enough times, eventually she'll give in and give it to me." These parents forget that they've taught their children to ignore their first "no," and their second, and their third—often because they are victimizing the children by automatically saying no to almost *all* requests, in hopes of saving themselves a little trouble or just to rub their "authority" in. These children know if they give up even for one second, they will lose out on their goals. Well, many victimizers, especially institutional and bureaucratic ones, are trying to be like these parents—and while it is certainly beneath your dignity to approach them like a whining, nagging child, they make it evident that you must apply the logic of the nagging child in dealing with them. While this is not an endorsement of nagging, you can see that it is sometimes extremely effective behavior. If you don't want to be nagged, stop reinforcing it. On the other hand, you can become a nagger, a pest, a thorn in the sides of big business. Don't give up. The second you hang back, you'll be whipped right into line, and join all the rest on the victim list.

> I hold to a doctrine, to which I owe not much, but all the little I ever had, namely, that with ordinary talent, and extraordinary perseverance, all things are attainable.
>
> Sir Thomas Fowell Buxton

ACTION VS. INACTION

Being creatively alive involves abandoning your posture of inaction in circumstances which have traditionally immobilized you. The name of the game is action. Doing. Overcoming your inertia and *acting* will give you a whole new lease on being creatively alive.

Action is the single most effective antidote to depression, anxiety, stress, fear, worry, guilt, and, of course, immobility. It is virtually impossible to be depressed and active at the same time. Even if you wanted to, you would find it difficult to keep on moping, complaining, lolling around and wallowing in self-pity if you got active and did something. Anything! Just doing is such an important part of being a fully functioning person.

You must also understand that lack of action is not a result of depression; it is the cause. And inactivity is most often a choice rather than an inescapable fact of life. Action is also a sure-fire way to avoid being victimized by yourself and others. If you decide to do something about your problem, rather than grumble about it, you'll be on the road to changing things around for yourself.

If you find yourself asking, "Yes, but what can I do?" the answer is really very simple. *Anything* is a lot more effective than nothing.

Julia was a client of mine who complained bitterly that she was depressed all the time. She defended her depression as if it were her close ally, rather than her worst enemy. Her reactions to my efforts to get her active were always the same. "Oh, I've tried that and it didn't work," or, "That's silly, my problem is a lot deeper than that, and just getting active won't change things around."

Julia wanted to find deep-rooted psychological explanations for her depressive behavior. But the answers were not very deep or involved. She had just become accustomed to feeling sorry for herself. She was sixty-seven years old, and couldn't handle "getting older," so she tried to escape by staying in bed half the day, refusing to leave her house, complaining to her children, and worrying about a gnawing feeling in her stomach that she feared was an ulcer.

Julia challenged me every time I suggested action as the most effective way to rid herself of her self-imposed victim status. I explained that being intensely involved in any life activity would be helpful for her, but her attitude had to be dealt with before she could even begin to take action. She had to give up wanting her depressive behavior, and realize that she was the only one suffering as a result of her choices. No one else was going to be affected very seriously, and certainly no one was going to join her in her psychological pits.

When she finally recognized that she really was doing all this to herself, she said she was ready to embark on an action course to help her become creatively involved in life, but at first she began to return to her depressive ways when I encouraged her to choose some specific actions. She complained that she didn't know what to do, and so she would do nothing. So I gave her the following list of potential activities, all of which she could do.

Walk around the block briskly.
Play catch with a ball.
Go to a library and talk to the librarian.
Introduce yourself to five strangers.
Take up yoga lessons.
Learn dance steps.
Take any adult education course.
Volunteer at a nursing home.
Go to an airport and observe goodbye behavior.
Organize a neighborhood lottery, play group, etc.
Ride a bike.
Go to the YWCA for a swim.
Get a massage.
See ten movies and critique them.
Throw a party and invite twenty people.
Play any game.
Write a poem or a short story.
Apply for ten jobs.
Start your own business in your home.
Begin a neighborhood newspaper, or advertising service, or block club.
Become a salesperson for any product.
Learn backgammon, checkers, canasta or any other card game.
Care for hurt animals.
Write ten letters.
Become a paid babysitter.
Go to a singles club.
Attend local lectures.
Go to every museum in town.
Learn a new vocation such as upholstering, flower arranging, or automobile mechanics.
Visit a new city.
Begin writing your life story.
Help sick children.

Any creatively alive person can come up with such a list of options which will launch idleness into action.

Julia soon began to get the message. As she took up some new activities, rather than constantly trying to explain why it was impossible for her to do so, she saw her depressive life style disappearing. She ultimately became free from her dependence on antidepressant drugs, which she had relied upon for almost three years. Whenever she found herself slipping into old depressing patterns, she talked to herself in new ways. Her thoughts shifted from, "Poor me, I guess I'm just old and stuck being depressed," to, "I won't stand for any self-pity, and I'm going to take some action steps to ensure that I don't just sit here feeling sorry for myself." It wasn't magic that brought Julia out of her depressive habits, it was action.

People who choose to be active are very seldom victimized. The action-oriented person will ultimately get injustices rectified, while the inactive person, or the passive observer, will find himself victimized a lot, complain to everyone, and scratch his head in dismay. This old proverb has a lot of truth in it:

> Even when you're on the right track, you'll get run over if you just sit there.

THE LOGIC OF PEOPLE WHO ARE NOT CREATIVELY ALIVE

The following two sentences express ways of thinking which will keep you from being creatively alive in almost any situation if you let them. They both furnish groundless excuses for giving up in the face of a little frustration experience rather than thinking or acting in creative new ways.

1. THERE'S REALLY NOTHING I CAN DO! Once you've said this to yourself, you are doomed for as long as you continue to believe it. There is *always something* you can do, and your job as a non-victim is to begin experimenting, testing, and developing alternatives. Change this sentence around so that you say to yourself, "While I'm not sure what to do, I'm damned sure going to do something, rather than just sit here and be victimized." With this kind of an attitude, you will at least be tackling the problem, and you'll be developing a new habit of action, rather than passivity and listlessness. Don't demand a successful answer from yourself right away or all the time. Instead, insist upon staying active and experimenting. With enough trial behavior, you'll strike on something that works. But you'll never have the opportunity to strike on anything if you tell yourself from the start that there is nothing you can do.

2. THAT'S JUST THE WAY THINGS ARE   This kind of resignation comes from the erroneous notion that because things are a certain way now, you have no power to change them. But most circumstances that victimize human beings are in fact created by human beings, and can be changed somehow. And if there is any possibility of changing things, you will negate it if you say to yourself that things are "just that way." If you stand in line for an hour at the supermarket check-out and simply say, "That's the way things go, nobody can do anything about it," then you guarantee your own victimization. But if you say, "Hold it right here! I am a customer in this store, and should not have to pay an hour of my valuable time for the privilege of giving it my business! I don't care what these other people will stand still for; I'm going to see what I can do about it," then all kinds of exciting alternatives open up to you. You can approach the manager, tell him you cannot wait, and ask him to check you out himself. Or you can tell him he's going to lose a lot of business, including yours, if he doesn't open new registers. If you get no satisfaction from him you can tell him you are leaving your cart where it is, walking out, writing a letter to the main office about long lines in his store, and urging other customers to do the same. Or you can even go up front and help bag groceries so as to move the line faster. But you will never even consider any of these alternatives or any others if you say to yourself, "Well, this is just the way things are nowadays." Once you change that attitude, you are in a position to take action and make things happen.

SOME EXAMPLES OF CREATIVELY ALIVE BEHAVIOR

Below are some specific examples, from clients, friends, literature, and my own life experiences, in which creatively alive behavior overcame victimization. They provide an overview of real-life situations that are applicable to anyone who decides to give up giving up and make things work.

SEEKING EMPLOYMENT   This is one area in which, especially in this era of high unemployment, many people become victimized because they think in narrow terms and go after jobs in traditional ways, relying solely on resumes, phone inquiries, endless trips to the same old places, and a lot of wishing. These are not the best ways to get a job, simply because these are the paths pursued by most people, and job seekers who behave like "all the others" stand little chance of distinguishing themselves as unique.

Sandra was a client who came to counseling for the express purpose of learning how to present herself to potential employers and get a job. She related her long, sad tale of how she had sent out hundreds of resumes, how she had managed to get a few interviews, and how she had never even had a nibble. She was interested in public-relations work, but she had no idea how to be effective in the job marketplace. I explained that job-getting is a measurable skill, just like performing on the job once you've got it. I encouraged her to abandon her traditional ideas about job-hunting and employment, and to begin a complete reappraisal of her goals and how to put new behavioral efforts into their attainment.

It was November when Sandra told me about a position that would be opening in late March, as public-relations director for a major department store, but she said she couldn't apply yet because the present director wouldn't retire until February, and she didn't want to offend him. I urged her to toss that nice-lady victim attitude into the garbage can, to begin to think of herself, and to size up the situation. As a result, Sandra took her first risk the second week of counseling; she went to the store and talked with the public-relations director about being his successor.

He was surprised and offered no encouragement, and in our next counseling session Sandra said she felt she'd jeopardized her chances by being too pushy.

Not so. Her next assignment was to talk to the personnel director, fill out an application, and let it be known that she was not only interested, but that she was determined. The final steps in her unorthodox approach to her job-hunting were to write to the president of the company detailing not her qualifications, but what she was going to do to upgrade the store's image in the community, and to put together a dynamic portfolio of public-relations plans for the coming year.

Sandra not only got the job, but at a salary that surpassed her most optimistic aspirations. She proved herself by abandoning the "right way" approach to job hunting and substituting creative, individualized behavior that brought results.

AN ALTERNATIVE TO BEING AN EMPLOYEE There are thousands of ways to earn a living without being employed by another person or a firm. Job victims generally get stuck because they can only imagine making money in a very few ways. If you've always worked for a salary, perhaps you should consider new ways of earning a living, particularly if you are dissatisfied with having your strings pulled by employers, or having to run your life on someone else's schedule. You can rid yourself of your stereotypical thinking and list some alternatives, assess the risk factors, and then pick the best bet and *do it*, rather than talking endlessly about "what if," "maybe," and "I'm not sure." No one can be sure about anything until they do it. But if you *believe* you can't do it, then forget it, because your belief will win out over reality.

The most effective technique for getting out of job victimization is to become your own marketing expert on your own idea. You can package an idea and sell it to anyone if you can demonstrate that it will work. Or perhaps you can turn your avocation into a vocation.

TURN YOUR HOBBY INTO A BUSINESS Here are several examples of creative approaches to earning a living of the type anyone could undertake for the reward of being his own boss.

• Marilyn was interested in macrame. She did it as a hobby until she saw the business opportunities available. Her friends wanted specialized items made, and they were willing to pay her. After one year, she had turned a hobby into a full-time fun job, and was making a very nice income.

• Louise had artistic talent and loved to paint T-shirts. Her friends were constantly asking her to make them for birthdays, special events, and the like. She decided to organize her hobby into a business. Her friends gladly solicited orders for her. In six months Louise was earning $2,000 a month painting T-shirts. She has now quit her job as a cashier, tripled her income, and she is having a ball.

• Joel was a tennis nut who played whenever he could get away from his hated factory job. As he got better and better, he started giving lessons to his friends. Then, at the suggestion of his counselor, he advertised group lessons on Saturday mornings. After three months he had set up his own business and retired from his factory job. His clientele has now grown to hundreds. Joel is loving every day of his life, because he is combining his interests with his earning capacity, and he has managed to double his income in one year.

• Ben was rendered an invalid in World War Two. He was confined to a bed, but he decided he wasn't going to stay there for the rest of his life just feeling sorry for himself. So he began his own newspaper-clipping service. He subscribed to twenty newspapers, cut items out of them, and sent them to the people, companies, etc., mentioned in the stories, along with requests for small payments if they wished to make them. Next he had regular clients, and before too long he was conducting a huge enterprise, all from his own bed. Ben literally became a millionaire by taking a creatively alive approach to overcoming adversity and making his own living.

• Sarah was an unemployed violinist, broke and desperate. She parked herself outside a theater in midtown New York and played beautiful music for theater patrons coming, going, or waiting in line. She had more money dropped into her violin case in two weeks than she had made in the previous six months. Once again, a creative approach to employment, rather than a complacently angry approach.

If you are a nay-sayer, you will be telling yourself that imaginative approaches like this may be fine for others, but they could never work for you. But *anything* can work for you if you are willing to take risks, to abolish your victimizing self-doubts, and *do* it. If you believe you need special licenses to do what you want, or that the restrictions must be too great, look again from a creatively alive point of view. There are always exceptions to the general rules of employment. Some of the most influential people in the field of psychology have had no specialized training. Two contemporaries are Gail Sheehy, who wrote a best-selling book about adult development based upon her interests as a journalist, and Werner Erhard, the founder and head of the *est* movement in America. In other fields, the examples of non-trained persons succeeding in "foreign" fields are legion: Larry O'Brien, with his credentials as the chairman of the Democratic party, becoming the National Basketball Association Commissioner; physics professors writing best-selling novels; lawyers becoming broadcasters, etc. If you want to work at something, and you are willing to ignore the way you're "supposed to do it," or the way "everybody else does it," and get on with doing it *your* way, with the expectation that you'll eventually succeed, then you will. Otherwise, you will stay stuck where you are, and do no more than defend your victimizing position by saying it can't be helped.

DEALING WITH THE COLLEGE ADMINISTRATION Gordon had been assessed a twenty-five-dollar fee by his university for late registration. Rather than simply paying it, he took a creative approach to avoiding the charge. He had the head of his department write a special letter indicating that he had been delayed in registering through no fault of his own, and requesting that the fee be dropped, which it was immediately.

FIGHTING THE COMPUTER LETTER Nick had two hundred dollars' worth of traveler's checks stolen from his motel room. They had been purchased three years earlier from a bank in Germany, so he didn't know the check numbers, nor precisely where he had bought them. He wrote to the traveler's-check company, and received in return a computer-written letter informing him that he would have to come up with the numbers or he couldn't be reimbursed. Obviously, "the computer" had not read his letter very closely. So he wrote a very specific letter to the president of the company, once again explaining his special circumstances, and making it clear that he did not want to receive a letter telling him that the company was "sorry, but . . ." He wanted the president to look into it personally, or Nick would have his lawyer adjudicate the claim in small claims court. The following week Nick received a check for two hundred dollars with a letter of apology. Because he was unwilling to be victimized by a standardized letter, and due to his assertively creative approach, he simply received what he was entitled to.

THE HORRORS OF A DAY IN TRAFFIC COURT   Eugene was forced to spend a day in court, waiting interminably, being shuffled around, constantly being exposed to inconsiderate "civil servants," and ultimately being declared guilty on a charge that he felt was unjust. He asked himself, "How is it possible to turn this into something positive?" He hit on the idea of writing an article about his experience, detailing the horrors of his day in court, and attempting to sell it. He did just that: A national magazine paid $1500 to publish his diary of a day in court in three installments. Furthermore, he was then contacted by other publishing houses, and his day in court turned into a new exciting career in freelance writing. By being creatively alive and looking for an opportunity even in the face of a day in a crowded traffic court, Eugene became a victor rather than a victim.

A LONG DELAY AT THE AIRPORT   Wesley arrived at the airport to learn that all air traffic had been canceled for the next six hours. As he looked around, he noted that everyone was upset and complaining about the snowstorm that had visited this injustice on their travel plans. He realized he was going to be stuck there until the next morning, since he had to be in another city the next day. He decided to make the most of the situation rather than to be victimized by the turn of events. He saw a woman he thought he would like to meet, so he took the risk and introduced himself to Penny, who was also stuck. They had dinner together at the airport restaurant, and spent the remaining six hours touring the airport. Wesley had the time of his life. In fact, he and Penny became very close friends, and three years later they are still seeing each other whenever possible. Almost everyone else at the airport that night chose to be upset, immobilized, and victimized by the weather, but Wesley instead created a new bond of human friendship out of the same circumstances.

WRITING A SCHOOL ASSIGNMENT   Elizabeth is a college student who not long ago realized that most of her assignments were meaningless. She was forced to write research papers on uninteresting topics and go through the motions of pleasing professors, instead of doing assignments relevant to her goal of becoming an oceanographer. She decided, after some help from a competent therapist, that she was going to see if she could shift this around. At the beginning of the next semester, she arranged meetings with each of her professors and offered specific alternatives to their standard assignments, which still met their course requirements. She was shocked to find that four of her five teachers agreed with her, and were very willing to have her complete the individualized assignments she had suggested. By taking a creative approach, she spent the whole semester doing things she enjoyed, that were pertinent to her own personal goals, and still received credit for her course work.

A DIVISION OF DINNER EXPENSES Andrew and Barbara were having dinner at a restaurant with another couple for the first time. The other couple ordered lavishly: drinks before, during and after dinner, to the tune of a forty-dollar bar bill alone, and all the most expensive dishes on the menu. Andrew and Barbara do not drink, and ordered slightly less expensive food. But when the dinner was over, one of the other couple told them casually (the way such things are always done), "Well, the bill comes to $104.00 plus tip. We'll split it down the middle. Make it $60.00 each."

Andrew and Barbara for many years had stayed silent during these kinds of circumstances, embarrassed about calling the other people on such obvious rip-offs. But this time Barbara simply announced, "Our share of the bill is $30.00, and that's what we'll be paying. Yours is $90.00." The other couple was stunned, but they didn't fight it. In fact, they readily agreed that it was the only fair way to divide the bill.

PURCHASING AN INFERIOR PRODUCT Kay bought a pack of cigarettes which contained hard strands of foul-smelling tobacco. She couldn't smoke them, so she wrote to the company and told them just how she felt about it. Within ten days she received a refund, three complimentary cartons of cigarettes, and a letter of apology.

REMAINING CREATIVELY ALIVE IN SUPREMELY CHALLENGING CIRCUMSTANCES In the novel *One Day in the Life of Ivan Denisovich*, Aleksandr Solzhenitsyn takes the reader on a guided tour through life in a forced-labor prison in Siberia. The novel tells of Ivan Denisovich Shukhov's day, which is filled with tales of bare survival and the almost incomprehensible atrocities visited upon the men in the frozen wasteland camp. Shukhov's attitude displays creative aliveness even under the worst of conditions. The book concludes with these lines:

> Shukhov went to sleep fully content. He'd had many strokes of luck that day: they hadn't put him in the cells; they hadn't sent his squad to the settlement; he'd swiped a bowl of kasha at dinner; the squad leader had fixed the rates well; he'd built a wall and enjoyed doing it; he'd smuggled that bit of hacksaw blade through; he'd earned a favor from Tsezar that evening; he'd bought that tobacco. And he hadn't fallen ill. He'd got a happy day. There were three thousand six hundred and fifty-three days like that in his stretch. From the first clang of the rail to the last clang of the rail. Three thousand six hundred and fifty-three days. The three extra days were for leap years.

Survival in these brutal labor camps depended upon taking a creatively alive approach to every present moment, and living each moment for whatever it was worth, rather than judging the experience, or even allowing oneself the punishment of feeling sorry for oneself and simply giving up.

The stories of people who have survived beastly experiences imposed by tyrants are almost always the same. Whether it be the POW's, the survivors of the Nazi concentration camps, or Papillon as he writes about his experiences on Devil's Island, all talk in their own ways about using their minds to be creatively alive in moment-to-moment contexts. Applying your own sense of self-worth to the present moment and refusing to let your own attitudes defeat you, seem to be the basic ingredients of survival, both in prison camps and, though less harshly, in everyday life, where the prison bars are most often self-imposed.

IN SUMMARY

You are the product of what you choose for yourself in every life situation. You do have the capacity to make healthy choices for yourself by changing your attitude to one of creative aliveness. By being ever alert for turning adversity around, by improving your attitudes and expectations for yourself, and by fearlessly implementing risk-taking alternatives, you'll soon be gratified by the way your life can take a turn for the better. Be fully alive while you're here on this planet; you'll have an eternity to experience the opposite after you leave.

10

Victim or Victor? Your Present Victim-Profile Based on 100 Typical Situations

A typical victim behaves typically.

Now that you've absorbed the philosophy and practice of non-victimization, and hopefully have started putting your personal freedom *into* practice with modified behaviors, you will want the chance to rate yourself on whether you typically choose to be victimized or not. The "test" below should help you do this. It is a checklist of 100 typical victimizing situations, each a normal sort of occurrence in life, along with two alternative ways of reacting. One is a victim response, the other a "victor's" or non-victim response. Check which response most typifies your ordinary reaction, or the way you probably would react, in such situations.

This checklist is not intended as a precise measure of anything. Rather it is for *your own evaluation*, to help you assess your own status or progress—and to give you a list of victim behaviors you want to work on changing. So don't worry about being absolutely "correct" in your answers. Simply read about the situation and "guesstimate" how you would normally behave. If a situation couldn't apply to you, then use a hunch. If you become obsessed with the test itself and the exact wording of its questions, you won't be applying the creatively alive approach to it. So just have fun with it.

GAUGING YOUR PRESENT
VICTIM-PROFILE

1. In a restaurant you feel that the food quality is inadequate and that the service has been poor.

   Victim Response
   _____ You tip the waiter the standard fifteen per cent and grumble about the food as you leave.

   Non-Victim Response
   _____ You do not leave a tip, and inform the management just why you are dissatisfied.

2. A relative (mother, in-law, son, etc.) asks you to talk on the telephone when you are very busy and just don't want to talk.

   Victim Response
   _____ You talk with the relative and feel hurried, harassed and upset.

   Non-Victim Response
   _____ You tell the relative you really are too busy and don't have time to talk.

3. The telephone rings while you are making love or otherwise personally engaged.

   Victim Response
   _____ You interrupt your personal activity and answer the phone.

   Non-Victim Response
   _____ You let the phone ring and go about your activity without interruption.

4. Your spouse (partner) unexpectedly changes his or her plans, causing a conflict for you.

   Victim Response
   _____ You change your plans and allow yourself to be inconvenienced.

   Non-Victim Response
   _____ You carry through with your original plans and don't even view the incident as a source of unease.

5. You are eating a meal and you feel pleasantly satisfied and full, even though your plate is only one third empty.

   Victim Response
   _____ You continue to eat everything on your plate and leave the meal feeling uncomfortably stuffed.

   Non-Victim Response
   _____ You stop eating the moment you no longer feel hungry.

6. Someone in the family has lost something and blames you.

   Victim Response
   _____ You become the detective and use up your present moments in a desperate search for someone else's belongings.

   Non-Victim Response
   _____ You simply go about your business, oblivious to the manipulation being directed at you in the name of blame.

7. You would like to attend a social function alone.

   Victim Response
   _____ You ask permission to go, and leave your decision up to other members of your family.

   Non-Victim Response
   _____ You tell your family that you're going, and if necessary, that you *are going alone.*

8. You notice someone trying to drag you down into his own personal gloom.

   Victim Response
   _____ You listen to the person's complaints and eventually feel just as lousy as the sourpuss.

   Non-Victim Response
   _____ You excuse yourself and leave, or you announce that you are not interested in discussing gloom right now.

9. A family member complains that the laundry is not done.

   Victim Response
   _____ You apologize and offer to do it right away.

   Non-Victim Response
   _____ You offer to teach the complainer how to run the washing machine, and let him do it for himself, or you simply ignore the complaints and teach him he is responsible for his own clothes.

10. You are rushed for time and you see a long line at a checkout counter in the grocery store.

    Victim Response
    _____ You wait in line, fuming over the lack of help and the fact that you are being unnecessarily delayed.

    Non-Victim Response
    _____ You insist that the manager open another line, or that he give you personal attention.

11. You arrive at a restaurant which has advertised its closing time as 10:00 P.M. It is 9:30 P.M. and the restaurant is locked up, although the employees are still inside.

    Victim Response
    _____ You turn around and leave, upset because you have been misled by false advertising.

Non-Victim Response

_____ You insist that the employees come to the door, and politely tell them you are a paying customer and you want to be served. If you are not served, you will inform the management.

12. Your motel air-conditioner is not working and you are uncomfortable.

Victim Response

_____ You don't say anything because you don't want to make a pest of yourself.

Non-Victim Response

_____ You insist that it be fixed right away, or that you be moved to another room.

13. In a job interview you are asked a series of tough questions.

Victim Response

_____ You squirm, excuse yourself, act scared, and apologize for being nervous.

Non-Victim Response

_____ You respond confidently and label efforts to intimidate you. "You're asking to get my reaction, not because you are interested in an answer. There is no clear-cut answer."

14. Your doctor informs you that you will need surgery; you have some personal doubts and fears.

Victim Response

_____ You "go along" quietly and subject yourself to the surgery.

Non-Victim Response

_____ You get second and third opinions from other specialists before consenting to surgery. You inform your doctor that you want this as a standard practice.

15. You feel that you deserve a promotion or a raise.

    Victim Response
    _____ You wait until your boss thinks to do something for you.

    Non-Victim Response
    _____ You ask for what you think you have earned, citing your reasons, being non-emotional and non-apologetic.

16. A distant relative has died and you don't want to attend the funeral.

    Victim Response
    _____ You grudgingly go along and dislike spending your time this way.

    Non-Victim Response
    _____ You do not attend.

17. Someone you do not want to kiss sticks his face at you in a greeting, expecting you to respond.

    Victim Response
    _____ You give the kiss and feel abused.

    Non-Victim Response
    _____ You extend your hand and simply refuse to kiss the person.

18. Everyone in the family is hungry and demanding to be fed, even though you are not hungry and do not feel like cooking.

    Victim Response
    _____ You go ahead and cook and feel angry at them.

    Non-Victim Response
    _____ You announce that you are not cooking tonight and you stick by your words, allowing the others to come up with a different alternative for dinner.

19. You are asked to make arrangements for an office party when you would rather not.

    Victim Response
    _____ You go ahead and do it, and feel upset that you are always the one who has to do the dirty work.

    Non-Victim Response
    _____ You say you are not interested in being the organizer, and follow through by refusing to do it.

20. You are going to a party where everyone else will be dressed up, but you don't want to dress up.

    Victim Response
    _____ You dress up, feel uncomfortable, and are mad because you are wearing clothes you'd rather not be wearing.

    Non-Victim Response
    _____ You wear casual clothes or don't go to the party.

21. Your house is cluttered with things left around by other family members.

    Victim Response
    _____ You go around and pick up after everyone.

    Non-Victim Response
    _____ You announce that you will not be a picker-upper, and leave the clutter alone.

22. You don't feel like having sex, and your partner does, even though you've just been treated poorly an hour before.

    Victim Response
    _____ You go ahead and have sex and feel abused.

    Non-Victim Response
    _____ You tell your partner you do not feel like having sex when you are mistreated, and simply refuse the advances.

23. Someone shouts out obscenities in your presence.

    Victim Response
    _____ You get angry and feel insulted.

    Non-Victim Response
    _____ You ignore it and refuse to allow someone else's behavior to control your emotions.

24. You have to use the bathroom at a party and everyone is within earshot of the room.

    Victim Response
    _____ You don't go to the bathroom because you don't want to be embarrassed by any bathroom sounds.

    Non-Victim Response
    _____ You use the facilities and you don't worry about what someone else thinks about you. You recognize that bathrooms are for normal human functions, and you shouldn't be ashamed of yourself for being human.

25. You are subjected to silly rules which have no meaning, but which are really harmless, such as being expected to wear white at a tennis court, or rituals like sitting in the bride's section of the church.

    Victim Response
    _____ You make a fuss, get upset, complain to everyone, and follow the silly rules anyhow because you haven't much choice.

    Non-Victim Response
    _____ You simply shrug your shoulders and go along without being upset, and without endorsing the rules. You are quietly effective.

26. A truck driver cuts in front of you on the highway.

    Victim Response
    _____ You fume, holler, and try to retaliate by cutting him off.

Non-Victim Response

___ ___ You forget it and remind yourself that you cannot control another driver's behavior by being upset about it.

27. A co-worker asks you to complete a chore that you don't want to do, and which you are not required to do.

Victim Response

_____ You go ahead and do it anyhow, and feel abused and manipulated.

Non-Victim Response

_____ You say no without making up any excuses.

28. You discover that you have been overcharged in a store.

Victim Response

_____ You don't say anything because you don't want to create a scene, or appear to be obnoxious.

Non-Victim Response

_____ You announce that you've been overcharged and that you want it corrected.

29. You check into a hotel and the clerk gives your key to the bellboy, who is going to accompany you to your room for a tip even though you have no need of his services.

Victim Response

_____ You don't say anything and have him go along, because you don't want to be embarrassed.

Non-Victim Response

_____ You tell the bellboy you don't need his services, but if he really must come along, he'll do so without being paid by you.

30. Your children want a ride to a friend's house to play, and expect you to cancel your own plans and chauffeur them.

    Victim Response
    _____ You cancel or alter your plans and chauffeur your children.

    Non-Victim Response
    _____ You tell your children they will have to figure out a way to get there without you, since you have important things to do.

31. You are being abused by a fast-talking salesperson.

    Victim Response
    _____ You sit there and listen patiently, waiting for the salesperson to dismiss you.

    Non-Victim Response
    _____ You interrupt and say you don't want the hard sell. If the person continues, you simply leave.

32. You are going to have a party, and you have three days to prepare.

    Victim Response
    _____ You spend all your time arranging, preparing, and worrying about things going well.

    Non-Victim Response
    _____ You make the necessary minimal arrangements and just allow things to go as they will—no extra cleaning, no special treatment, simply letting things happen in a relaxed fashion.

33. Someone criticizes your work.

    Victim Response
    _____ You get nervous, explanatory and upset.

    Non-Victim Response
    _____ You either ignore the criticism or accept it without having to defend yourself to your critic.

34. Someone is smoking next to you, and it is distracting and discomforting.

    Victim Response
    _____ You sit there and take it.

    Non-Victim Response
    _____ You politely request that the person not smoke. If he refuses, then you either move or ask that he do so.

35. You receive a well-done steak in a restaurant when you asked for it rare.

    Victim Response
    _____ You eat it well done because you don't want to cause a problem.

    Non-Victim Response
    _____ You send it back and ask for a *rare* one this time.

36. Someone pushes ahead of you in a line.

    Victim Response
    _____ You say nothing and let him stay, but you are furious.

    Non-Victim Response
    _____ You tell the person you don't let people push ahead of you.

37. Someone has borrowed money and has neglected to repay you.

    Victim Response
    _____ You agonize over the inconsiderate behavior, but you say nothing.

    Non-Victim Response
    _____ You firmly inform your borrower that you expect to be repaid now.

38. You are a stranger at a social gathering.

    Victim Response
    _____ You hang back and hope that someone will invite you to partici-
    pate in the discussion. You are uneasy.

    Non-Victim Response
    _____ You walk up to people, introduce yourself, and avoid the uneas-
    iness that comes from hanging back.

39. You are dieting and a well-intentioned friend insists that you have some
    dessert made especially for you. Or you have given up drinking and
    someone insists on buying you a drink.

    Victim Response
    _____ You take the dessert or the drink because you don't want to hurt
    your friend's feelings.

    Non-Victim Response
    _____ You refuse the drink or the food and say that you appreciate the
    kindness, but that you simply will not be talked into changing
    your mind.

40. You are confronted by a sidewalk weirdo who is pushing a product or a
    point of view.

    Victim Response
    _____ You stand and listen, hoping he'll soon stop. Or you buy the
    product to get away from him.

    Non-Victim Response
    _____ You turn around and leave without one word of explanation.

41. Someone asks you to apologize for something you don't feel sorry about.

    Victim Response
    _____ You go ahead and ask forgiveness and allow yourself to be ma-
    nipulated.

Non-Victim Response

_____ You state what you believe and then you turn your thoughts to your life, rather than being upset because someone else refuses to understand your point of view.

42. A real estate person continues to hound you about showing you property that you don't want to see.

Victim Response

_____ You go along and look anyway, because you feel obliged to be nice to someone who has gone to all that trouble.

Non-Victim Response

_____ You say forthrightly that you are not interested in seeing any property, and you refuse to be bulldozed by high-pressure sales tactics.

43. You order a soft drink in a restaurant. You receive three-fourths ice and one-fourth soft drink.

Victim Response

_____ You pay for the glass of ice and don't mention your displeasure.

Non-Victim Response

_____ You politely tell the waitress that you want a little ice and a full glass of soda pop, since that is what you are paying for.

44. Someone says to you, "You don't trust me! You must think I'd cheat you!"

Victim Response

_____ You deny that you don't trust the person, and proceed to be victimized by the feigned hurt feelings.

Non-Victim Response

_____ You say that being cheated is a very real possibility when dealing with people, and that you are being effectively skeptical. If the person can't handle your skepticism, then you'll deal with someone else.

45. Your doctor tells you to return for a second visit for some problem. You do not want to pay for a second office call, and you are feeling just fine.

Victim Response

_____ You return on schedule, report that you are doing fine, and pay for the unnecessary visit.

Non-Victim Response

_____ You only return to the doctor if you feel there is a need to do so. You trust yourself, particularly if it is a minor matter, and you know that the check-back visit is more ritual than necessity.

46. You are seeing a therapist, but you want to terminate the therapy because you feel you no longer need it.

Victim Response

_____ You believe you owe your therapist an explanation, and so you spend several sessions talking about it, and paying him to participate in the ritual of ending therapy. You are seduced into staying and talking about it, and every time you give a reasonable reason, it is countered with such statements as, "You must be angry. That proves you aren't ready to leave." You put yourself into a no-win situation by discussing it.

Non-Victim Response

_____ You call your therapist and announce that you are terminating, but that you would like the option of returning at a future date if necessary. You refuse to pay him to tell him that you are finished for now, and you understand that you owe your therapist nothing.

47. You are requesting a loan from a bank, and the lender is acting in supercilious, intimidating ways.

Victim Response

_____ You say, "Yes, sir," a lot; you are begging and acting meek.

Non-Victim Response

_____ You instantly request an interview with another bank official, and announce that you will not tolerate intimidating tactics.

48. You are having a prescription filled, but you do not know the cost or the contents of the drug in advance.

    Victim Response
    _____ You take what the druggist gives you and say nothing, and you pay whatever price he charges.

    Non-Victim Response
    _____ You ask both the doctor and the pharmacist about the ingredients, and you ask what the price will be. If it seems too high, you go to other drug stores and check out prices before deciding where to buy. If you do not like the ingredients, you ask your doctor to provide data on the drug, why he is giving it to you, and what results he expects.

49. You find after returning home from the store that the garment you purchased isn't satisfactory.

    Victim Response
    _____ You don't return the garment. Or you do so, but you are rebuffed by the cashier who refuses to take it back, so you leave unsatisfied.

    Non-Victim Response
    _____ You return the garment and insist on a refund. If you are rebuffed, you take it all the way to the president of the company if necessary.

50. You are invited to an event that you don't want to attend, and you are expected to purchase a gift even if you don't go.

    Victim Response
    _____ You go out and buy a gift, and feel resentment.

    Non-Victim Response
    _____ You politely send regrets, and you do not buy a gift.

51. You are confronted with the dilemma of sending out greeting cards during the holidays when you'd rather not do it.

Victim Response

_____ You buy the cards, address the envelopes, pay the postage, and hate every minute of it.

Non-Victim Response

_____ You do not send out any cards, nor do you offer explanations.

52. A nearby radio or stereo is playing loudly enough to cause you physical discomfort.

Victim Response

_____ You simply endure it without saying anything. Or, you protest loudly and get into an argument about it.

Non-Victim Response.

_____ You turn the sound down yourself, or you ask the offending party to do so. If he refuses, then you leave the premises, or notify the manager that you won't return unless the decibels are reduced, or whatever fits the situation.

53. A neighbor's dog is barking loudly in the morning and disturbing your sleep.

Victim Response

_____ You lie there and get angry.

Non-Victim Response

_____ You call your neighbor and tell him that his dog's barking is disturbing you. If he doesn't try to stop it, you call him in the middle of the night whenever the dog barks. If that doesn't work, you notify the police and file a complaint about noise pollution.

54. At a closing meeting on a home purchase, you are confused about all the hidden charges, and feel as though you are being victimized.

   Victim Response
   _____ You say nothing for fear of appearing stupid, but you continue to feel abused.

   Non-Victim Response
   _____ You hold up the transaction until you are given a full accounting that satisfies you. You refuse to be intimidated by your ignorance.

55. The heat has been turned off in a movie theater and you are uncomfortably cold.

   Victim Response
   _____ You sit there and freeze.

   Non-Victim Response
   _____ You ask for the manager and insist on a full refund, because you did not pay to sit in an unheated theater.

56. You notice that you have been overcharged a few pennies' sales tax on your grocery bill.

   Victim Response
   _____ You go ahead and pay it, because people will think you are cheap to complain about such a tiny amount.

   Non-Victim Response
   _____ You pay only what you owe.

57. You are trying to make a long-distance phone call and you encounter a surly, uncooperative operator.

   Victim Response
   _____ You engage in a long dialogue with the operator and end up frustrated.

   Non-Victim Response
   _____ You hang up and dial again for another operator.

58. A drunk at a party is pestering you with meaningless chatter.

    Victim Response
    _____ You sit there and feel abused, wishing he would go away

    Non-Victim Response
    _____ You leave and refuse to be around him.

59. You are at a gas station and the attendant ignores your dirty windshield.

    Victim Response
    _____ You say nothing and get mad at him for not doing his job.

    Non-Victim Response
    _____ You ask him to wash the windshield and forget about the fact that you had to ask him. Your goal is a clean windshield, not a reformed gas-station attendant.

60. You hate the prospect of fertilizing your lawn and don't even believe in it, but you are expected to do it because everyone else has a shiny green lawn.

    Victim Response
    _____ You go ahead and buy the fertilizer and use up your time, hating yourself for giving in to such silly pressures.

    Non-Victim Response
    _____ You simply don't fertilize your lawn, rather than looking to the neighbors to see how you should behave. If yours isn't as green as everyone else's, then you accept that rather than worrying about what the neighbors will think.

61. Your doctor keeps you waiting for an appointment when you've arrived on time.

    Victim Response
    _____ You say nothing, because you understand how busy and important doctors are.

Non-Victim Response

_____ You tell him how you feel about being kept waiting and request a reduction in fee to compensate you for your lost time.

62. You receive a grade that you believe is unjust.

Victim Response

_____ You do nothing and get mad at the teacher.

Non-Victim Response

_____ You make an appointment with the teacher and explain your feelings. If you get no results, you write a letter to the principal, dean, or other administrator. You follow the appeal procedures. You persist.

63. A funeral director tries to manipulate you into purchasing more expensive funeral arrangements by capitalizing on your grief.

Victim Response

_____ You go ahead and order the expensive funeral, because you don't want him to believe that you didn't love the recently departed.

Non-Victim Response

_____ You label what the funeral director is attempting to do, and insist upon being treated squarely, rather than with maudlin condescension.

64. You are enrolled in a class in which the teacher or professor is dull and uninformed, and you are wasting your time and money.

Victim Response

_____ You stay enrolled in the class and suffer in silence.

Non-Victim Response

_____ You complain to the department chairman or administrative superior. You insist on withdrawing and getting your money back and say that if you are refused, you promise to carry it to the courts, public newspapers, and even write a story about it for publication.

65. Someone doesn't send you a thank-you note for a favor you've done.

    Victim Response
    _____ You get upset and complain a lot about the ingrate.

    Non-Victim Response
    _____ You ignore it and remind yourself that you didn't do the favor for the person because you expected to be thanked. If he doesn't practice the same approach to manners that you do, it doesn't mean that he is bad, and it certainly doesn't mean that you should be upset.

66. You need one onion at the grocery store, but all the onions are in three-pound bags.

    Victim Response
    _____ You either get no onions or buy three pounds which you don't need.

    Non-Victim Response
    _____ You break open a bag and take the one onion you want to buy.

67. You are sleepy after a huge meal.

    Victim Response
    _____ You stay awake and suffer because you are not supposed to take a nap, according to someone else's rules.

    Non-Victim Response
    _____ You lie down without feeling guilty about wanting to take a nap.

68. Your boss asks you to stay late, and you have a very important personal date.

    Victim Response
    _____ To please the boss, you break your personal date and work.

    Non-Victim Response
    _____ You tell your boss that your engagement is important, and that working late with such short notice on this occasion is impossible.

69. You would like to stay in a nice hotel, but it is too expensive.

    Victim Response
    _____ You go to a cheaper place because you can't bring yourself to be extravagant now and then. Everything must always be a bargain.

    Non-Victim Response
    _____ You splurge on yourself and don't worry about it. Instead you decide to enjoy it, because you are worth it.

70. You are about to speak, and someone interrupts to speak for you.

    Victim Response
    _____ You let it pass, and allow the other person to speak for you.

    Non-Victim Response
    _____ You announce that you have just been interrupted, and that you'd prefer to speak for yourself.

71. Someone asks you, "Why don't you have any children?"

    Victim Response
    _____ You go into a lengthy, embarrassed explanation, and feel abused.

    Non-Victim Response
    _____ You tell your inquisitor that it is a personal matter, and that he has no business prying into your private life.

72. You arrive at an airport to pick up your rented car, and are informed that the car you were promised is not available, or not at the rates you were promised.

    Victim Response
    _____ You take a more expensive car and pay the difference.

    Non-Victim Response
    _____ You insist that you be given a car at the quoted price or you'll go to a competitor, and you'll write to the company stating your shift of allegiance. You are adamant about being serviced properly.

73. You are given a monitored allowance for household expenses, and you have no freedom to spend money on yourself without asking permission.

    Victim Response
    _____ You complain a lot, but you go along with being a financial slave.

    Non-Victim Response
    _____ You allow household items to run low when you don't have the money, and you let the financial wizard figure out how to get them into the house. You open your own checking account, even if it is only for a few dollars, and you refuse to account for yourself monetarily.

74. You believe you have been overcharged by the phone company.

    Victim Response
    _____ You go ahead and pay the bill to avoid the hassle.

    Non-Victim Response
    _____ You deduct the amount in question and include a letter with your payment. You insist on a detailed accounting of the charges in question, and if they are not provided, you don't pay.

75. You are a vegetarian, and you sit down to a meal as a guest, where meat is being served.

    Victim Response
    _____ You eat the meat offered so as not to offend your hosts, or you apologize for being an inconvenience and then feel bad because you have exercised your option to be a vegetarian.

    Non-Victim Response
    _____ You eat only the vegetables, without saying a word, or with a mild explanation. You feel no guilt, and you stick to your commitment to yourself to be a vegetarian, with pride.

76. At a dinner with several couples, the check is handed to you, and no one offers to pay.

    Victim Response
    _____ You go ahead and pay the check and resent those who don't volunteer to pay their shares.

    Non-Victim Response
    _____ You tell each person what his share is and ask them to ante up.

77. You lose your money in a coin telephone.

    Victim Response
    _____ You go away angry.

    Non-Victim Response
    _____ You call the operator, tell him you lost money, and request that it be sent to your home.

78. Someone is insisting that you accompany him to an event that you don't want to attend.

    Victim Response
    _____ You go along and resent it.

    Non-Victim Response
    _____ You say you are not going, and you stick to your guns with behavior rather than words.

79. You arrive at a restaurant serviced by a parking valet, but you don't want to have an attendant drive your car.

    Victim Response
    _____ You reluctantly watch the attendant drive your car away and do God knows what with it.

    Non-Victim Response
    _____ You tell the valet attendant that you will park your own car, and if he refuses, you take it up with the restaurant manager.

80. You are being subjected to a lecture which you don't want to hear.

    Victim Response
    _____ You sit there and take it, seething inside, but hoping that the person will soon stop.

    Non-Victim Response
    _____ You politely tell your victimizer that you aren't interested in being lectured, and if he continues, you calmly walk away or otherwise tune out.

81. You feel a hunger pang, but you are working at losing weight.

    Victim Response
    _____ You eat something fattening and then feel lousy.

    Non-Victim Response
    _____ You reward yourself for resisting with a strong pat on the back.

82. You have more things going on than you have room to accommodate in your busy calendar.

    Victim Response
    _____ You get tense, irritable, and try to do everything, devoting a minimal amount of time to each thing, and giving nothing your complete attention.

    Non-Victim Response
    _____ You calm yourself down by allocating responsibilities to others, and giving yourself some relaxation time.

83. You are subjected to nagging.

    Victim Response
    _____ You sit there and take it and are annoyed.

    Non-Victim Response
    _____ You remind the nagger that you don't want to hear this, and if it persists, you dismiss yourself without feeling guilty.

84. Your children are asking you to resolve their disputes, and they are obviously just looking to monopolize your time.

    Victim Response
    _____ You have a long conversation with them, and you act as the referee, but resent the whole thing.

    Non-Victim Response
    _____ You tell them you are not interested and then leave and allow them to work it out for themselves.

85. Your friends invite you over and you don't want to go.

    Victim Response
    _____ You volley back and forth with noncommittal responses, and eventually end up being talked into going over.

    Non-Victim Response
    _____ You say, "No, thank you."

86. Someone is prying into your personal life by using such tactics as, "Well, maybe I shouldn't be asking, but . . ."

    Victim Response
    _____ You tell him the private information because you don't want to hurt his feelings.

    Non-Victim Response
    _____ You tell him that he is prying, and that the information is confidential and will remain that way.

87. Someone is giving you a dose of unwanted advice.

    Victim Response
    _____ You take the advice and feel bad because you didn't stand up to him.

    Non-Victim Response
    _____ You inform him that you are capable of running your own life, but that you appreciate his concern nevertheless.

88. Someone tells you how much you should tip, even though it is your money he is willing to spend.

    Victim Response
    _____ You do what he tells you, so he won't feel bad.

    Non-Victim Response
    _____ You tip what you think is justified and tell the person he can leave as much of his own money as he chooses.

89. You receive a bill for a service that you believe to be overpriced.

    Victim Response
    _____ You go ahead and pay the amount and feel cheated.

    Non-Victim Response
    _____ You call or arrange a meeting with the person charging you the high price and go over every detail of the bill. You tell the person precisely what you disagree with, and that you want to renegotiate the charges.

90. You are filling out a job application that asks questions that are discriminatory and illegal to ask.

    Victim Response
    _____ You put down exactly what the application asks for, and you probably don't get the job.

Non-Victim Response

_____ You ignore the discriminatory sections, or provide information that will be favorable for you.

91. You would like to tell your children, spouse, parents, siblings, that you love them.

Victim Response

_____ You stop yourself from doing it because you would feel silly.

Non-Victim Response

_____ You force yourself to say, "I love you," right to their faces.

92. Your children want you to play children's games with them, but you don't really enjoy the games.

Victim Response

_____ You go ahead and play "Barby," "Kandyland," or some such game, and constantly look at your watch to see when this will be over.

Non-Victim Response

_____ You do things with your children that all of you enjoy. You seek out mutual fun activities and leave the things that you don't enjoy alone. Just as your children aren't willing to play adult games with you because they are not interested, so can you make a similar choice.

93. The members of your family expect you to be a waiter or waitress by regularly asking you to get up and get things for them.

Victim Response

_____ You take on the role of a waiter.

Non-Victim Response

_____ You tell them you are not going to wait on people, and then you follow through by simply not getting up when the "hey, waiter" signals start.

94. Someone says he doesn't understand you.

> *Victim Response*
> _____ You attempt to explain yourself again, or you feel bad because you are a failure at communication.

> *Non-Victim Response*
> _____ You stop trying to explain yourself, with the full knowledge that the person will probably never understand you anyhow.

95. Someone says he dislikes your hairdo, clothes, etc.

> *Victim Response*
> _____ You fret about it and reexamine whether you like it, based on the other person's opinion. You change your hairstyle, clothes, or whatever.

> *Non-Victim Response*
> _____ You ignore the comments, because you understand that everyone can't think the same way and that other people's opinions have nothing to do with how you should feel or behave.

96. Your privacy is continually being interrupted.

> *Victim Response*
> _____ You yell at the intruders and get upset because no one lets you have any time for yourself. You give up trying to be alone.

> *Non-Victim Response*
> _____ You put a lock on your door and you take the telephone off the hook. You refuse to violate your privacy by getting up every time someone wants something of you.

97. You are ready to leave a party. Your partner is drunk, but insists on driving anyhow.

> *Victim Response*
> _____ You get in the car and fret all the way home.

Non-Victim Response

_____ You insist that you drive, call a cab, or just stay at the party. In any event, you absolutely refuse to get into the car when a drunk is behind the wheel.

98. The temperature climbs to 105 degrees.

Victim Response

_____ You complain to everyone about the oppressive heat, and you suffer a lot.

Non-Victim Response

_____ You ignore the heat, refuse to talk continuously about it, and focus on enjoying the day rather than complaining about it.

99. Someone you love has died.

Victim Response

_____ You become a wreck. You are out of control, immobilized for a long time, and refuse to get on with living. You constantly say, "This shouldn't have happened."

Non-Victim Response

_____ You express your sadness at losing a loved one, and then you turn your thoughts to your need to be alive. You refuse to be endlessly gloomy and depressed.

100. You feel a cold, influenza, cramps, etc., coming on.

Victim Response

_____ You expect to be immobile, and you get ready for the misery. You tell everyone you see what is about to happen, and you bitterly complain aloud and to yourself about your impending infirmity.

Non-Victim Response

_____ You stop thinking and talking about being sick. You stop expecting the disease and turn your thoughts to being involved in your life. You push out "sick" thoughts and focus on "alive" thoughts.

There you have 100 common kinds of circumstances in which people often turn out to be victims. If you scored high on this victim test, then you have work to do to regain control of your own strings. Here is a scoring guide to help you in determining your own victim index:

90 victim, 10 non-victim	Your strings are out of your control. You are the total victim.
75 victim, 25 non-victim	The hard-pressed victim, with a few minor exceptions.
50 victim, 50 non-victim	Half your life is under the control of other people—you are a non-string-puller.
25 victim, 75 non-victim	You are in charge of your life for the most part, but you are still prone to having your strings pulled a great deal.
10 victim, 90 non-victim	You are in charge of your own life, and are rarely victimized by others.
0 victim, 100 non-victim	You have mastered the contents of this book—or, if you were that way before buying this book, then you were victimized in spending your money for it, and your score reverts to 1 victim, 99 non-victim.

You have the power within you to reduce your victim index significantly. The choice is yours: Either pull your own strings and enjoy being in charge of your brief life here on Earth, or let others do it and spend your life being upset and controlled by the victimizers of the world. If you let them, they'll do it gladly, but if you refuse to let them, the victim game will end completely as far as you are concerned.

Index

Prices and postage and packing rates shown below were correct at the time of going to press.

FICTION

All prices shown are exclusive of postage and packing.

GENERAL FICTION

☐ THE AFFAIR OF NINA B.	Simmel	£1.20
☐ H.M.S. BOUNTY	John Maxwell	£1.00
☐ TY-SHAN BAY	R. T. Aundrews	95p
☐ A SEA CHANGE	Lois Gould	80p
☐ THE PLAYERS	Gary Brandner	95p
☐ MR. FITTON'S COMMISSION	Showell Styles	85p
☐ CRASH LANDING	Mark Regan	95p
☐ SUMMER LIGHTNING	Judith Richards	£1.00
☐ THE HALO JUMP	Alistair Hamilton	£1.00
☐ SUMMERBLOOD	Anne Rudeen	£1.25
☐ PLACE OF THE DAWN	Gordon Taylor	90p
☐ EARTHLY POSSESSIONS	Anne Tyler	95p
☐ THE MASTER MECHANIC	I. G. Broat	£1.50
☐ THE MEXICAN PROPOSITION (Western)	Matt Chisholm	75p

CRIME/THRILLER

☐ THE TREMOR OF FORGERY	Patricia Highsmith	80p
☐ STRAIGHT	Steve Knickmeyer	80p
☐ THE COOL COTTONTAIL	John Ball	80p
☐ JOHNNY GET YOUR GUN	John Ball	85p
☐ CONFESS, FLETCH	Gregory Mcdonald	90p
☐ THE TRIPOLI DOCUMENTS	Henry Kane	95p
☐ THE EXECUTION	Oliver Crawford	90p
☐ TIME BOMB	James D. Atwater	90p
☐ THE SPECIALIST	Jasper Smith	85p
☐ KILLFACTOR FIVE	Peter Maxwell	85p
☐ ROUGH DEAL	Walter Winward	85p
☐ THE SONORA MUTATION	Albert J. Elias	85p
☐ THE RANSOM COMMANDO	James Grant	95p
☐ THE DESPERATE HOURS	Joseph Hayes	90p
☐ THE MOLE	Dan Sherman	95p

NON-FICTION

☐	THE HAMLYN BOOK OF CROSSWORDS 1		60p
☐	THE HAMLYN BOOK OF CROSSWORDS 2		60p
☐	THE HAMLYN BOOK OF CROSSWORDS 3		60p
☐	THE HAMLYN BOOK OF CROSSWORDS 4		60p
☐	THE HAMLYN FAMILY GAMES BOOK	Gyles Brandreth	75p
☐	LONELY WARRIOR (War)	Victor Houart	85p
☐	BLACK ANGELS (War)	Rupert Butler	£1.00
☐	THE SUNDAY TELEGRAPH PATIO GARDENING BOOK	Robert Pearson	80p
☐	THE COMPLETE TRAVELLER	Joan Bakewell	£1.50
☐	RESTORING OLD JUNK	Michèle Brown	75p
☐	FAT IS A FEMINIST ISSUE	Susie Orbach	85p
☐	AMAZING MAZES 1	Michael Lye	75p
☐	GUIDE TO THE CHANNEL ISLANDS	Janice Anderson and Edmund Swinglehurst	90p
☐	THE STRESS FACTOR	Donald Norfolk	90p
☐	WOMAN × TWO	Mary Kenny	90p
☐	THE HAMLYN BOOK OF BRAINTEASERS AND MINDBENDERS	Ben Hamilton	85p
☐	THE HAMLYN CARTOON COLLECTION 2		70p
☐	WORLD WAR 3	edited by Shelford Bidwell	£1.25
☐	THE HAMLYN BOOK OF AMAZING INFORMATION		80p
☐	IN PRAISE OF YOUNGER MEN	Sandy Fawkes	85p
☐	THE HAMLYN FAMILY QUIZ BOOK		85p
☐	BONEY M	John Shearlaw and David Brown	90p
☐	KISS	John Swenson	90p
☐	CARING FOR CATS AND KITTENS	John Montgomery	95p
☐	PUDDINGS AND DESSERTS (500 Recipes)	Monica Mawson	85p
☐	THE HAMLYN PRESSURE COOKBOOK	Jane Todd	85p
☐	HINTS FOR MODERN COOKS	Audrey Ellis	£1.00

COOKERY

☐	MIXER AND BLENDER COOKBOOK	Myra Street	80p
☐	HOME BAKED BREADS AND CAKES	Mary Norwak	75p
☐	EASY ICING	Marguerite Patten	85p
☐	HOME MADE COUNTRY WINES		40p
☐	COMPREHENSIVE GUIDE TO DEEP FREEZING		40p
☐	COUNTRY FARE	Doreen Fulleylove	80p
☐	HOME PRESERVING AND BOTTLING	Gladys Mann	80p
☐	WINE MAKING AT HOME	Francis Pinnegar	80p

All these books are available at your local bookshop or newsagent, or can be ordered direct from the publisher. Just tick the titles you want and fill in the form below.

NAME...

ADDRESS ....

....

Write to Hamlyn Paperbacks Cash Sales, PO Box 11, Falmouth, Cornwall TR10 9EN
Please enclose remittance to the value of the cover price plus:

UK: 25p for the first book plus 10p per copy for each additional book ordered to a maximum charge of £1.05.

BFPO and EIRE: 25p for the first book plus 10p per copy for the next 8 books, thereafter 4p per book.

OVERSEAS: 40p for the first book and 12p for each additional book.

Whilst every effort is made to keep prices low it is sometimes necessary to increase cover prices and also postage and packing rates at short notice. Hamlyn Paperbacks reserve the right to show new retail prices on covers which may differ from those previously advertised in the text or elsewhere.